Justice in the Shadow
of Death

Justice in the Shadow of Death

Rethinking Capital and Lesser Punishments

Michael Davis

ROWMAN & LITTLEFIELD PUBLISHERS, INC.
Lanham · Boulder · New York · London

ROWMAN & LITTLEFIELD PUBLISHERS, INC.

Published in the United States of America
by Rowman & Littlefield Publishers, Inc.
4720 Boston Way, Lanham, Maryland 20706

3 Henrietta Street
London, WC2E 8LU, England

Copyright © 1996 by Rowman & Littlefield Publishers, Inc.

British Cataloging in Publication Information Available

Library of Congress Cataloging-in-Publication Data

Davis, Michael.
Justice in the shadow of death : rethinking capital and lesser
punishments / Michael Davis.
p.   cm.
Includes bibliographical references and index.
1. Capital punishment—United States—Moral and ethical aspects.
2. Punishment—United States. 3. Criminal justice, Administration
of—United States. I. Title.
HV8699.U5D29   1996   364.6'0973—dc20   96-8129   CIP

ISBN 0–8476–8269–2 (cloth : alk. paper)
ISBN 0–8476–8270–6 (pbk. : alk. paper)

Printed in the United States of America

∞™ The paper used in this publication meets the minimum requirements of
American National Standard for Information Sciences—Permanence of
Paper for Printed Library Materials, ANSI Z39.48–1984.

Contents

Acknowledgments

A book is seldom the work of its author alone. Certainly this one is not. Well before editors, printers, and binders joined the enterprise, secretaries turned rough drafts into typescripts, librarians helped prepare lists of possible sources, predecessors (some long dead) had to be consulted, critics heard out, and the skinny questions of colleagues, friends, family, and students picked clean of insight. Those who have paid the bills (especially my employers and my lawyer wife) have also contributed. Even my computer-loving son who, after some urging, watched TV instead of watching me, has contributed. "Intellectual property" is a legal category; for academics, there is only debt, unrepayable except by the attempt.

To these common debts, I must add a set that many books avoid. *Justice in the Shadow of Death* grew out of eleven papers written over two decades (and published over a decade and a half). Many of the chapters are better because I took a journal editor's (or reviewer's) advice, even when I spurned the advice initially and only saw my error after publication; none is the worse for it. Editors protect writers from themselves, much as a straitjacket protects a madman, except that editors must work by reason, authority, pleading, or (if all else fails) threat to withhold publication, not by the more immediately effective (and satisfying) application of animal, mechanical, or pharmacological force. Since some editors gave useful comments while rejecting the work, the following acknowledgments should be understood as implicitly recognizing their contribution as well as that of the editors of the journals explicitly credited.

Most of chapters 1 and 2 originally appeared as a single article, "Death, Deterrence, and the Method of Common Sense," in

vii

Social Theory and Practice 7 (Summer 1981): 145-177; most of chapter 3, as "The Death Penalty, Civilization, and Inhumaneness," *Social Theory and Practice* 16 (Summer 1990): 245-259; chapter 4, as the body of "The State's Dr. Death: What's Unethical about Physicians Helping at Executions?" *Social Theory and Practice* 21 (Spring 1995): 31-60; chapter 5, as "Is the Death Penalty Irrevocable?" *Social Theory and Practice* 10 (Summer 1984): 143-156; half of chapter 6, in a review of Bedau's *Death is Different* in *Law and Philosophy* 8 (December 1989): 412-419; chapter 7, as "Arresting the White Death: Preventive Detention, Confinement for Treatment, and Medical Ethics," *APA Newsletters* 94 (Spring 1995): 92-98; most of chapter 8, as "Guilty But Insane?" *Social Theory and Practice* 10 (Spring 1984): 1-23; chapter 9, as "Punishment as Language: Misleading Analogy for Desert Theorists," *Law and Philosophy* 10 (August 1991): 310-322; chapter 10, as "Setting Penalties: What Does Rape Deserve?" *Law and Philosophy* 3 (April 1984): 62-111; chapter 11, as "How Much Punishment Does a Bad Samaritan Deserve?" *Law and Philosophy* 15 (November 1996) forthcoming; and chapter 12, as "Criminal Desert and Unfair Advantage: What's the Connection?" *Law and Philosophy* 12 (May 1993): 133-156.

Justice in the Shadow of Death takes precedence over the papers it incorporates. Having learned much in two decades, I have refined my arguments accordingly, adding here and there, never allowing the original text an authority it could not still earn. To my surprise, I have had to withdraw no significant claim. My original arguments seem to have survived their first test. Now, strengthened both by small improvements in each and by integration into one compact body, they must face another. I wish them equal success.

Introduction

We punish criminals in order to pay them back, and we execute the worst of them out of moral necessity.

—Walter Bern, *For Capital Punishment* (1987)

Here hang I, and right and left,
Two poor fellows hang for theft:
All the same's the luck we prove
Though the midmost hangs for love.

Comrades all, that stand and gaze,
Walk henceforth in other ways;
See my neck and save your own:
Comrades all, leave ill alone.

— A. E. Housman,
from "The Carpenter's Son,"
A Shropshire Lad (1895)

Now is a good time to rethink the death penalty. Only two decades ago, the United States Supreme Court seemed ready to rule death a "cruel and unusual punishment" forbidden by the Constitution. Two centuries of work for abolition awaited only the capstone. Today, however, the United States seems less likely to abolish the death penalty than at any other time in this century. Public opinion, most state legislatures, Congress, and even the Supreme Court all favor retention. For a decade now, the number of executions—though small compared either to the number a half-century ago or to the number of death sentences imposed—has increased each year. In 1994, Congress added more than sixty crimes to what had until then been a short list of those for which the federal government could ask death. This reversal of

1

prospect, remarkable both for suddenness and scale, is also re-markable for at least two other reasons:

First, the better part of the world has continued to move in the opposite direction. Europe, most English-speaking countries, and most of Latin America have abolished the death penalty; none of these countries seems likely to reverse itself soon. Each year our legal system resembles that of Sweden, Canada, or Brazil less and that of Nigeria, Bangladesh, and China more.

Second, the debate has remained both static and emotional. There are few new arguments, none in favor of the death penalty. What seems to have changed is the persuasiveness of old arguments.

Political debates generally do not last because opportunities to act generally do not last. A longstanding political debate is a prodigy worth a look just because it is still there. But a political debate at once longstanding *and philosophical* is a prodigy of another order, a forty-ton dinosaur stamping about in rush-hour traffic. Debate over the death penalty is such a prodigy, a mass of misunderstanding locked against misunderstanding, of seem-ingly convincing argument confronting seemingly convincing ar-gument, just what always attracts philosophers. But unlike many debates that attract philosophers, this one is of practical impor-tance. It may change laws—and help to decide when and how some people die.

We should, however, not claim too large a part for philoso-phy in the debate. If the same arguments that seem to have car-ried most countries in one direction have carried the United States in another, reason alone cannot count for much. Perhaps under-standing the debate means visiting dark powers that cry out not for light but blood, subterranean creatures whose language be-longs to history, sociology, or psychology rather than to philos-ophy. Perhaps philosophy can only observe and comment, shedding light where the blind lead the sighted well enough.

While I doubt philosophy is so powerless, I believe that, even if it were, philosophers should try to understand the death-penalty debate. Understanding is an independent good. While few political debates can repay a substantial work of philosophy, debate over the death penalty should be able to—for at least three reasons. One is that almost any debate at once ancient and active, scientific and practical, cerebral and passionate, is likely to benefit from the clarifications philosophy typically provides. Another reason is that the death penalty has already generated enough significant philosophical work to show that more is needed. A third reason to believe that the debate will repay a philosopher's attention is the debate's special connection with philosophy, a connection most political debates lack.

Like Christianity, philosophy claims a founder whom law put to death. "The Carpenter's Son" reminds us of the ambiguities of the death sentence, its power to beguile its victims and defeat its champions, to raise heroes as well as denounce villainy. The gallows is a confusing stage in this world as well as a convenient doorway into the next. Philosophers should find much that is familiar from other contexts, much they already understand, much that will allow them to transform Walter Bern's simple assertion into something both useful and true.

We should not begin an examination of such a longstanding debate by assuming that time has settled who has the best arguments or even that much we suppose true (or false) actually is. We should start with an open mind. But since we are human, we start instead with a mind shuttered, as if against a storm, the door opened a crack to see what the wind is blowing our way. We cannot avoid prejudgment (a polite term for "prejudice"). We can, however, admit our prejudgments, allowing others to discount accordingly. I shall now admit two of mine. One admission will, I fear, displease those favoring the death penalty; the other, those opposing it. But together the two should give those who have read this far reason to read on.

The first admission is that I favor abolition. I do not, however, favor it on moral grounds, as is usual, but on relatively indecisive practical grounds: I lived in Michigan for seven years while a graduate student. Before that, I had lived in Ohio. Ohio had always had a death penalty; Michigan abolished its death penalty in 1817. While Michigan seemed no more dangerous than Ohio, it did differ. Murder trials seemed shorter than in Ohio. They received less publicity. What publicity they did receive focused less on the accused than on the crime. The murderer disappeared from public consciousness with the announcement of sentence. The murderer's punishment was without drama; his or her person, never an object of pity. Bern's "moral necessity" was not obvious. Michigan's system of criminal justice seemed in balance in a way that Ohio's did not. I have now lived almost two decades in Illinois, another state with the death penalty. I have seen nothing to change my opinion: the death penalty seems to distort a system of criminal justice in ways better avoided.

That is my first admission, the opinion of a citizen. The second is that, as a philosopher (as well as a citizen), I find the other side's arguments to be better than my side's. Indeed, admitting the superiority of their arguments is, it seems to me, the beginning of wisdom on this vexed and vexing subject. Much of what I shall try to do here is demonstrate that superiority. Yet— though it may often seem otherwise—my purpose is not to win support for the death penalty but to spy out the strengths (and weaknesses) of its supporters, to map strongholds often remarked but almost as often unappreciated, to prepare the way for successful assault. If rational argument has any substantial part to play in abolition, we who oppose the death penalty must do better than we have at making rational arguments. To discover in what that "more" consists, we may have to go behind the enemy's lines. We shall have to examine their position with a care that they have not. Now and then, we may even have to do their work for them, risking both friendly fire and the ironic triumph of helping the wrong side to a victory. Like most spies, we shall not follow a straight line. The twelve chapters of this book approach many subjects from an unusual direction (and sometimes only after a strange turn or two).

The first six chapters defend the death penalty against various criticisms. Chapter 1 examines the main premise of the chief argument, the "argument from deterrence"; chapter 2, three subsidiary premises. We must, I argue, agree that the death penalty is a better deterrent than life imprisonment until we have *decisive* proof to the contrary (something we are unlikely to get). Chapter 3 evaluates an argument newly revived, one attacking the death penalty on grounds of inhumaneness. Chapter 3 also responds to criticism made of the argument of chapter 1 (and of an earlier version of the argument of chapter 3). Chapter 4 considers the proper role of physicians in executions (focusing on a recent innovation, lethal injection). Why should physicians object to participating in executions? What relation, if any, do those objections have to the moral status of the death penalty? Chapter 5 considers arguments for abolition resting on the supposed irrevocability of the death penalty. None of these arguments shows the death penalty to be more irrevocable than imprisonment.

Chapter 6 reviews the arguments for abolition that Hugo Bedau, the most important (and gifted) philosopher-abolitionist writing today, brought together in his recent *Death is Different* (1987). Though inventive in parts, as a whole *Death is Different* displays not the bounty of abolition's arsenal but its empty vaults and exhausted accounts. Chapter 6 is, however, not a mere review of old arguments for abolition; it offers as well an argument for the death penalty that Bedau (and almost everyone else) overlooks—that high penalties for other crimes makes death attractive as a way of distinguishing murder from lesser crimes. This argument from proportion provides a bridge from the (largely negative) first half of *Justice in the Shadow of Death* to the more positive—but much wider-ranging—second half.

The first six chapters together form a coherent critique of abolitionist arguments today. The second six make a start at understanding the criminal justice *system* with which arguments for or against the death penalty must reckon. Here considerations of desert become increasingly prominent, though death is never long out of sight.

The second half has two related purposes. One is to strengthen the analysis of the first half, especially the argument from proportion, by connecting it with a general theory of punishment. The other purpose is to provide a vocabulary for arguing for general reduction in punishments. Though few of the conclusions drawn in the second half are themselves controversial (among abolitionists at least), they are important nonetheless. They are important because the theory from which they are drawn is retributive (and retribution is often supposed to be what drives punishment toward severity). The second half offers a theory of punishment in which retribution is a "side constraint," requiring proportionate punishment but leaving legislators free to take many other considerations into account in setting maximum penalties.

Chapter 7, "Preventive Detention," argues that both preventive detention of the dangerous and medical quarantine presuppose a right to punishment (a response to Schoeman's well-known argument against such a right and the theory of criminal desert of which it is part). Among the conclusions to draw from this chapter is that we cannot justify execution as mere incapacitation. The criminal always has a right to punishment.

But do the insane? Chapter 8, "Guilty but Insane?" deals with the possibility of punishing the insane, arguing that, while conviction is morally permissible, punishment is not. The insane cannot deserve punishment.

Chapter 9, "Punishment as Language," considers the use of punishment to send a message. While every punishment carries certain information (for example, such-and-such an act was legally wrong), strictly speaking only statutes, judicial sentences, and other *linguistic* acts carry messages (for example, "Murder is punishable by death"). Neither sending a message nor transmitting information can, as such, justify otherwise unjustified punishment.

Chapter 10, "What Does Rape Deserve?" shows that treating individual crimes as part of a *system* of criminal justice having many distinct penalties and requiring some proportion between crime and penalty sets severe limits on what punishment can be deserved. Because rape is a form of battery, relative desert sets a low limit to its morally justifiable punishment. Rape cannot deserve death—or even penalties appropriate for murder, armed robbery, or arson of an occupied dwelling.

Chapter 11, "Punishing the Bad Samaritan," uses a somewhat different approach to explain why *allowing* death deserves less punishment than *causing* it. The argument makes clear that *lex talionis* has little or nothing to do with justifying criminal penalties. "Life for life" is a slogan, not an argument.

Chapter 12, "Criminal Desert," connects these last two chapters with my general theory of deserved punishment, clarifying a number of points and responding to recent criticism.

The conclusion I draw from these twelve chapters—and argue in chapter 6—is that while justice does not require that murder (or any other crime) be punished by death, considerations of justice (or at least of proportion and deterrence) do push in the direction of having the death penalty as the punishment for murder *once punishment for lesser crimes becomes sufficiently severe.* The purposes of the criminal law demand, or at least urge, a scale of penalties with enough steps to distinguish, for example, between aggravated murder and simple murder, murder and attempted murder, attempted murder and manslaughter. The steps should embody significant differences in severity. Where simple murder already gets life imprisonment (or its practical equivalent, say, a term of sixty years without parole), aggravated murder will seem to require the death penalty. Making a good case for eliminating the death penalty in a jurisdiction where other crimes are punished very severely probably presupposes drastically reducing other penalties. Since such a drastic reduction is unlikely until the rate of crime drops sharply (or until enough Americans come to understand how expensive high penalties can be and how little effect they have on the rate of crime), those who want the United States to join the better part of the world in abolishing the death penalty need to think hard about how to reduce crime, especially violent crime. Making arguments against the death penalty stronger seems to require changing both the arguments themselves and the context in which they are made; such changes seem, in turn, to require paying more attention than is commonly done to the *system* of criminal justice in which death is but one punishment among many.

One

Is Death the Most Effective Deterrent?

To deter is to turn away (by fear). To claim that death is the most effective deterrent is to claim that legal provision for a penalty of death *both* a) would (all else equal) turn any potential criminal from a crime if any penalty would *and* b) would (all else equal) turn some potential criminals from some crime when no other penalty would.

When people debate the justification of the death penalty, sooner or later, they almost inevitably argue "deterrence." Those favoring the death penalty argue that death deters better than life imprisonment (or some lesser term); those opposed, that it does not. Deterrence remains central to the debate over the death penalty; other considerations radiate from it like streets leading from a town's center. The argument for the death penalty that relies on deterrence—what I shall call *the argument from deterrence*—may be stated in this way:

1. The state should, all else equal, provide as penalty the most effective deterrent among those humanely available;
2. (The penalty of) death is the most effective deterrent (among those humanely available);
3. (The penalty of) death is humanely available:
4. All else is equal (for murder and perhaps for certain other crimes);

So: The state should provide death as penalty for murder (and perhaps for certain other crimes).

This chapter's subject is premise 2. I shall argue: that premise 2 requires a method of proof I call "the method of common sense"; that anyone who accepts the criminal law as a reasonable means of controlling certain human behavior ought to accept the method of common sense in the proof of premise 2; and that the method does prove death to be the most effective deterrent among those humanely available.

To admit that death is the most effective deterrent is, of course, not to admit that the death penalty is justified unless premises 1, 3, and 4 are also justified. In the next chapter, I shall survey prospects for justifying one or another of those three premises.

DETERRENCE AND COMMON SENSE

Debates over deterrence often go something like this: Those opposed to the death penalty appeal to the statistics of social science to prove that there is no established relation between statutory provisions for death and the actual rate of capital crime. Those favoring the death penalty respond, "So what? We don't need social science. Our claim is just plain common sense." That response earns nothing but unconcealed condescension from death-penalty opponents. To those who appeal to social science, the appeal to common sense sounds old-fashioned and therefore outmoded. Yet the debate over the death penalty has regularly taken this form at least since the French debated abolition in 1791.[1] *Both* appeals are old-fashioned. Some deep misunderstanding divides the two sides, leaving each talking almost entirely to its own.

Consider, for example, what Justice Brennan had to say about the argument from deterrence in a classic 1972 death-penalty case, *Furman v. Georgia*. Brennan's attack (the part of concern here) is clearly against premise 2. The attack has two stages. The first stage treats premise 2 as a claim to be supported by ordinary scientific evidence. There is, he points out, no such evidence. Comparative statistics give no reason to believe death a more effective deterrent than a long prison term.[2] (That is so, but the defense of premise 2 has rarely relied on such empirical evidence, though those attacking the death penalty usually suppose that it should.)

Having thus pushed through the outworks, Brennan reaches the citadel, common sense:

> The States argue, however, that they are entitled to rely upon common human experience, and that experience, they say, supports the conclusion that death must be a more effective deterrent than any less severe punishment. Because people fear death the most, the argument runs, the threat of death must be the greatest deterrent.[3]

Brennan treats this second defense as a continuation of the first (scientific) defense by other means. Though the claim is arguable, he does not deny that people fear death the most (supposing that torture and other inhumane penalties are not among the alternatives). He merely tries to explain why that fear does not appear from the evidence and why, therefore, it is irrelevant. He supposes he must explain away that "common human experience" because he does not know what else to do with it. He has two explanations: *First*, the defense makes an unrealistic assumption about potential criminals:

> [The] argument can only apply to . . . the rational person who will commit a capital crime knowing that the punishment is long-term imprisonment . . . but will not commit the crime knowing that the punishment is death. On the face of it, the assumption that such persons exist is implausible.[4]

Second, Brennan explains, the defense also makes an unrealistic assumption about the legal system:

> Proponents of this argument necessarily admit that its validity depends upon the existence of a system in which the punishment of death is invariably and swiftly imposed. Our system, of course, satisfies neither condition. . . . The risk of death is remote and improbable; in contrast, the risk of long-term imprisonment is near and great. . . . Whatever might be the case were all or substantially all eligible criminals quickly put to death, unverifiable possibilities are an insufficient basis upon which to conclude that the threat of death has any greater deterrent efficacy than the threat of imprisonment.[5]

Brennan is twice mistaken. The argument from deterrence is independent of the assumption that potential criminals calculate risk like graduates of a business school. Defenders need only assume that the threat of death will guide the action of a potential criminal somehow or other. The threat of death may give forbidden acts a special fearfulness that the less calculating appreciate without understanding. The threat of death may reinforce social practices that in turn steer the potential criminal away from even conceiving of the forbidden act. And so on. The argument's defenders have said as much many times.[6]

The argument from deterrence is also independent of the unrealistic assumption that our legal system (or any other) invariably and swiftly imposes death upon those guilty of capital crimes. The argument does perhaps assume that the death penalty is not mandatory upon conviction.—If it were mandatory, a potential criminal could rationally gamble that judge or jury would find him not guilty in order to escape having to condemn him to die.—However, except where there is a mandatory sentence of death (a possibility we may hereafter ignore), the potential criminal should look upon death as a risk to be added to the risk of imprisonment. The possibility of a (nonmandatory) death sentence, however improbable, is no more than one more bad consequence that may follow upon the crime. Where there is no death penalty for murder, he risks imprisonment. Where there is a death penalty for murder, he risks imprisonment or death. As long as death is worse than imprisonment, the risk of death, no matter how much smaller than the risk of imprisonment, adds to the reasons against committing a capital crime. A potential criminal may in fact ignore that risk, but he cannot rationally do so. Thus, Brennan's second explanation returns us to his first, the sense of assuming that the potential criminal will adjust his acts to accord with the threat of punishment (whether he does that consciously or not).

Though Brennan is twice mistaken, it does not much matter. The argument from deterrence does not gain its strength from either of the assumptions that Brennan foists on the defenders or even from the alternatives I mentioned. The argument no more needs armchair social science than it needs comparative statistics. The argument's strength is out of all proportion to the delicate evidence upon which such social science would have to found it. The argument stands like a granite wall set in bedrock: *Because people fear death the most, the threat of death must be the greatest deterrent.* Brennan's attack, like so many before it, rushes past that stronghold chasing a phantom.

All right, you say, let us admit that Brennan has misunderstood the argument from deterrence. How, then, is it to be understood? If premise 2 does not rest on the evidence of social science, on what does it rest? On what *could* it rest? My answer is "common sense." I must now explain how that can be.

SOCIAL SCIENCE OR COMMON SENSE?

Common sense (as I use that term here) does not name a source of knowledge different from that of social science. Common sense is not intuition or revelation. Both common sense and social science draw from the same well of human experience. The difference between them is like that between social science and judicial fact-finding, a difference in what is drawn and how it is drawn, a difference in method of noting and assessing experience. Each method serves certain human interests, but not even the method of social science can serve all. In this section I justify using common sense to establish the deterrent value of penalties. I do that in three steps. First, I describe the method of common sense. Second, I contrast it with the method of social science. And last, I show that, for purposes of criminal law, common-sense conclusions about deterrence serve better than those of social science.

The *method of common sense* is familiar. We ask ourselves what we would do if thus-and-so were true, what we would think if such-and-such happened, and so on. We do not have to pump the world for information. As long as we ask the right questions, the answers readily pour from us. Who is this "us"? What is it we do? This "us" is all of us, more or less, the same "us" that does science or follows rules. Common sense is *common* because we all share in it. But common sense is *sense* only because what we share is rationality. Rationality (as I use the term here) includes reason, that is, the capacity to observe, generalize, hypothesize, infer, plan, predict, and do those other calculated acts characteristic of both scientific research and everyday life. Rationality is, however, not only reasoning. The man who methodically sets about to maim himself with no further object is, though perhaps technically gifted and ultimately satisfied, not rational. He is mad. Besides reason, rationality includes certain basic evaluations, for example, that (all else equal) loss of limb, life, or freedom is to be avoided. What we, as rational persons, do is reason from those basic evaluations. That is the method of common sense.

The method is fallible. You and I make mistakes. The more complicated the reasoning, the more likely that we will err. We are well advised to compare our basic evaluations with those of others to make sure we have them right, and also well advised to open our reasoning to public examination. Multiplying reasoners, though it cannot make error impossible, can at least make it unlikely.

Though fallible, the method of common sense is neither unreliable nor "subjective." Consider an analogy. You and I both speak English. Sometimes what we say comes out gibberish. Sometimes we are mistaken about what we can correctly say. Our speech sometimes benefits from the criticism of others. Nevertheless, we are generally right about what is correct English. While the capacity to speak English does not guarantee performance in every case, it does guarantee it in general. Being a native speaker makes one an authority on what a native speaker would say. Being rational is a capacity like being an English speaker. The rational person's knowledge of what is rational is as reliable as her knowledge of her own language; rationality itself is no more "subjective" than language is. The method of common sense works well for the same reason the linguist finds that the best way to learn a language is to ask a native speaker what she would say. The rational person is in the same position with respect to what is rational that the native speaker is with respect to what it would be correct to say.

The particular truths of common sense are, therefore, at once conceptual and contingent. They are conceptual because they follow from premises all rational persons share. The premises include (beside the basic evaluations already mentioned) such facts about ourselves as everyone knows, for example, that we (both you and I) may be injured, that we plan, that we are rational, and that we may act upon our plans. The truths of common sense are nevertheless contingent insofar as the premises and principles of reasoning are no more necessary *a priori* than the principle of induction or the deep structure of human language. We could, it seems, have been beings who, though rational (in the sense explained above), would not come to know that others could suffer injuries, that we could plan, that we were rational, and so on.[7] The method of common sense yields knowledge of rational agents only insofar as we are rational agents and only because rational agents are what they are.

The *method of social science* is to assume nothing about those to be studied, to collect relevant data, and to draw only such conclusions as the data support. The social scientist pretends to be an outsider, to know nothing about the subject of research except what he culls from his data. While he may use his own experience to help plan research or formulate hypotheses, he must treat that experience as mere hunch or subjective impression. That pretence is what is supposed to make the method "value free." The collected data consist of records of "behavior," that is, of records of acts and events described as an outsider would describe them insofar as that is practical. The social scientist may simply gather existing records of behavior (police records of suicides, homicides, and so on) or may actively generate data by taking surveys or staging experiments. Because the data are in terms of behavior, the conclusions drawn from the data must be too. Social science (so described) is merely a science of behavior. Its standard of proof is both difficult to satisfy and highly specialized.

I do not claim this description of social science accurately describes social science generally. While a positivist might not object to that calumny, all I claim is that I have accurately described the method of social science implicit in much of what the opponents of the death penalty say. Consider, for example, the following passage from H. L. A. Hart's discussion of the argument from deterrence.

> If we turn from the statistical evidence to the other "evidence," the latter really amounts simply to the alleged truism that men fear death more than any other penalty, and that therefore it must be a stronger deterrent than imprisonment. . . ."[8]

The use of the word "scientific" or "empirical," like Hart's contrast between statistical evidence and the (scare-quoted) "evidence" of common sense, is a sure sign that the special method of social science is being treated as the only appropriate one.

The method of social science is, however, only appropriate for some questions. For example, suppose that you make "Brand X" bagels and want to increase sales. You want people to ask for your bagels, put money on the counter, and walk off, bagels in hand. You do not care why they do it as long as they do; you would as soon have them do it for bad reasons as for good. You do not even care whether the buyers would have to be mad to pay your price so long as you can get them to do it. You are concerned only with getting a certain behavior. If that is all you are concerned about, then the method of social science may be just what you need.

Suppose instead that you are a linguist about to study a human language. To be a linguist is to assume that those you study have a capacity for language. To go somewhere to study a certain language is to assume that the language spoken there is one you can learn. The linguist is never altogether an outsider. Because she knows a good deal about her own language (as well as those she has already studied as a linguist), she begins work on her next language with at least one foot in the door. Pretending otherwise would be a waste of time. Perhaps the method of social science would, in time, approximate the results that the linguist's method gets much sooner. Whether that is actually so is a tangled question in philosophy of language that I need not unravel here. My point is simply that, whatever might in time be possible, using the method of social science instead of the linguist's method would be a waste of time. If what you want is to learn the language as soon as possible, the method of social science is not what you need. What you need is to ask a native speaker what he would say.

Which method is preferable for deciding the deterrent value of penalties? The method of social science may at first seem preferable. After all, are we not, like the bagel-maker, concerned only with getting certain behavior? Do we care why people obey the law so long as they do? If raising the penalty for breaking a certain law would mean fewer crimes, would we not have a reason to raise the penalty? And if raising the penalty had no visible effect, could we justify the higher penalty? The method of social science seemingly tells us just what we need to know. The method of common sense seems, in contrast, to offer only (in

Justice Brennan's words) "unverifiable possibilities" or (in Hart's words) "alleged truisms." Seeming, unfortunately, does not make it so. The method of social science seems preferable only while we see the criminal law as nothing more than a system for controlling behavior generally. The instant we notice that it is more than that, that it is a particular system for controlling a special kind of behavior, social science no longer seems preferable to common sense.

The criminal law is a system for controlling the acts of rational agents by making certain acts rationally less appealing. Criminal laws differ from laws that simply provide for official action if something happens (for example, a health law requiring quarantine of anyone with contagious tuberculosis). The criminal law is supposed to consist of rules that a potential criminal can follow or not as she chooses. Every criminal law has a penalty for its violation. The penalty is supposed to give the potential criminal a reason to follow the rule. The potential criminal is supposed to be someone who, though perhaps immoral and heartless, can still recognize the penalty as a reason for not violating the law. If we do not think of the potential criminal as someone who can be guided by law and penalty, we are at a loss to justify any punishment whatever. We can, of course, justify something like punishment, for example, sending the law-breaker to a mental hospital as if she were insane, or caging her as if she were a wild animal, or disposing of her altogether as if she were a rabid dog. We cannot, however, justify fining a law-breaker, warning her, or locking her up for a set time only to turn her loose again whatever she was or has become. The criminal law makes no sense unless we suppose the potential criminal to be more or less rational. On that at least, both deterrence theorists and retributive theorists have always agreed.

Indeed, even reform theorists agree that the criminal law makes that supposition. It is for just that supposition that they criticize the criminal law. Beneath debate of the death penalty swim luminous doubts about the criminal law as we know it. The same statistics that fail to show death to deter better than long imprisonment also fail to show long imprisonment to deter better than brief imprisonment. I shall not fish up those doubts here. The purpose of this chapter is to clarify the argument from deterrence. Both those who make the argument and most of those who attack it accept the criminal law as is, agree that certain penalties deter better than others, and disagree only about whether death deters better than any alternative penalty. While they do not think social order depends entirely on the criminal law, they do think that the criminal law makes a substantial contribution. Still, since doubts are easier to extinguish than to evade, let me briefly make four points to clarify how relatively uncontroversial should be the claim that the potential criminal is rational.

First, the claim is not that all *lawbreakers* are rational. We may admit that some lawbreakers are insane (or otherwise incompetent). The admission merely commits us to controlling those lawbreakers differently than the rest. We commit ourselves to excluding them (more or less) from criminal justice (although, as we shall see in chapter 8, this is a more complicated matter than is commonly supposed). The sane may be punished; the insane may not. We need not claim that rational persons constitute any particular percentage of potential or actual lawbreakers.

Second, we need not claim that people have "free will." We may admit (for what it's worth) that we are all prey to the dance of atoms, that the perfect physicist could predict our every motion, or that society makes us what we are. We need claim only that the prospect of penalty is a factor that may help to guide a potential criminal away from this or that prohibited act.

Third, we need not claim that only the prospect of penalty keeps rational persons from committing crimes. We may admit that there are other good reasons to obey the law (for example, the opinion of one's neighbor or the lack of opportunity or motive). We may also admit that habit, superstition, awe of authority, and other blind sentiments help to keep us law-abiding even when we do not stop to think. The judge does not wear his long black robe in vain. We may even accept the distinction between good citizen and potential criminal. The good citizen would obey the law (for good reason or from blind sentiment) even absent a penalty for disobeying. The potential criminal would disobey if there were not some penalty (and some chance of suffering it). Though the distinction between good citizen and potential criminal is probably relative to the law in question, we may admit that any society with many potential criminals will have trouble keeping order. What we must claim is that a rational person *could* commit a crime. The proof of that is easy enough. We have only to examine ourselves to find someone who would, though rational, break the law *under easily imaginable circumstances* if either the penalty itself or the risk of suffering it were not sufficiently high. Some of us, perhaps, have even contemplated murder.

Fourth, we need not claim that a criminal *act* must be rational for the agent to be subject to punishment. Rational agents sometimes act irrationally; that is, they do what they have good reason not to do, because they did not stop to think, because they misjudged the chance of capture, or because they did not appreciate the penalty. Such persons remain fit subjects of punishment because they should not have done the act even if there were no penalty (or no chance of suffering it). They cannot complain because *they* miscalculated. "Okay, I made a mistake: I should have known I couldn't get away with that!" is an admission of guilt, not a plea of excuse. Such miscalculation is not to be confused with temporary inability to act rationally (for example, when acting under posthypnotic suggestion) or reduced ability to reason (for example, when acting under extreme provocation). Such inability constitutes full or partial excuse exactly insofar as it could lead anyone, good citizen as well as potential criminal, to commit the crime.

Since the criminal law presupposes that the potential criminal is rational, it presupposes as well that we have much in common with him. He shares with us certain basic evaluations, and he can reason as we do. We can assess options as he can, plan as he can, and even act as he can. We may reasonably ask ourselves what we would do if such-and-such and expect an answer that is also the answer of the potential criminal. To accept the criminal law as a reasonable means of social control is then to presuppose that we are in a position to use the method of common sense to determine the deterrent value of penalties. Rationality is itself the "common human experience" upon which the argument from deterrence is supposed to rely. The only question remaining is whether we should prefer the method of common sense to the method of social science. There are, I think, at least four reasons why we should:

First, social science has nothing conclusive to report. The findings of social science to date—"no established correlation between death penalty and murder rate"—are consistent with any findings common sense is likely to make.[9] The inability of social science to establish a correlation does not entail the inability of other methods of discovery to do better. The method of social science has no monopoly on knowledge about what rational agents will do.

Second, social science is admittedly working under conditions unfavorable to it. The data are rough and incomplete, consisting as much of police reports of crime as of judicial sentences and official announcements of executions. Categories of crime vary from jurisdiction to jurisdiction, from period to period. The rate at which crimes get reported varies as well. There have been few surveys and no controlled experiments. Statistical analysis requires controversial assumptions about the independence of variables.[10]

Third, social scientists are not now in position to interpret better data even if they had it. There is no adequate theory of society. Social scientists would not know how to distinguish the effect on their data produced by a change in statutory penalty from the effect produced by a change in rates of reporting crime, by a change in knowledge of penalty, by a change in the pool of potential criminals, by a change in success of prosecution, or by a change in any number of other factors. Social scientists do not even know all the factors to check for. All they know is how to start searching out such things and, even so, they do not know how long the search will take.

Last, there is no reason to believe that, when social scientists have better data and are in position to control for extraneous factors, they will come to conclusions about rational agents inconsistent with those that the method of common sense yields now. An inconsistency between the method of social science and that of common sense is no more to be expected than an inconsistency between the method of social science and that of the linguist. The method of common sense is, after all, conceptual. The most the method of social science could show is that potential lawbreakers are never rational (an unlikely discovery) or that the pool of potential criminals is much smaller than commonly supposed (a less unlikely discovery). No such discovery would undermine the claims of common sense about what it is rational to do, though it would make those claims of less practical importance. Social science does have a special place in the debate over the death penalty. But as I shall explain in chapter 2, that place is premise 4, not premise 2. The discoveries of social science cannot affect the findings of common sense concerning what would deter rational agents.

When we consider how little the method of social science has to offer, we must conclude that the method would have no appeal here were it not for a misunderstanding of the method of common sense. I have, I hope, now cleared up that misunderstanding. If so, we are ready to examine the defense of premise 2 ("Because people fear death the most, the threat of death is the greatest deterrent"). If I have not yet cleared up that misunderstanding, perhaps the following will. What better way to see that the method of common sense works than to see it at work?

COMMON SENSE ON DEATH

In this section, I apply the method of common sense to the defense of premise 2. The method applies to people only insofar as they are rational agents (just as the linguist's method applies to people only insofar as they are speakers of the language under study). I must therefore restate the defense of premise 2 so that it is explicitly an argument about rational agents. Here is that restatement:

2a. Rational agents fear their own death more than any other evil (that is, any rational agent would prefer any other evil if given a choice between it and death);[11]

2b. If rational agents most fear a certain evil, they would (all else equal) do their best to avoid it (that is, each rational agent would try to avoid that evil where he would try to avoid every other and also sometimes where he would not try to avoid every other);

2c. If rational agents would do their best to avoid an evil, making that evil the penalty for a crime would (all else

equal) turn each rational agent from that crime if any
penalty would and would (all else equal) turn some
rational agents from that crime even if no other penalty
would;

2d. If making an evil the penalty for a crime would have
that effect, that penalty is the most effective deterrent;

So: Death is the most effective deterrent.

The defense is now an argument about rational agents, not actual people. The argument is valid. Is it sound? Premises 2b and
2d are unobjectionable. Premise 2b is true because (all else equal)
suffering an evil that one could avoid without suffering one as
bad or worse would be irrational. Premise 2d simply restates the
definition of "the most effective deterrent" given above. But while
premises 2b and 2d seem unobjectionable, premises 2a and 2c
do not. Let us now consider what objections might be made to
them and how good those objections are, beginning with premise
2a.

The first objection to premise 2a is that, as stated, it is false.
Death is not the greatest evil. Death combined with any other
evil is worse than death alone. A rational agent would, for example, prefer immediate death to death by slow, painful torture.
More important, a rational agent may prefer death to some evils
not involving death. We have only to think of the living dead of
Dachau: on one side, hard labor, beatings, hunger, hopeless waiting, the steady contraction of humanity; on the other, quick death
on an electrified fence. Who would say that those who chose the
fence acted irrationally? Here rational people may disagree about
what it is better to do. What, then, are we to make of the claim
that rational agents fear their own death more than any other
evil?[12]

Obviously, the claim must have a limiting context. The alternative to death cannot include death by slow, painful torture,
confinement in a concentration camp, or any other radically inhumane punishment. That, indeed, is the context in which debate over the death penalty goes on. The alternatives to death
range only from several years to life in a relatively humane pris-

on. We may, then, escape this first objection simply by rewriting premise 2a to make that context explicit:

2a'. Rational agents fear their own death more than any other evil *humanely available as penalty.*

(Rewriting premise 2a in this way will, of course, mean that the conclusion will have to be rewritten accordingly; hence, the second set of parentheses in my initial statement of premise 2.)

There is another objection to premise 2a. We may put it this way: Is it irrational to prefer death to life in prison? Arguably not. Death, at least, is the end of trouble. Life in prison is an indefinite childhood under harsh rules, in bad company, and without privacy, family, or future. Consider how you would choose if you had two lives before you: a life of thirty years ending with death by electrocution; or the same life until age thirty followed by fifty years more, all in prison. Are you sure you would not choose death at thirty? Is there any decisive reason why you should not? Surely (the objection concludes), here too rational agents may disagree about which to choose.

This second objection is wellfounded but beside the point. The objection is wellfounded because common sense has little to say about comparative value. The only settled cases are extreme. It would, for example, certainly be irrational (all else equal) to prefer death to a pin prick. Every rational agent would agree that the mild pain of an instant is the lesser evil. The problem here is that we are not comparing a great evil with a small one. We are comparing two great evils, death and life-long loss of freedom. Common sense does not say which to prefer. A rational agent may prefer either. The objection is nevertheless beside the point because we should not be comparing these two evils. Death has a property that life in prison does not: finality. The objection presents life in prison as if the whole fifty years were as final as death. The fifty years in prison are, of course, not final until the last year is served. In the meantime, the prisoner might escape, die, be pardoned, or in some other way not serve out her term. The same, it must be observed, is not true of death. The sentence of death, executed in an instant, is thereafter final.

That observation, though often made, is as often misunderstood. Thus, Brennan says:

> The unusual severity of death is manifested most clearly in its finality and enormity. Death, in these respects, is in a class by itself. . . . Death forecloses even the possibility [of regaining the right to have rights].[13]

The severity of death as a penalty is not, as Brennan says, merely "manifested" in its finality. The finality is almost all there is to death. Take that away, and the "enormity" disappears, too. A little science fiction should make this clear. Imagine a world where it is possible to put a person in a box that suspends his mental activity while permitting his body to age normally and his mental activity to resume once he has left the box (if he leaves the box before his natural death). The criminal penalties in that world, let us suppose, include (beside death and imprisonment as we know them) the novel penalty of suspension of mental activity for life. Obviously, choosing death over suspension would (all else equal) not be rational. Suspension is the rational choice because the only difference between suspension and death is that suspension holds out the hope of pardon, parole, or other clemency while death does not. Is it not equally obvious, then, that prison would have to be a relatively comfortable place before choosing it over suspension could be rational? Insofar as prison is bearable only because it holds out the hope of coming to an end, suspension is preferable, holding out the hope without the burden.

This observation suggests yet another objection to premise 2a, the last I shall consider here: Even if we compare the penalty of death (remembering its finality) with the penalty of life in prison (remembering its tentativeness), we cannot conclude that preferring death to prison is irrational. We could, perhaps, draw that conclusion if the world were somewhat different—if, that is, prisons today were the reformatories described in our high-school civics texts. One would, indeed, have to be irrational to prefer death to a gentle detention hardly worse overall than a pin prick. However, prisons today, though varying widely, are never that gentle, and the worst are terrifying. A prisoner may have to live in an overcrowded cell, eat bad food, and do hard, boring labor.

He may live in fear that the guards will torture him, that his fellow prisoners will rape him, or that he will be caught in a war between prison gangs. Life in prison can (so the objection runs) be lonely, grim, futile, oppressive, and ultimately crushing. What does it matter that the prisoner might get out some day if that day is at least years away and might well never arrive?[14] The enormity of death hardly exceeds the enormity of such imprisonment.

This last objection, like the one before it, is at once wellfounded and beside the point. The objection is wellfounded because choosing death instead of prison is not always irrational, even taking into account the tentativeness of prison. The objection is nevertheless beside the point because what makes prison a lesser penalty than death is just that a prisoner *can* choose death instead of prison while the dead can*not* choose prison instead of death. The finality of death cuts off choice; the tentativeness of prison does not. If a prisoner comes to prefer death to prison, he can (in any ordinary prison) find a way to kill himself (or at least to get himself killed). He therefore has a guarantee that being sent to prison will never be worse than being put to death.[15] Death is his benchmark, the known position from which he can survey life. A rational agent most fears the penalty of death not because he most fears death itself, but because the penalty of death takes from him something no other (humane) penalty can. Any (humane) penalty other than death leaves him two options, that penalty or death, but the penalty of death leaves him to choose between death and death. Any rational person would (all else equal) prefer to have more choice than that.

We should, then, rewrite premise 2a' to make clear that our concern is not death itself but the *penalty* of death:

2a". Rational agents fear *the penalty of* death more than any other evil humanely available as penalty.

(Rewriting premise 2a' in this way will, of course, mean another rewriting of the conclusion; hence, the first set of parentheses in the original premise 2.)

Premise 2a (now 2a") is therefore unobjectionable after all. What of premise 2c ("If rational agents would do their best to avoid a certain evil, threatening that evil as penalty for a crime would turn each rational agent from that crime if any penalty would and would turn some rational agents from that crime even if no other penalty would")? There are two objections: one concerns what the potential criminal *can* appreciate (her capacities), the other, what she *would* appreciate (her performance). I shall discuss the objections in that order.

The *objection from capacity* might be put this way: The threat of death is too remote to be distinguished from the threat of life imprisonment. Even a rational agent can, it seems, handle only so much information, can make only so many discriminations, and so cannot be expected to tune his acts as finely as the legislature can tune its penalties. At the moment before he acts, the potential criminal has to take into account the chances of capture, indictment, and conviction, the vagaries of sentencing, the hope of appeal, pardon, or parole, the possibility of escape, and so on. The distinction between life imprisonment and death *must* (so the objection runs) sink from sight in such a welter of considerations, the inevitable consequence of any system of criminal justice. If life imprisonment would not turn the potential criminal from his crime, neither would death. The potential criminal is, under the circumstances, incapable of seeing the distinction.

This objection must be understood within the context of the criminal law. Gradation of penalty is essential to that law. Every system of criminal law today makes distinctions like that between one-year imprisonment and two, one-to-ten years imprisonment and one-to-twenty, one-to-twenty years imprisonment and life. The lower penalty is assigned to the less serious crime. The gradation of penalty is supposed to give the potential criminal a reason to prefer the lesser of two crimes should she have the opportunity to choose between the lesser and the greater. The distinction between life imprisonment and death is one gradation among many, but it is *not* like these others. The other distinctions are distinctions of degree. The distinction between life imprisonment and death is more like a distinction in order of magnitude. The penalty of death is, as explained above, necessarily worse than life imprisonment (no matter how bad life in prison is in fact), because the penalty of death takes from the convicted criminal the power to choose between death and any number of years in prison. To suppose that such a distinction *must* sink from sight is, it seems to me, either to call into question all gradation of penalty or to promise to justify gradation of penalty without deterrence.[16] At least three reasons, each sufficient, require us to reject that supposition and to maintain that some potential criminals can sometimes make the distinction between life imprisonment and death when deciding to commit a crime:

First, the distinction between life imprisonment and death is not always a fine distinction. To the criminal who is serving a life sentence, for example, the distinction between a *second* life sentence and a death sentence would, of course, be as crude as can be. To argue that no potential criminal could make that distinction seems (to turn Justice Brennan's phrase against him) "on the face . . . implausible." Indeed, it is inconsistent with what we, as potential criminals, know we can do.

Second, the distinction between life imprisonment and death is cruder than distinctions we make all the time amid a storm of considerations no worse than that which might toss a potential criminal. Think what you take into account, for example, when deciding to cancel a life-insurance policy, when choosing between buying a house and renting an apartment, or when considering several job offers. The objection must either portray us as unable to make the fine distinctions necessary for the long-term planning we in fact do or exclude us from the class of potential criminals. Either way, the objection would require us to suppose what we know to be false.

Third, a lawbreaker incapable of making the distinction between life imprisonment and death when deciding to commit a crime would (all else equal) not be a criminal at all. Anyone so feeble-minded (or so steadily and irresistibly preoccupied) that he *could not* take into account that distinction would also be incapable of taking into account most or all gradations of penalty within the criminal law. He would be deaf to its threats. He would not be insane; nor would he necessarily be incompetent in the strict sense. He might be able to manage his everyday life satisfactorily. He would nevertheless be someone to be excluded from criminal justice. His breaking any important law would show his bad character. His inability to distinguish one penalty from another would show him to be someone who might commit several crimes if he committed one and the worst crime as easily as a bad one. He would be a dangerous animal. There would be nothing to do with him but lock him up in some "place of safety," keeping him there until he was no longer dangerous. The objection from capacity assimilates all persons potentially guilty of a capital crime to this special case. The objection leads to an absurdity.

The second objection to premise 2c, *the objection from performance*, is that though some potential criminals may in fact be capable of making the distinction between life imprisonment and death when deciding to commit a crime, there is no reason to believe any *ever* would. The objection must (as an objection to premise 2c) take this extreme form. "Often" or "usually" will not do. If there were only one case where (all else equal) a potential criminal would exercise his capacity to make that distinction and would be turned from a crime because he did not want to risk the death penalty, but would not be turned from the crime by any lesser penalty, the death penalty would (by definition) deter more effectively than any other and premise 2 would be secure.

We cannot, however, respond to the objection by fetching such a case. That would take us beyond the method of common sense (take us, that is, from what everyone knows to what some are privileged to find out). Nor can we respond that the objection makes such an extreme claim that it is unlikely to be true, that a claim's being unlikely is a reason for believing otherwise, and that therefore there is a reason to believe that potential criminals would sometimes distinguish between life imprisonment and death and act accordingly. Such a response is as certain as the probabilities upon which it rests. If the probability is ordinary probability, it is subject to change and so not something all rational persons would agree about. We would again have stepped beyond common sense. If, on the other hand, the probability is somehow conceptually necessary, it would be necessary to explain how that can be.

Common sense provides another response (dependent only on what we mean by "capacity"): Claiming that there is often a slip between capacity and performance is one thing; claiming that there always *would* be is quite another. The former claim might well be true, but the latter is *necessarily* false. To talk of a capacity to do *x* (in certain circumstances) that has yet to be realized makes sense. A startling series of misfortunes might cause such a state of affairs. To talk of the same capacity as one that never *will* be realized, though raising problems of proof, still seems to make sense. To talk this way would be to project that startling series of misfortunes forward until the end of time. But to talk about the same capacity as one that never *would* be realized is fundamentally different. To talk about a capacity to do *x* that never would be realized is to talk about a capacity to do *x* that is *not* a capacity to do *x*. The objection from performance relies upon that contradiction.

The objection from performance is, I think, actually not an objection to premise 2 but part of an objection to premise 4. As part of an objection to premise 4, it may well be stated with "often," "usually," or some weaker term; and, so stated, it is both plausible and important to arguments concerned with the net cost of the death penalty (as we shall see in chapter 2). Premise 2 is secure. We may turn to the rest of the argument from deterrence.

NOTES

I read the first draft of this chapter before the Philosophy Colloquium, Illinois State University, 13 September 1978 and parts of the second and third sections of a later draft before a session of the Conference on Capital Punishment, Atlanta, Georgia, 19 April 1980. I should like to thank those present at the two readings for many helpful comments. I should also like to thank Nelson Potter and certain anonymous referees at *Ethics* for their detailed criticism of the penultimate draft.

1. Finn Hornum, "Two Debates: France, 1791; England, 1956," in *Capital Punishment*, ed. Thorsten Sellin (New York: Harper & Row, 1967), 62–64, 68–69.

2. *Furman v. Georgia*, 408 U.S. 238, 92 S. Ct. 2726 (1972), 301–303.

3. *Furman v. Georgia*, 301.

4. *Furman v. Georgia*, 302.

5. *Furman v. Georgia*, 302.

6. See, for example, Ernest van den Haag, "On Deterrence and the Death Penalty," *Ethics* 78 (July 1968); 280–289, or John Stuart

Mill, "Speech in Favor of Capital Punishment," in *Philosophy of Law*, ed. Joel Feinberg and Hyman Gross (Encino, California: Dickenson Publishing Company, 1975), 620–621. If some of these "sociological" defenses seem to appeal to so-called "non-deterrent preventive effects" (for example, reenforcing social practices), I can only say that there is nothing in the "sociological" form of the argument from deterrence to require the fear of death to operate through any particular mechanism. For a strong attack on van den Haag's (and so on Mill's) statistical argument, see Hugo Adam Bedau, "The Death Penalty as Deterrent—Argument and Evidence," *Ethics* 81 (April 1972): 205–217. For an attack on van den Haag's betting argument, see David A. Conway, "Capital Punishment and Deterrence," *Philosophy and Public Affairs* 3 (Summer 1974): 431–443. Such attacks make clear how delicate the "sociological" arguments are (and how easy it is to confuse them with the argument from common sense) while leaving the argument from common sense untouched.

7. Bernard Gert has argued that the content of rationality is a good deal less contingent than I have made it out to be here. I find his argument at least tempting. See his *The Moral Rules* (Harper Torchbooks: New York, 1973), 23–25 and 164–171.

8. H. L. A. Hart, "Murder and the Principles of Punishment: England and the United States," *Northwestern Law Review* 52 (September 1957): 458. If this quotation leaves any doubt about whether Hart believes the "*alleged* truisms" of common sense to be at all plausible, the context does not.

9. Compare *Furman v. Georgia*, 456–458. The Supreme Court's discussions of the statistical evidence (not only this one discussion but those of all the justices in *Furman*) are, compared to Hart's, so sloppy as to be almost embarrassing to read.

10. For an interesting description of the problems associated with such data, even within a single state, see Hugo Adam Bedau, *Death is Different* (Boston: Northeastern University Press, 1987), 195–216.

11. By "fear" I mean a recognition that a certain state, event, or outcome is positively undesirable, dangerous, or otherwise something to be avoided because of what it is. Fear (in this sense) does not necessarily involve agitation, panic, or any other distress beyond the mere apprehension of the possibility of suffering what one does not want to suffer. The expression in parentheses is, then, supposed to be a paraphrase of premise 2a. The argument from deterrence, as I understand it, is primarily a conceptual argument, not a psychological or sociological argument. It is important to keep the human's fear (which belongs to premise 4) distinct from the rational agent's fear (which belongs here in premise 2).

12. Rational people also disagree about whether their own death or that of someone they care about—a parent, friend, or child—would be worse. I ignore this sort of disagreement here not because I suppose people to be egoists generally but because the question before us, the effectiveness of death as a penalty, does not implicate other people directly. No humane system of punishment has open to it the choice of putting someone to death or punishing him in some way through those he cares about. In a humane system of punishment, vicarious punishment is always marginal, involving minor crimes and light penalties.

13. *Furman*, 289–290. Brennan, it should be noted, overstates his point. Even the dead have some rights, for example, the right to a decent burial, the right to have their will carried out, and the right to survival of an action in tort. Whatever the death penalty does deprive one of, it does not deprive one of the right to have rights. I shall have more to say on this point in chapter 5.

14. For a helpful discussion of the problems that a rational person may face when trying to choose between death and a set of relatively unsatisfactory prospects, see Richard B. Brandt, "The Morality and Rationality of Suicide," in *A Handbook for the Study of Suicide*, ed. Seymour Perlin (New York: Oxford University Press, 1975), 61–76. For an analysis of what makes death an evil similar to the one I give here, see L. S. Summer, "A Matter of Life and Death," *Nous* 10 (May 1976): 153–163. I came upon Summer's article only after I had completed the first draft of the paper out of which this chapter grew. The independence of our work provides additional support for our common conclusion.

15. This is not, as Justice Brennan would perhaps think, a question of rights. There is no legal right to kill oneself, much less a legal right to get oneself killed. The availability of death is merely a fact about the regime of most prisons, a fact that perhaps cannot be changed without invading the few legal rights prisoners have, but a mere fact all the same. My point about choosing death has nothing directly to do with Brennan's point about "the right to have rights."

16. Even a retributivist cannot, I believe, justify the schedule of penalties without appeal to deterrence. To say this is not, let me add, to say that retributive theory is just a confused form of the utilitarian theory of punishment. I certainly would not say that. For my reasons, see chapter 12 below and my *To Make the Punishment Fit the Crime* (Boulder: Westview Press, 1992), chapter 4.

Two

The Rest of the Argument
from Deterrence

Chapter 1 kept clear of premises 1, 3, and 4 for a reason. Those three premises belong more to issues other than deterrence. To have entered upon other premises before we finished with premise 2 would only have complicated what was already complicated enough. Now, finished with premise 2, we may safely go to the others. My purpose is not, however, as it was for premise 2, to prove these other premises true (or false). Premise 2 states a conceptual truth in need of proof. The others either state conceptual truths in no need of proof or raise issues too complex to settle here. My purpose in discussing the other premises here is simply to distinguish the difficulty of attack on them from the difficulty of attack on premise 2; to show that certain attacks are more likely to succeed than others; and to point out what must be done before there can be a successful attack. This is a scouting mission, not a full-scale assault. I shall discuss the three premises in order.

WHAT SHOULD THE STATE DO?

Premise 1 seems to make two claims: *first*, that it is morally permissible for the state, all else equal, to provide as penalty the most effective deterrent among those humanely available; and *second*, that it is prudent for the state to provide such penalties. Premise 1 must be understood to make some claim about what is morally proper because the argument from deterrence is in part an argument *against* the claim that the death penalty is immoral. Premise 1 need not be understood to claim more than moral permissibility. Few defenders of the death penalty take the position that a government—such as that of the United Kingdom or the State of Michigan—that does not have the death penalty is failing to do something morally required of it. Instead, they generally take the position that moral considerations do not decide the question of whether to retain or abolish the death penalty. Morality permits the death penalty; other considerations, especially preventing crime, make the death penalty attractive.[1] Premise 1, then, must also be understood to make a claim about what is prudent. Otherwise, given our understanding of its moral content, its "should" would be pointless.

So understood, premise 1 seems entirely unobjectionable. Everyone but an anarchist would agree that the state should, *all else equal*, provide as penalty the most effective deterrent among those humanely available. Even the anarchist would object to the state itself rather than to the state's choice of punishment. Premise 1 is just a special case of a conceptual truth in no need of proof (that, all else equal, we should use for a good end the best means permitted). When there are doubts about premise 1, they are roused by the two weasel phrases "all else equal" and "humanely available." I shall postpone discussion of the first phrase until I come to premise 4 ("all else is equal"). I shall say something about the second now.

A penalty may be humanely unavailable either *absolutely* (by being too cruel to be used for any crime) or only *relatively* (by being too cruel for this crime but not for all, that is, by being out of proportion to the crime). Since I intend the phrase "humanely available" to mean "absolutely humanely available," I may postpone discussion of absolute unavailability until premise 3 ("Death is humanely available"). The doubt I shall discuss now concerns only relative unavailability and may be put this way: Premise 1 would be false if there could be a penalty that is both the most effective deterrent and not absolutely inhumane but still out of proportion to even the worst crime possible under the legal system in question.

There could, it seems, be such a penalty. Consider, for example, a system of criminal law prohibiting *only* various forms of theft (the worst being theft of a large sum without the use of force). Suppose the penalty for the worst form of theft were death.

Surely (it will be said), death for theft, even in that system, would be out of proportion to the crime (whatever we may think of death as a penalty for murder in our own system). If so (the doubt concludes), premise 1 must be false.

That doubt is not worth pursuing. To make anything of it, we would have to argue that even in a legal system like our own, one not radically truncated, the harshest penalty could be out of proportion to the worst crime. There are two reasons not to argue that.

First, the argument would require us to prove that proportion is independent of deterrence (a respectable retributivist view), that there is a standard of proportion independent even of the structure of a legal system like ours (a less common but still respectable retributivist view), and that such a standard is also independent of absolute inhumanity (a dubious view indeed).

Second, if having to argue all that were not bad enough, we would also have to find another example. The one above seems to work only because the legal system in question is radically incomplete. The system does not prohibit most of those acts that people fear (for example, deliberate and unjustified maiming, torture, kidnapping, and killing). Of course we can explain why death is too harsh a penalty even for the worst crime in that system. We need only complete the list of crimes (by borrowing from *our* criminal law), assign appropriate (absolutely humane) penalties to the new crimes, and then observe that theft was assigned a penalty worse than crimes considered worse. When, however, a system is complete enough to punish murder, we could not say that death as a penalty is out of proportion to murder (though we might still say that the penalty is absolutely inhumane). If the law of retaliation has any appeal, it is when the "worst evil" (murder) is given the "worst penalty" (a sentence of death). Further, even if we were willing to say that the death penalty is out of proportion to murder, we could not explain why as we did before. Having assigned worst to worst already, we would have exhausted what we need to show disproportion. We would have to find a new way to show it or keep quiet.

Since debate over the death penalty normally concerns (relatively) complete legal systems, and since the argument from deterrence may reasonably be read as taking such completeness for granted, there is no point to challenging premise 1 by examples from incomplete systems. Since there does not seem to be much to say about relative inhumanity within a complete legal system that assigns the worst penalties to the worst crimes, and there is no third point of attack, premise 1 seems safe. (If I seem to have been too quick with proportion, notice that I deal with it again later in this chapter.)

IS DEATH HUMANELY AVAILABLE?

Everyone seems to agree that what is humane changes but not on why it changes. Some explain the changes by "progress." But progress hardly explains why, for example, mutilation and torture spread through Europe as the Middle Ages *ended*.[2] Others explain the changes by what people are themselves willing to suffer. They do not, however, tell us why people are willing to suffer a certain evil one year and not the next. Nor do they tell us why, for example, we consider flogging inhumane when most of us would prefer fifteen or thirty lashes of the whip to life imprisonment. Still others explain the changes in what counts as humane by changes in what judges and juries are willing to do to others. But they do not tell us why such fashions exist. Nor do they explain why debate over humaneness usually takes for granted that judges and juries should do as the debate decides.

For us, the importance of such disagreements is that they affect the argument from deterrence. Disagreement in what explains changes in humaneness reappears as disagreement in how to decide whether death is inhumane. I shall therefore suggest another explanation of the changes in our conception of inhumaneness. Unlike the others, this explanation, if correct, will tell us why we do not today agree about whether death is inhumane, why we think it important that we should agree, and when we shall come to agree. The explanation will do that at some cost, however. If I am right, the dispute over the humaneness of death may *today* not be subject to rational resolution.

Humaneness is, I think, a function of shock. We do not object to a penalty simply because of what it is. The penalty, considered as a physical act—a certain quantity of pain or harm—never changes, though our objections do. Nor do we object to a penalty because of what we are willing to suffer. We are sometimes willing to suffer inhumane penalties ourselves (for example, a few lashes of the whip to avoid long imprisonment). We seem to object to a penalty as inhumane only when use of that penalty on anyone, especially someone else (against his will), shocks us; when, that is, we cannot comfortably bear its general use. Shock, of course, is neither rational nor irrational. The person who is not shocked by what shocks everyone else is eccentric, insensitive, or callous—but not necessarily irrational. We think he needs to let go more, to feel more, or to live better, not to be cured or caged. Shock at this or that is not a basic evaluation all rational persons must share; nor is it the inevitable consequence of what all rational persons share. Blood pouring from a bull's neck will not shock a butcher, though a Hindu might faint at the sight. What shocks us seems to be a consequence of how we live, of what we do and do not experience.

Though I may say a penalty is inhumane because it shocks me, a penalty is not inhumane just because *I* am shocked. To say a penalty is inhumane is to claim much more. If I think a penalty is inhumane, I expect you—and everyone else—to be as shocked by it as I am. I am surprised, even bewildered, when I find my expectation disappointed. We expect our feelings, especially the strongest and least personal, to be like those of others. If those near us share such a feeling, we expect everyone to. So, a penalty is inhumane (in a particular society) if its use shocks all or almost all (in that society); humane if its use shocks at most a few; and neither clearly humane nor clearly inhumane if its use shocks many but far from all.[3] We suppress inhumane penalties (in part, at least) because we do not want to be shocked by their use.

But shock as such is morally indifferent, while humaneness seems to be morally important. What is the connection between shock and morality? The connection seems to be this. If we treat someone in a way we find shocking, we do not treat her as a person. We bring upon her something that does not usually happen to those we know, something so bad that the sight of it (or perhaps even the contemplation) makes us uncomfortable. To treat a person in a way that we find shocking is, then, to treat her as we ourselves do not want to be treated, as we would not treat most other persons, as we might not even be willing to treat our own animals. It is, in short, to degrade her, to treat her as less than a person. If morality requires us to treat each person as a person (and that, it seems to me, is relatively uncontroversial), then if we inflict on a person (against her will) a penalty we find shocking, we do something (at least prima facie) morally wrong.

Making humaneness a function of shock in this way may seem puzzling. Shock, I said, is neither rational nor irrational. If what shocks us depends on how we live, why should we who live so differently ever come to the same conclusion about what is shocking? If what is inhumane depends upon most of us agreeing about what shocks us, how does it happen that there is so much agreement about what is inhumane?

The puzzle is not hard to solve. A certain way of life shapes our sensibilities in a certain way. A shared way of life, because it shapes a common sensibility, also forges a standard of humaneness. We are made to agree. The courts, I think, make too much of what *they* do when telling us why a certain penalty is inhumane ("cruel and unusual"). Whether a penalty is humane or inhumane has little to do with how often courts impose it. The courts contribute little to our common experience. The courts would do better to consider how often people experience, day in and day out, the evil corresponding to the penalty in question. Flogging does not shock a society in which parents beat their children, masters beat their servants, and everyone beats an animal. In such a society, flogging is not inhumane.[4] In a society of nomads, however, imprisoning someone for months or years would shock most people; in such a society, the gentlest detention would be inhumane. Imprisoning does not shock us, I am suggesting, only because we are every day penned in houses, workshops, and offices and often spend years in the same city or town. So, although we admit imprisonment to be a great evil (even apart from its perversions), we do not think it is an inhumane punishment. What the courts do largely reflects what goes on outside.

There is, then, some relationship between "progress" and what is or is not humane. Insofar as technological progress has coincided with the disappearance of certain evils from daily life, it should also have coincided with a change of sensibility and so with a change in what society should lay aside as too cruel. Public executions came to shock our humanity about the time it became rare for ordinary people to die in the street. During the last two decades, a majority of states switched from execution by (private) hanging or electrocution to execution by (private) lethal injection. Why? Perhaps because death by injection is more like the hospital death we have become accustomed to (hanging and electrocution resembling more the industrial accidents that, happily, are becoming relatively rare).[5]

What, then, of the death penalty itself? If what I have said so far is right, the death penalty will shock enough of us only when it has become rare enough for people to die unwillingly before old age (that being the evil the death penalty imposes). How rare is "rare enough"? That is a question for social science. All I dare say is this: Certainly the rate of early death has dropped much in the last two hundred years, especially among the upper and middle classes. To that seemingly irrelevant statistic we may attribute both the enormous increase in those who find the death penalty shocking and their uneven distribution among social classes. But just as certainly, the death rate has not yet dropped enough (or, at least, not remained low enough long enough). If it had, there would be almost no one to say that the death penalty is humane.[6]

We seem to have before us one of those strange controversies that, though not to be concluded by reason, will nevertheless be concluded by time. With respect to death, our standard of humaneness is still half-forged. Death is, for now, neither clearly inhumane nor clearly humane. All we can do, it seems, is wait for murderers (or the absence of murderers), wars (or the absence of wars), traffic accidents (or the absence of traffic accidents), and deadly diseases (or the absence of such diseases) to work upon our sensibilities until we are all made to agree one way or the other. If so, premise 3 is in limbo.

That, however, may not be so. Premise 3 does not claim that death is a humane penalty, only that death is humanely *available*. The difference, though small, is important here. "Humane availability" presupposes a rule for resolving unclear cases. If there is such a rule, premise 3 is either clearly true or clearly false. The two obvious candidates for that rule are: a) "A penalty is humanely available if, and only if, it is humane"; and b) "A penalty is humanely available if, and only if, it is not inhumane." The former rule would make premise 3 false today; the latter, true. How do we decide between these two candidates? Frankly, I don't know. Indeed, it seems to me that the problem of deciding between these two candidates resembles another apparently insoluable political-philosophical problem: deciding whether the fetus is a person for purposes of deciding the moral status of abortion. The problem seems to call for an arbitrary stipulation of some decision rule. But since the stipulation would itself decide everything in controversy, and since each side has strong feelings about how the controversy should be decided, neither side can look upon the stipulation as arbitrary.[7]

Though I do not know how to decide between those two decision-rules, I do have a suggestion. Perhaps the problem of deciding may be resolved by appeal to some higher principle, for example, the *liberal principle* "Resolve disputes over stipulation by preferring that rule the adoption of which would impose the least restraint on action" or the *conservative principle* "Resolve disputes over stipulation by preferring that rule the adoption of which would permit the fewest actions people find shocking." But the results of such appeal may not be altogether happy. The *liberal* principle would force the *conservative* conclusion that premise 3 is true (though forcing the liberal conclusion that abortion is not murder). The conservative principle would force the liberal conclusion that premise 3 is *false* (though forcing as well the conservative conclusion that abortion is murder). Deciding between these principles will not be easy. Attacking premise 3 will be no easier.

IS ALL ELSE EQUAL?

We assume that all else is equal absent some reason to conclude otherwise. There is good reason for that. The ways in which all else *might* not be equal are many, but what count are the ways in which all else *is* not equal, and those are always few or none. To prove that all else is *not* equal is relatively easy. We have only to prove this or that particular difficulty to exist. But to prove all else *is* equal is hard indeed. We have to prove that none of an indefinitely large number of possible difficulties exists in fact. It is only reasonable then to put the burden of proof on those who claim that all else is *not* equal. They should at least present some reason to believe that this or that particular difficulty exists rather than any other or none at all. They should raise real doubts, not mere speculative doubts or hyperbolic shadows. That, surely, is a fundamental principle of reasoning, as appropriate here as in science or law.

I shall now consider two ways in which all else may not be equal for which reasons have been given. The first concerns gradation of penalty; the second, costs.

The argument from deterrence can, I think, justify the penalty of death for no more than a few crimes. For the rest, all else is not equal. Penalties should be graduated so that potential criminals have reason to prefer the lesser of two crimes when in a position to choose. There are, of course, limits to how far gradation can go. We may not be able to distinguish between the brutal murder and the very brutal murder, between the fourth killing and the fifth, and so on. Still, within limits, the importance of gradation is plain enough: If death is the most effective deterrent humanely available, it should be reserved for the worst crimes (the worst crimes simply being those rational persons fear most).

Murder is certainly among the worst crimes (for the same reason the death penalty is the most effective deterrent). The hard question is whether any other crimes are. There is good reason to think none are, certainly not rape, kidnapping, or drug-dealing (the few crimes besides murder and treason still sometimes punishable by death).[8] Consider, for example, whether kidnapping should be a capital crime. To make kidnapping a capital crime is to say to the kidnapper, "Once you have kidnapped someone, he is as good as dead. We no longer care what you do with him." Except under extraordinary circumstances, that will not be what we want to say. The general rule is that, if murder can be added to another crime and thereby make that crime *much* worse, the crime should not be punishable by death. Perhaps treason would escape this rule. I do not think any other crime would.

Therefore, to be safe from attack on grounds of gradation, premise 4 (and the conclusion) should be amended to include the proviso "for murder and perhaps for certain other crimes." But so amended (as in the original statement of it in chapter 1), premise 4 seems secure from attack here.

The costs of a penalty may exceed the benefits society actually receives from it. This is a second way in which all else might not be equal. By "costs" I understand all the bad consequences a penalty may have (without supposing them commensurable). The costs of the death penalty may include the following: *public expense*—where the state must spend more for trial in capital cases, for maintenance of a death row, and so on; *injustice*—where the penalty of death in fact prevents the correction of error; and *disorder*—where the penalty of death provokes crimes, whether by glamorizing capital crimes or by outraging those close to the criminal. Nothing I have said so far rules out such possibilities. What is ruled out is a) treating bare possibilities as actualities without good reason and b) setting bare possibilities against deterrence.

The following argument treats bare possibilities as actualities without good reason: "We have reason to believe death does not deter. Illinois and Michigan are similar in population, urbanization, and wealth. Illinois has a death penalty for murder: Michigan does not. Yet the murder rates are about the same." This argument does "suggest" that the death penalty has no effect upon the murder rate. But the argument hardly meets the standard of proof appropriate to arguments from social statistics. The most that it proves is that the effect of the death penalty is not large and proves that only if there is no reason to doubt the data or the similarity of the two states. Many critics of the death penalty have, I am afraid, confused suggestion with proof.[9]

The following argument sets bare possibilities against deterrence: "We have no reason to believe that the death penalty has any deterrent value at all. If some people fear death, others may be attracted to it. We have no way of knowing whether those deterred outnumber those attracted." Bare possibilities cannot be set against the deterrent value of death because that deterrent value is, though a conceptual truth, a proven truth nonetheless (as chapter 1 showed). We know that death deters (by the method of common sense), though we do not know how much effect the death penalty in fact has on the murder rate. On the other hand, we do not know whether any people (who would not kill otherwise) are sufficiently attracted to government-administered death to kill. There is nothing rational in such attraction—except in special circumstances. Since we do not know what special circumstances are operating, we are in no position to use the method of common sense. We have suspicions, but suspicions cannot themselves shift the burden of proof. Because critics of the death penalty have rarely recognized the method of common sense as a distinct (and reliable) method of proof, they have often thought that they could answer the conceptual argument for deterrence with the possibilities of armchair social science. They cannot.

To prove all else less than equal will take much more work than anyone has yet done. Even to be in position to show that the death penalty has any substantial costs, we need more information about society than we are likely to have soon. Today we are not in a position even to prove, say, that any innocent person could be put to death given contemporary standards of procedure, proof, and appeal, much less to estimate the likelihood of discovering the error if that person were instead to be sentenced to life imprisonment. Premise 4 is, no doubt, the weak wall in the citadel of death. But for now, the defenders can still look down even from that wall and smile. It will be some time before those of us looking up from below have the engines and towers necessary for serious assault.

NOTES

1. See, for example, Ernest van den Haag, *Punishing Criminals* (New York: Basic Books, 1975), 207: "That leaves but one moral and one utilitarian justification for the death penalty. Moral: death may be required, or at least permitted, by considerations of justice; utilitarian: capital punishment may be a more effective deterrent than the alternatives." For someone who clearly does take the view that moral considerations require the death penalty, though perhaps without realizing how counterintuitive that makes his defense of the death penalty, see Igor Primoratz, *Justifying Legal Punishment* (Atlantic Highlands, New Jersey: Humanities Press Internation, Inc., 1989), 158–169.

2. Torture, though known in all nations of the ancient world (except perhaps the Hebrew) fell into relative disuse in Europe (as a means of inquiry or official punishment) during the Dark Ages, perhaps because Christian teaching was against it, perhaps because it was associated with a relatively sophisticated notion of proof. Torture began to revive only in the thirteenth century, perhaps because of a revived interest in Roman law, perhaps because of the church's new interest in uncovering heresy by inquisition. Torture thereafter remained commonplace throughout Europe well into the Age of Enlightenment. For a useful scholarly history of torture, see Malise Ruthven, *Torture: The Grand Conspiracy* (London: Weidenfeld and Nicolson, 1978), especially chapters 2 and 3. Though Ruthven makes much of the connection of torture with judicial inquiry, torture, once revived, also came to be used in punishment. The torture and execution of Damiens for the attempted assassination of Louis XV is perhaps the best-known instance. See Peter N. Walker, *Punishment: An Illustrated History* (New York: Arco Publishing Company, 1973), 93–94. The career of mutilation is somewhat different. The Germanic tribes of northern Europe seem to have managed well enough during the Dark Ages by fining for violent crimes and executing for theft. Mutilation—when introduced into England by Canute in the eleventh century—was a substitute for execution. William the Conqueror actually went so far as to abolish the death penalty altogether in favor of mutilation! See Walker, 30–31.

3. This broad band of unclear cases corresponds to a certain looseness in the move from talk about individuals to talk about "society" or the "we" who govern. It is, I think, unavoidable.

4. These remarks suppose a society of relative equality. The situation might be more complicated where there were castes or rigid class distinctions. For example, in a society of honor where it is an insult for one free man to strike another, the flogging of a free man might well be inhumane even though the flogging of a servant is not.

5. Compare David D. Cooper, *The Lesson of the Gallows* (Athens, Ohio: Ohio University Press, 1974). Cooper apparently thinks the arguments against public executions to be the better arguments in themselves. But though he lays out the arguments for and against public execution with great care, what is striking (apart from the close analogy to the debate over abolition of the death penalty itself) is how arguments that in 1768 seemed to win over almost no one in England could, in 1868, carry the day. Almost as striking is the constant use of the terms "barbaric," "uncivilized," and "debased" in these arguments.

6. Perhaps the substantial increase in murder in the United States since the 1950s explains the substantial increase in support of the death penalty—an increase in support otherwise hard to explain when the rest of the industrial world has, during that period, moved decisively toward abolition.

7. Roger Wertheimer, "Understanding the Abortion Argument," *Philosophy and Public Affairs* 1 (Fall 1971): 67–95. Though I mention Wertheimer's argument here, I do not necessarily endorse his conclusion with respect to abortion. It seems to me that this dispute, unlike the one over the humaneness of the death penalty, has a resolution. See my "The Moral Status of Dogs, Forests, and Other Persons", *Social Theory and Practice* 12 (Spring 1986): 27-59.

8. Those offenses in which death is caused, whether by recklessness, negligence, or mere accident, present a somewhat more complicated problem. Felony-murder statutes—whether so-called or not—do not threaten deterrence as directly as does punishing with death mere kidnapping, rape, or robbery. On the other hand, once a death has occurred in the course of a crime, however incidentally, the criminals no longer have any incentive to avoid murder. I doubt that the threat of death will deter enough criminals or, failing that, convince enough of them to take adequate precautions to avoid causing death, to make up for whatever deterrence is lost once a death has occurred. Of course, my doubts are no substitute for evidence of the sort the social sciences should supply but generally cannot. Without such evidence, it is, I think, hard to make a strong deterrence argument one way or the other. If there is an adequate justification for extending the death penalty to such death-causing crimes, it must rely on other considerations. What other considerations? I have no idea!

9. In this category belongs research like Thorsten Sellin's classic study *The Death Penalty* (Philadelphia: American Law Institute, 1959). The continuing weakness of social science is best seen by comparing Sellin's study with that of Isaac Ehrlich, "The Deterrent Effect of Capital Punishment: A Question of Life and Death," *American Economic Review* 65 (June 1975): 397–417. Ehrlich comes to conclusions inconsistent with Sellin's by analyzing much the same data in a different (but seemingly equally respectable) way. For a critical but nontechnical comparison of the two methods, see Jon K. Peck, "The Deterrent Effect of Capital Punishment: Ehrlich and his Critics," *Yale Law Journal* 85 (January 1976): 359–367.

Three

The Argument from Inhumaneness

This chapter's subject is (what I shall call) *the argument from inhumaneness*. The argument purports to show that the death penalty should be abolished even if some criminals deserve death. Since the argument is not consequentialist, we should not be surprised that it is enjoying a revival at a time when consequentialist arguments are out of favor. Two important punishment theorists, Hugo Bedau and Jeffrey Reiman, have each recently published a substantial article making the argument.[1] Reiman's article has already been included in several anthologies.[2]

I will focus on Reiman's version of the argument here, commenting on Bedau's only in footnotes. I take this approach for three reasons. First, Reiman's version is both simpler and less tentative, making exposition briefer and easier to follow. Second, only Reiman's article specifically criticizes the argument of chapter 1, my "common sense" argument for the claim that death is a more effective deterrent than life imprisonment.[3] And third, Bedau has recently endorsed that criticism: "Davis's essential claim has been nicely refuted by Reiman."[4]

These reasons are connected. Reiman's criticism rests on a misunderstanding of my argument. A proper understanding of it reveals crucial weaknesses in his version of the argument from inhumaneness, including some that Bedau's version shares. Chief among these is an analysis of inhumaneness that cannot both fit common intuitions and include death among inhumane penalties.

TWO ARGUMENTS, NOT ONE

We may formalize the argument from inhumaneness in this way:

1. The state should not use an inhumane penalty without weighty reason.
2. The death penalty is inhumane.
3. Preventing serious harm to innocent people is a weighty reason for using a particular penalty (as is doing justice), provided we can show that using the penalty does prevent serious harm.
4. But, on the evidence we have, we cannot show that the death penalty prevents harm to innocents more effectively than the (more) humane penalty of life imprisonment.
5. There is no other weighty reason relevant here (justice having been shown to allow punishing murder by life imprisonment as well as by death).

So: All things considered, the state should not use the death penalty.

Reiman's article begins with a long discussion of retributivism. Its purpose is to show that the moral insights underlying retributivism are consistent with (and, indeed, seem to imply) the first premise.[5] The state has a right to give the criminal the punishment she deserves, and some criminals deserve death. But the state's right is limited by its duty to treat even criminals with the respect every moral agent deserves. Treating a criminal inhumanely without good reason is inconsistent with that duty. Hence (according to Reiman), no matter how bad the crime, the state should not treat the criminal inhumanely without good reason. The only good reasons to treat a criminal inhumanely are that justice requires it or that such treatment would prevent harm to innocent people that more humane punishment would not. The rest of Reiman's article tries to show that death is an inhumane penalty that today satisfies neither condition. Hence, the death penalty is not justified today.

That is the unimposing skeleton of Reiman's imposing argument (the parenthetical phrases in the argument's formal state-ment refer to parts not relevant to what follows). Reiman reach-es my common-sense argument only as part of his defense of the fourth premise. The death penalty would, Reiman admits, be justified if it could be shown to protect the innocent from harm that they would otherwise suffer at the hands of criminals.[6] The primary means by which the death penalty might prevent such harm is by deterring potential murderers whom the penalty of life imprisonment would not deter. Hence, an argument showing that the death penalty is a more effective deterrent than life im-prisonment would refute Reiman's argument by showing premise 4 to be false.

Reiman treats my argument as if it posed such a threat:

> Davis claims that it is *rational* to fear the death penalty more than lesser penalties and thus *rational* to be more deterred by it. Thus, he concludes that the death penalty is the most effective deterrent *for rational people.* . . . To bring [this argument] back to the actual crim-inal-justice system that deals with actual people, Davis claims that the criminal law makes no sense unless we suppose the potential criminal to be (more or less) rational.[7]

Reiman then points out that "[the] problem with this strategy is that a deterrence justification of a punishment is valid only if it proves the punishment actually deters actual people from com-mitting crimes."[8] If my argument were, as Reiman supposes, addressed to his fourth premise, this criticism would be deci-sive. His first two premises put the burden of proof on those arguing that the death penalty in fact prevents harm. My argu-ment cannot bear that burden.

Fortunately, it need not. The argument is *not* addressed to Reiman's fourth premise. Although, like Reiman's, my argument is concerned with both deterrence and inhumaneness, it is not a mere variant or subsidiary of his. Recall our formal statement of *the argument from deterrence* (chapter 1):

1. The state should, all else equal, provide as penalty the most effective deterrent among those humanely available. [A penalty is "humanely available" if it is not inhu-mane—or, at least, not clearly inhumane.]

2. The penalty of death is the most effective deterrent (among those humanely available).

3. The penalty of death is humanely available.

4. All else is equal (for murder and perhaps for certain other crimes).

So: The state should provide death as a penalty (for murder and perhaps for certain other crimes).

Reiman's criticism does not address any premise of this argument. That is obvious for premises 1 and 3. So let us look at premises 2 and 4. Premise 2 is a conceptual truth—as chapter 1 showed. Since Reiman finds no fault with the argument by which I show premise 2 to follow from what rationality requires, his criticism must fail for exactly the reason my argument must (as he says) fail as criticism of his premise 4.

My first three premises, like Reiman's first three, establish a burden of proof. The only difference is that, given my first three, the burden falls on those who (like Reiman) claim that the death penalty will *not* prevent more harm than life imprisonment, not (as in Reiman's argument) on those who claim it *will*. Reiman is no more prepared to carry that burden than I am to carry the corresponding burden that his argument would assign me.

It is, I think, worth stressing that Reiman and I do agree about the empirical evidence relevant here. Like Reiman, I recognize (and expressly so state in the course of my argument) that the deterrent effect of the death penalty seems at best too small to measure. Whatever tendency the death penalty has to guide the conduct of rational agents might, for all we know, be swamped by the irrational impulses of those same agents (or by the irrational impulses of irrational agents).[9]

What Reiman and I disagree about here is not an *empirical* question but a *conceptual* one. My argument purports to show that, absent proof (or at least strong evidence) that the deterrent tendency of the death penalty is swamped in some way or other; common sense requires us to suppose some deterrent effect, and so, all else equal, to provide death as a penalty. Reiman's quite different argument purports to show that, absent proof to the contrary, we must suppose no deterrent effect and so, all else equal, abolish the death penalty. We disagree about who must carry the burden, not about whether it can be carried. But that disagreement does not doom us to talk past each other. Our opposed arguments rest in part on a common foundation: humaneness. That brings me to the crucial weakness in Reiman's argument, his analysis of inhumaneness.

TWO ANALYSES OF INHUMANENESS

Both Reiman and I agree that inhumaneness is relevant to the justification of the death penalty. Even so, we have a significant disagreement. As I understand the argument from deterrence, a penalty must be humane (or at least, not clearly inhumane) if we are to be justified in using it. Inhumaneness rules out justification. For Reiman, a penalty can be justified even if it is inhumane, provided it has some practical advantage, such as preventing harm to innocents. For Reiman—but *not* for me—inhumaneness can be a routine and widespread feature of justified penal practice. What explains this difference?

The answer is that Reiman and I do not share an analysis of inhumaneness. Indeed, the term is mine (chosen to avoid the overly constraining legal history of "cruel and unusual"). Reiman talks instead about "the horrible things we tolerate doing to our fellows," "barbaric" penalties, and so on. (Reiman also avoids the legal term "cruel and unusual.")[10] Still, I think it clear enough that Reiman and I are talking about a single concept.[11] The differences between us are therefore striking.

For me, a penalty is inhumane if (and, I think, only if) its use on anyone, especially someone else, would normally shock us (that is, would shock us unless we ignored his status as a rational agent). To treat someone in a way that would normally shock us is to disregard our common humanity, to treat him as less than a person, and so to deny him the minimum respect that morality requires us to show all rational agents. Given this (essentially Kantian) analysis of what is wrong with inhumaneness, an inhumane punishment might occasionally be excused, but it cannot be justified. We can never justify treating a rational agent as less than a rational agent. To describe a penalty as "inhumane" is, on this analysis, to condemn it in the strongest terms that morality permits.

Everything then depends on what shocks us ("us" referring to a social consensus, not to what absolutely everyone in a society thinks or to what any particular percentage of individuals think). What shocks may, as chapter 2 argued, vary from society to society and from time to time even in the same historically continuous society. No punishment is necessarily shocking, no particular criterion necessarily good across all rational agents. For example, even intense pain is not necessarily shocking, and so even intensely painful penalties are not necessarily inhumane.

The claim that no penalty is *necessarily* shocking is, however, consistent both with explaining why a certain penalty shocks a certain society while others do not and with predicting what will be shocking in a certain society. Indeed, chapter 2 offered the (empirical) hypothesis that what penalties shock in a particular society is a function of what life in that society is like generally. For example, after dying in the streets became uncommon in England, public executions began to shock, and so public executions became inhumane—"barbaric"—and soon disappeared.[12] What I deny is that such an explanation, as opposed to the shock itself, is relevant to justification.

For Reiman, the death penalty is inhumane because it is "horrible" (a term seemingly close to my "shocking"). But for Reiman, there are universal criteria for what is horrible. A penalty is horrible insofar as it involves both "intense pain" and the "spectacle of one human being completely subject to the power of another."[13] Reiman does not merely claim that these two criteria describe what we find horrible. Had he claimed only that, his claim would have been much more plausible. Instead, he claims that his criteria of inhumaneness apply in all societies through all of time. That is no mere slip of the pen. Reiman's article requires a fundamentally universalist analysis of inhumaneness. For Reiman, humaneness matters not because morality requires us to treat each other humanely but because treating people humanely is—note the language—"part of the civilizing mission of modern states."[14] And what is "civilization"? For Reiman, civilization is—again, note the language—the progressive "taming" of the human animal, a slow process older, perhaps, than recorded history.[15]

Though such language was common in the nineteenth century, it is now rare enough to sound old-fashioned (in much the way "white man's burden" does). Why is it so rare? Perhaps because this century has seen modern states enslave, torture, and murder vast numbers of their own subjects or subjects of neighboring states with a fierceness Victorians thought only dark-skinned people in loincloths still capable of. While speaking of "technological progress" still seems unproblematic, speaking of "moral progress" does not.

Reiman's talk of the modern state's "civilizing mission" may seem old-fashioned for another reason as well. This century has been the great age of anthropology. Most of what we know about "uncivilized" people we have learned since 1900. Today we understand how much variety, intelligence, and humanity was concealed under the pejorative "uncivilized"—and its near synonyms "primitive," "barbaric," "savage," and "wild." Many a "savage race" turned out far "tamer" than we are; only a few turned out to be much wilder. Anthropology has also taught us to appreciate that the same physical act can have a different meaning in another society. So, for example, while a few months in jail may seem a relatively mild punishment to us, for a nomadic people it might seem more horrible than branding or whipping. This, I think, is the truth in Nietzsche's paradox, quoted by Reiman, that "[in early times] pain did not hurt as much as it does today."[16]

Reiman's analysis of inhumaneness must, like mine, eventually fit the facts, especially the facts of history and anthropology. We might then expect Reiman, in defense of his analysis, to array some of this century's work in the history or anthropology of punishment. What we find is something else. Reiman makes no reference to anything written in this century. Indeed, he refers to only one work to support his empirical claim, a 23-page article published in 1900.

Its author, Emile Durkheim, though trained as a philosopher, is, of course, a founder of modern sociology. He is certainly someone whose opinions concerning his society still deserve respect. But he is hardly a trustworthy guide to history or anthropology. He did no field studies himself. He simply organized the little information about earlier societies then available (relying heavily on a few secondary sources). The sample was biased.

Most of the societies belong to Western Civilization (including ancient Greece, Rome, Egypt, and Assyria). Even the sampling of Western societies seems unaccountably biased. While Durkheim draws many examples from French history, he entirely ignores English, Swedish, and Russian developments (many of which seem not to fit his scheme).

Durkheim's use of his (biased) sample is suspect as well. He claims to establish two universal "laws" governing the "evolution of the apparatus of punishment" (for example, "The intensity of punishment is the greater the more closely societies approximate to a less developed type—and the more the central power assumes an absolute character").[17] A historian today might well draw a far less daring conclusion from the same evidence. The most Durkheim's evidence seems to establish is a "tendency" for intensity of punishment to decrease as power becomes less absolute or the society more developed.

Durkheim's weighing of evidence also seems to me less persuasive than Reiman finds it. For example, Durkheim declares the "city state . . . without doubt a more advanced type of society [than the kingdom of ancient Israel]."[18] He gives no reason. Not only do I doubt the claim, I also doubt that it could be plausibly decided. Yet much of Durkheim's evidence for the "two laws" would be evidence against them were our ratings of social advancement to differ much from his.

Such criticism of Durkheim would be irrelevant here if Reiman had shown that Durkheim's conclusions fit the new evidence that historians and anthropologist have compiled in the nine decades since Durkheim wrote. He does not. Reiman does not even try to show that our understanding of the penal practices of societies that Durkheim cites remains unchanged. Reiman rests the entire weight of his argument on one outdated article. Yet even that article supports Reiman's claim for the modern state's "civilizing mission" in a most equivocal way.

For Durkheim, punishment tends to become milder because certain crimes—what he calls "religious crimes"—tend to disappear as society becomes more developed or more equal: "The offense of man against man cannot arouse the same indignation as the offense of man against God."[19] The crimes remaining after religious crimes have disappeared are the ones that were tra-

ditionally punished less severely. The two "laws" Durkheim identifies do not imply that penalties will approach zero as societies
continue to develop, only that they will approach the range assigned crimes of "man against man."[20] Durkheim's two laws imply
nothing about the death penalty, except insofar as that penalty's
appeal rests on religious feeling. Reliance on Durkheim seems
to force Reiman to equate "the advance of civilization" with
making people less religious. Making people less religious seems
an odd mission for modern states, certainly one few Americans
are likely to feel called to.

Reiman's argument for abolition falls apart if he cannot establish that "the reduction in horrible things we do to our fellows is in fact part of the advance of civilization."[21] Yet his
attempt to establish that empirical claim is surprisingly feeble.
Why? Could he find no respectable historian or anthropologist
more recent than Durkheim from whom to draw even the equivocal support Durkheim provides?[22]

Reiman's argument and mine come into direct conflict over
the analysis of humaneness (and perhaps only there). Reiman rests
the defense of his analysis on the work of one nineteenth-centu-
ry scholar. I, at least, cite more recent work.[23] Until Reiman
shows that his argument is consistent with what we now know
about the history of punishment, the argument remains in empirical limbo.

When I first made this criticism, Reiman offered three replies.
The first enlarged the field of empirical evidence from which he
could draw:

> [My] claim about the progress of civilization is more than a
> claim about the history of punishment. It covers all the things that
> we tolerate having done to ourselves and to others, including,
> for instance, the passing out of fashion of such entertainments as
> bare-knuckle boxing and throwing Christians to lions, as well as
> the passing of such punishments as public whipping or beheading
> or drawing and quartering.[24]

Having enlarged the field, he leaves us to guess what a patient
search might yield.

Reiman's second reply softens the empirical claim without
actually changing it: "[My] claim is not that history presents an

unbroken trend in this direction without reverses, but rather
its overall trend is that way—which seems to me to remain
true even if the anthropologists show us that some 'less advanced' societies were more merciful than some 'more advanced'
societies."[25] Of course, what such softening gains in truth, it
loses in interest. Reiman's original claim was daring because
it was easy to disprove; this one is much safer because it is
almost empty.

Reiman's third—"and most important"—reply completes the
retreat by begging the question. His claim of progress is, he tells
us, "not a simple empirical generalization, but a complex
empirical-and-normative proposition."[26] It is not simply a claim
about what tends to happen in history but about those things
that have "tended to happen which are good."[27] Understanding
his claim in this way renders it, he tells us, "less vulnerable to
contrary historical examples than it would be if it were merely
an empirical generalization about what has tended to happen
in history."[28] Indeed, understanding his claim in this way seems
to render it altogether invulnerable. What could we not prove
about the progress of history if we were allowed to exclude all
negative instances as Reiman does?

Having thus begged the question, he nonetheless concedes that
"there is much more I would have to do to make good on the
civilization tenet of my argument." He has, as far as I know, yet
to redeem that promise. Until he does, his argument must lan-
guish in logic's oubliette.

WHAT'S WRONG WITH TORTURE?

Though serious enough, Reiman's lack of empirical evidence is,
I think, only a part of what is wrong with his analysis of humaneness. The analysis also seems to bar the simple moral criticism of inhumane penalties that mine permits. Indeed, Reiman's
criticism of inhumane penalties generally—and so ultimately his
criticism of the death penalty—seems curiously muted. For example, the worst Reiman says about torture (apart from defining
it as "horrible") is that imposing it "demonstrates a kind of hardheartedness that a society ought not to parade."[29] If inhumaneness is a moral criticism for Reiman, it is so only because the

hardheartedness required is the antithesis of a moral virtue like kindness or mercy. For Reiman, it seems, torture is at worst morally bad, not morally wrong.[30]

This way of understanding what is wrong with torture explains why Reiman thinks that torture (and other inhumane penalties) can be justified. Justifying a failure in kindness or mercy is relatively easy so long as one does not build too much into those virtues.[31]

Understanding what is wrong with torture in this way seems to leave out something important, however. For most of us, at least, a punishment involving torture would be unjustified even if it deterred crime more than imprisonment does. Torturing people is objectionable not simply because we should refuse to endorse the hardheartedness necessary to torture someone. Torturing is objectionable, in large part at least, because we cannot both treat a person with the respect morality requires and put him to torture. We seem to reserve "inhumaneness" for criticism of this relatively severe sort, not for objections to mere failures of kindness or mercy, however great. Reiman's analysis of humaneness thus seems to leave out an essential element of inhumane penalties or, at the very least, an essential element of what makes torture so morally objectionable.

THE ANALOGY BETWEEN TORTURE AND DEATH

Reiman's argument for abolition of the death penalty relies on an analogy with torture. Having argued that his analysis of inhumaneness explains why torture is inhumane, Reiman tries to show that the death penalty is enough like torture to be inhumane as well:

> The death penalty is the last corporal punishment used officially in the modern world [except, of course, in certain Islamic countries]. And it is corporal not because administered via the body, but because the pain of foreseen, humanly administered death strikes us with the urgency that characterizes intense physical pain, causing grown men to cry, faint, and lose control of their bodily functions. There is something to be gained by refusing to endorse the hardness of heart necessary to impose such a fate.[32]

If, as I have argued, the characteristics of torture on which this analogy between torture and the death penalty relies do not explain our objection to torture, they cannot explain a similar objection to the death penalty. Reiman's argument for abolition is radically incomplete. He lacks what used to be called "a middle term."

But that is not all that is wrong with his argument. While torture is shocking to most of us in a way (or to a degree) that the death penalty is not (or at least is not yet for most of us), Reiman's analogy between torture and death misleadingly suggests the opposite. So, for example, Reiman himself objects to execution by lethal injection because:

> Execution shares [with torture] this separate feature [subjection], since killing a bound and defenseless human being enacts the total subjection of that person to his fellows. I think, incidentally, that this accounts for the general uneasiness with which execution by lethal injection has been greeted. Rather than humanizing the event, it seems only to have purchased a possible reduction in physical pain at the price of increasing the spectacle of subjection—with no net gain in the attractiveness of the death penalty. Indeed, its net effect may have been the reverse.[33]

What is wrong here? Let's begin with the obvious: Does killing a bound and defenseless human being "enact the total subjection of that person to his fellows"? Not necessarily. It would not, for example, if the killing were euthanasia of someone wild with incurable rabies. What, then, if the killing were a lawful execution where those involved clearly act as agents of an impersonal law, a law that the criminal herself would endorse insofar as she is rational? The answer, it seems to me, is that execution under those circumstances would likewise not be a "spectacle of subjection." Can a penalty be administered in this way? While I don't think we can any longer administer torture in this way, it seems to me quite possible to administer death in this way. Indeed, the practices surrounding the death penalty—the last meal, the chaplain, the solemnity, the preference for less painful means of execution, even the practice of some states of letting the condemned choose between modes of execution—do suggest something other than total subjection.[34]

But the crucial question is not whether killing a bound and defenseless human being *necessarily* enacts the total subjection of that person to his fellows but whether it does in fact. Reiman's criticism of execution by lethal injection would stand even if we actually thought of execution by lethal injection as he claims we do. How people actually think is an empirical matter, one about which Reiman needs to provide evidence. What he does is something else.

Reiman merely claims that there is "a general unease with execution by lethal injection." He gives no evidence; I know of none. Though, like Reiman, I favor abolition, I do not share his unease. Medical doctors are, of course, concerned that medical technology is used to kill, a concern rising from their professional ethics (though, as we shall see in chapter 4, even this concern is harder to defend than commonly supposed). But in Illinois at least, the only obvious opposition to lethal injection—apart from that of medical doctors—was from abolitionists afraid that the death penalty, appearing less horrible, would be harder to repeal; and from law-and-order advocates afraid that, being less horrible, death by lethal injection would deter less than death by electrocution. I have not heard anyone suggest that death by lethal injection is more horrible than death by electrocution.[35]

Here again Reiman needs evidence. If he is right about the general attitude toward execution by lethal injection, my analysis of inhumaneness is probably mistaken; if (as I think) he is wrong, then his analysis is.

CONCLUSION

Reiman's argument for abolition of the death penalty seems to rely at several crucial points on empirical claims for which he has offered inadequate evidence and for which adequate evidence seems unlikely to exist. Reiman might escape these empirical difficulties by switching to another analysis of inhumaneness, one closer to the facts and our intuitions. I have suggested that my analysis is closer to the facts and intuitions we have. But Reiman cannot save his argument simply by taking over my analysis. On my analysis, the humaneness of the death penalty is (as explained in chapter 2) today more or less undecidable.[36]

The argument from inhumaneness addresses nonconsequential-
ists in their own terms without entanglement in questions of
desert. This makes the argument attractive to abolitionists today.
But the attraction may be deceptive. The argument can be made
only with an analysis of inhumaneness narrow enough to permit
the strong moral criticism we save for inhumane penalties and
yet broad enough to include death among inhumane penalties.
We cannot simply suppose that such an analysis exists. To make
the argument from humaneness is to come under an obligation
to invent such an analysis. Reiman and Bedau have each contributed to our understanding of the argument by trying to invent one. What we can learn from their failed attempts is that
inventing one will not be easy. We need not conclude that it
cannot be done.

NOTES

I should like to thank Paul Gomberg for helpful comments on an
early version of this chapter.

1. Hugo Adam Bedau, "Thinking About the Death Penalty as a
Cruel and Unusual Punishment," *U. C. Davis Law Review* 18 (Summer 1985): 873–925, reprinted as chapter 4 of Bedau's *Death is Different* (Boston: Northeastern University Press, 1987); and Jeffrey
Reiman, "Justice, Civilization, and the Death Penalty: Answering van
den Haag," *Philosophy and Public Affairs* 14 (Spring 1985): 115–148.

2. See, for example, Robert M. Baird and Stuart E. Rosenbaum,
eds., *Philosophy of Punishment* (Buffalo, NY: Prometheus Books, 1988),
109–140; and A. John Simmons et al., eds., *Punishment* (Princeton,
New Jersey: Princeton University Press, 1995), 274–307.

3. See Michael Davis, "Death, Deterrence, and the Method of
Common Sense," *Social Theory and Practice* 7 (Summer 1981): 145–
177. Since this article is an early version of chapters 1 and 2, I shall,
for convenience, cite those chapters rather than the original article.

4. *Death is Different*, 269 n.7.

5. Reiman, "Justice," 119–134.

6. Reiman, "Justice," 142.

7. Reiman, "Justice," 144 n.

8. Reiman, "Justice," 144 n.

9. Chapter 1, 20–21.

10. While Bedau sticks with the term "cruel and unusual punishment," the context makes clear that he does not consider himself

bound by legal usage. He is clearly involved in the same all-things-considered enterprise as Reiman and I are.

11. Or so I thought when I published this criticism in 1990. Reiman's reply has left me bewildered. See Jeffrey Reiman, "The Death Penalty, Deterrence, and Horribleness: A Reply to Michael Davis," *Social Theory and Practice* 16 (Summer 1990): 261–272. Reiman still contends that when he claims that the death penalty is "horrible" he means "mainly that it causes the recipient extreme pain." He correctly observes that I suppose his term "horrible" to mark a *"normative status achieved by activities that cross a forbidden moral boundary."* He does not, it turns out, think of "horribleness" in this way. Doing horrible things is, he tells us, like killing (rather than like murder), *"prima facie* morally wrong—but not more than that." ("Reply," 269–270.) What I find bewildering about this reply is that it makes much of his argument unnecessary. Who would deny either that causing others pain or killing them is *prima facie* morally wrong? Indeed, the reason everyone agrees that the death penalty requires a justification is precisely that unjustified killing is morally wrong. Why then shift discussion from killing to (extreme) pain—when we generally suppose killing morally harder to justify than causing pain? Since debate about the death penalty begins precisely at the point at which Reiman now says he wants to end it, I can only conclude that he did not say what he meant. I have therefore preserved my original argument, since the position it criticizes is more interesting than the one to which Reiman now seems to have retreated.

12. Chapter 2, 38.

13. Reiman, "Justice," 139–140. What is Bedau's position? On the one hand, he can seem to reject Reiman's universalism. For example, early in the article, he declares, "The concept of cruelty is social, moral, and cultural, rather than physiological, organic, or in some other manner essentially unhistorical" (Bedau, 102). On the other hand, he ultimately endorses a conception of inhumaneness like Reiman's: "[The] very 'heart of cruelty' is best described as 'total activity smashing total passivity.'" Both want to think of inhumaneness as a certain "power-relationship" (though Bedau denies that intense pain is necessary for a penalty to be inhumane). This might suggest that Bedau's position is that what counts as "total activity smashing total passivity" is determined by social, moral, and cultural factors. Actually, history comes into his analysis of humaneness only at a very odd place, the concept of the person: "For several centuries—and in particular, since the Age of Enlightenment—philosophers have struggled to enunciate a conception of the person as fundamentally social, rational, and autonomous, and as immune to change in these respects by virtue of

any contingencies of history or circumstance" (Bedau, 127). It is this concept of the person, ahistorical though itself a product of history, that, according to Bedau, leads to the conclusion that "even the worst and most dangerous murderer is not a fit subject for annihilation by others" (Bedau, 127). Given how many philosophers have accepted this theory of the person and yet defended the death penalty, I am at a loss to understand why Bedau (who knows their work at least as well as I do) should suppose that the theory leads to that conclusion. Unfortunately, he is very brief at this point in the argument.

14. Reiman, "Justice," 142.

15. Reiman, "Justice," 136.

16. Reiman, "Justice," 135.

17. Reiman, "Justice," 136.

18. Emile Durkheim, "Two Laws of Penal Evolution," *Economy and Society* 2 (1973): 285–308. This is a translation by T. Anthony Jones and Andrew Scull of an essay originally published in *Année Sociologique* 4 (1899–1900). Cited passage is at 290–91.

19. Durkheim, "Two Laws," 303.

20. Durkheim, "Two Laws," 306.

21. Reiman, "Justice," 137.

22. Apparently not. Though Reiman's reply repeats some of his claims, he adds not a single source for them. He seems to be engaged in *a priori* history. Like Reiman, Bedau relies heavily on one source to support his analysis of cruelty. For Bedau, that source is Phillip P. Hallie, *Cruelty* (Middletown, CT: Wesleyan University Press, 1982). While Hallie's work is timely in a way Durkheim's is not, it is, like Durkheim's, equivocal in its support. As Bedau frankly admits, "Hallie mentioned the death penalty once . . . in passing; he makes no attempt to decide whether the death penalty was or is a cruel punishment." *Death is Different*, 264 n.76.

23. Chapter 2, n. 15.

24. Reiman, "Reply," 268.

25. Reiman, "Reply," 268.

26. Reiman, "Reply," 269.

27. Reiman, "Reply," 269.

28. Reiman, "Reply," 269.

29. Reiman, "Justice," 141.

30. I am giving Reiman the benefit of the doubt here. What he actually says suggests that the condemnation even of torture may rest on arbitrary commitment of the sort existentialists used to talk about. So, for example, he describes "reduction in the horrible things we do to our fellows" as an advance in civilization "we are called upon to continue *once we consciously take upon ourselves* the work of civilization" (Reiman, "Justice," 139—my italics).

31. Though Bedau does not think that inhumane penalties can be justified, his criticism of them can occasionally come out sounding almost as muted as Reiman's. For example: "Bringing [deliberate, institutionalized, lethally punitive cruelty] to an end in all human affairs heads the list of *desiderata* for any society of persons who understand themselves as moral agents" (*Death is Different*, 127—my italics). Why just "desiderata"? Why not "requirements"? Has Bedau so stretched the concept of inhumaneness that he feels uncomfortable with the concept's normal vocabulary?

32. Reiman, "Justice," 141.

33. Reiman, "Justice," 140.

34. Despite some historical references, Bedau—like Reiman—makes no attempt to connect his concept of inhumaneness with the historical record. He certainly gives no argument for his fundamental claim that the death penalty is inhumane because of its "unalterable nature . . . even when carried out in the most dignified fashion." *Death is Different*, 128.

35. Though Bedau mentions "lethal injections" once in the article we are considering, he expresses *no* "unease." Indeed, his statement on lethal injection strongly suggests that he views it much as I do: "With death carried out by the state in a manner that does not disfigure the offender's body, apparently causes no pain whatever, and brings about death within a few minutes, it is extremely difficult and maybe even impossible to construct a convincing argument that condemns the practice based on its 'indignity,'" *Death is Different*, 124–125.

36. Chapter 2, 39–40. Bedau has exactly the same problem. Though I have already argued otherwise, suppose he is right that "[what] is most compelling about the concept of cruelty understood as a 'power-relationship' in the manner described is that it focuses our attention on the salient common factor in all situations where the death penalty is inflicted, however painlessly, and whatever the condemned person has done." *Death is Different*, 124. What would follow from that supposition? Nothing—unless he could also distinguish this power relation from those thought morally unobjectionable (or at least less so). Why, for example, is imprisonment not exactly the same sort of "power-relationship"? Why does Bedau's version of the argument from inhumaneness not lead to the counterintuitive conclusion that imprisonment is no more morally justifiable than the death penalty? Bedau's argument, like Reiman's, seems to *pre*suppose that death is different from imprisonment (but not from torture). We shall return to that supposition in chapters 5 and 6.

Four

What is Unethical About Physicians Helping at Executions?

Since 1983, an Illinois statute has provided that "[a] defendant sentenced to death shall be executed by a continuous, intravenous administration of a lethal quantity of an ultrashort-acting barbiturate in combination with a chemical paralytic agent until death is pronounced by a licensed physician according to accepted standards of medical practice."[1] Until 1992, the statute also required that at least two "physicians" be present as "witnesses" (along with six other people). The statute was (and is) silent concerning whether a physician is to order the drugs and equipment, insert the needle into the condemned prisoner's vein, open the drip lines leading to the barbiturate and paralytic, or regulate their mix and flow to achieve death. The only hint is that the prison *warden* is to "supervise the execution."[2]

Unless declared unconstitutional, lethal injection is Illinois's only means of lawful execution. Thus, between 1983 and 1992, no one could be legally executed in Illinois without the voluntary participation of at least two physicians. Even today, a physician must determine that the execution has achieved its purpose. At some point during the execution, this "physician-monitor" will be asked whether the prisoner is dead. If, upon examination, she finds that he is not, she must inform the warden, who would then have to allow the execution to continue. The execution can end only when the physician-monitor pronounces death.[3]

At least twenty states and the federal government now have similar arrangements.[4] The factory-like gallows, guillotine, electric chair, and gas chamber are giving way to the hospital's wheeled bed, plastic tubes, and transparent bags of transparent fluid; the executioner in black, to the executioner in white.

Illinois first used its new method of execution in 1990.[5] The official announcement indicated that three physicians had participated (apparently three medical residents from Southern Illinois University).[6] The Illinois State Medical Society then asked for the names of the physicians, indicating that it believed there may have been a breach of medical ethics. The state declined to release the names. The physicians did not identify themselves. The investigation stalled, leaving the question: What, if anything, did the physicians in question do wrong?[7]

THE MEDICAL ETHICS BACKGROUND

In 1980, the American Medical Association (AMA) adopted Opinion 2.06:

> An individual's opinion on capital punishment is the personal moral decision of the individual. A physician, as a member of a profession dedicated to preserving life when there is hope of doing so, should not be a participant in a legally authorized execution. A physician may make a determination or certification of death as currently provided by law in any situation. (I)[8]

This opinion is remarkable for at least five reasons.

First, the forbidden "participation" is left undefined (except that certifying death "as currently provided by law in any situation" is allowed). "Participation" would seem to include actually administering the drug, witnessing the execution (as a physician), and even monitoring bodily signs to determine when the execution is complete. In December 1992, the AMA issued a new opinion that makes it clear that "participation" also includes ordering the necessary drugs, signing for them, training others to administer them, and any other act that "would contribute to the ability of another individual to directly cause the death of the condemned."[9] The AMA clearly intends to erect a wall between medicine and the death penalty.[10]

Second, Opinion 2.06 *assumes* that the medical profession is "dedicated to preserving life when there is hope of doing so." The parenthesized Roman numeral "I" at the end of the opinion indicates that the assumption derives from "Principle I" of the AMA's "Principles of Medical Ethics." Yet, Principle I dedicates physicians only to the more modest enterprise of "providing competent medical service with compassion and respect for human dignity." Opinion 2.06 seems to rely on the unstated (and undefended) premise that assisting in a lawful execution is inconsistent with competent medical service, with compassion, or with respect for human dignity.

Third, Opinion 2.06 is near Opinion 2.01. Opinion 2.01 *allows* physicians to perform abortions (which, of course, destroy life where there is hope of preserving it). Together, these two opinions remind us that physicians today are debating many questions concerning the propriety of not preserving life just because it can be preserved, whether by withholding treatment (for example, by an order not to resuscitate), by withdrawing treatment (for example, by removing a respirator or feeding tube), or even by killing (for example, by helping a patient commit suicide, whether by providing a deadly drug or instructing in its lethal use).[11] Preserving-life-when-there-is-hope-of-doing-so is today at best a controversial purpose of medicine. Certainly, nothing else in the AMA's code of ethics suggests otherwise.[12] Opinion 2.06 has the look of novelty; it is not (as its text makes it seem) an explication of a long-standing assumption.[13]

Fourth, Opinion 2.06 is designated a "Social Policy" (and stated with the "should" of counsel rather than the regulatory "shall" of the AMA's Principles). The Opinions' "Introduction" declares: "In matters strictly of a policy nature, a physician who disagrees with the position of the American Medical Association is entitled to freedom and protection of his point of view." We might then suppose that Opinion 2.06 (or its Illinois equivalent) could *not* be used to discipline a physician who acted contrary to its recommendation (though it might support private judgments of unethical conduct). Yet if Opinion 2.06 cannot be used to discipline a physician-executioner, what could? No other provision of the AMA's code of ethics has more than a remote connection with the death penalty.[14]

Fifth, Opinion 2.06 (indeed, the entire AMA code of ethics) purports to govern "physicians" in general, not just the minority of American physicians who are members of the AMA. It is a professional standard, not just a standard for members of a professional society. It justifies condemning the three physicians, if it does, not because they are AMA members (which they might well not be) but because they are physicians. This generality, though a common feature of professional codes, raises a fundamental question of professional ethics: On what authority can the AMA claim to tell physicians what medical ethics requires, allows, or forbids?

We may distinguish four common approaches to medical ethics: "the philosophical," "the casuistic," "the therapeutic," and "the social" (as I shall call them). All four are alike in assigning the AMA no special moral authority. For each of these approaches, the AMA, though perhaps a depository of medical wisdom, is otherwise exactly like any other group of physicians, indeed, like any group of philosophers, lawyers, clergy, or other lay people, who undertakes to examine a question of medical ethics.

The first three approaches—the philosophical, casuistic, and therapeutic—are also alike in assuming that physicians are held only to the same moral standards as nonphysicians. The philosophical and casuistic differ from the therapeutic in relying solely on the facts of the particular situation to transform universal standards into specific directives. They differ only in the way they determine the standards. The philosophical appeals to some moral theory (utilitarianism, Kantianism, or the like) to determine what should be done. The casuistic appeals instead to ordinary moral standards (either explicitly, for example, by citation of moral rules like "Don't kill" or "Don't torture," implicitly by comparison of cases, or—most often—by some combination of these).

The therapeutic approach differs from the philosophical and casuistic approaches insofar as it relies (instead or in addition) on special "principles of medicine" derived from the "nature" of medicine (or the "therapeutic context"). These special principles (together with ordinary morality and the specific facts of a situation) determine what should be done in a particular situation. The nature of medicine may be timeless (a Platonic idea) or a product of history (like a Darwinian species), but it is not changeable in the way a law or contract is.[15]

The social approach resembles the therapeutic in that it attributes some special quality to physicians. It differs from the therapeutic in understanding this special quality as (at least in

part) a product of social decision (the role society has construct-
ed for physicians). For the social approach, the standards of
medical ethics derive not from the nature of medicine as such
but from a "contract" with society (or much less often, from
society's unilateral dictate). Appeal to a "contract" with society
may seem out of place when, as with physician participation in
executions, society (or at least its agent, the state) seems so unaware of the contract's terms that it has passed a law—over the
loud objection of physicians—allowing physicians to do what the
"contract" supposedly forbids. It is, I think, proof of the tenaci-
ty of the idea of contract that, however out of place it may seem,
it has nonetheless been invoked to justify prohibiting physician
participation in executions.[16]

To these four common approaches, I would add a fifth, my
own approach to professional ethics. It resembles the social insofar as both recognize a certain arbitrariness in what may turn
out to be "ethical" for physicians. My approach differs from the
social in placing that arbitrariness in the profession of medicine
rather than in the decisions of society as such or in some agreement that physicians have wrested from society. For me, society
(like morality or the nature of medicine) is a "side constraint,"
not the primary (or even coequal) party in determining the content of medical ethics. We might, then, call my approach "professional" to emphasize the central place the profession has in
defining professional standards. The professional approach alone
provides a way to recognize a special moral authority in an AMA
Opinion on a question of medical ethics.

The professional approach may also explain why we must look
beyond the AMA's official code of ethics to find a sustained argument for disciplining physicians who participate in an execution—indeed, even for an argument condemning their conduct as
a breach of medical ethics. Legislators do not need arguments in
the way private physicians, philosophers, or others seeking to
influence legislation do. The only sustained argument for condemning physician participation in executions was published in
the *New England Journal of Medicine* about the time the AMA
adopted 2.06.[17] The authors—William Curran, a lawyer, and Ward
Casscells, a physician—were both on the faculty of Harvard

Medical School. Their article remains the classic statement of the argument against physician participation.[18] It is to that argument we must now turn.

The argument of Curran and Casscells may be divided into two subarguments, one depending on international statements of medical ethics, the other on a (supposedly) fundamental principle of medical ethics. Both arguments combine therapeutic and casuistic elements. I dispose of the first subargument in the next section and of the second in the one following that. I then formulate what I take to be the concern underlying them, a misfit between typical medical practice and physician-assisted executions. Next, I show that physicians could respond to that (therapeutic) concern without ruling out all physician participation in executions. Physician participation in executions can be made enough like typical medical practice (arguably) to satisfy Principle I. If physicians are to be disciplined for participating in executions, it will have to be under Opinion 2.06, interpreted as a regulation rather than as a (mere) social policy, not under Principle I or any other "fundamental principle of medical ethics." Last, I will sketch an argument for the special moral authority of Opinion 2.06, an authority providing a basis for professional discipline as well as private criticism.

INTERNATIONAL STATEMENTS

Curran and Casscells promise to show that "the ethical principles of the medical profession worldwide should be interpreted to unconditionally condemn medical participation in this new form of capital punishment."[19] In fact, they show nothing of the kind. Their arguments fail for one of two reasons. First, most "principles" they refer to, while certainly widely accepted rules both of medical ethics and ordinary morality, are silent on the crucial point. Second, the one "principle" that seems on point is not really a widely accepted "principle" of medical ethics.

Here, perhaps, is the place to prevent a terminological confusion. In medical ethics, "principle" is sometimes used to mean a reason, something that should carry weight in deliberations without necessarily being decisive. Principles (in this sense) can be neither obeyed nor disobeyed. They can only be given "due consideration" or not, whatever we actually do. That is how I generally use "principle." But "principle" can also be used to mean a relatively abstract rule from which specific (disciplinary) rules derive. Principles—in this second sense—do require (or forbid) certain acts; they can be obeyed or disobeyed; they do not simply weigh in deliberations. "Principle" may also be used in a third sense, to mean an ideal ("high principle"); that is, an objective that it is good to aim for but not bad to fall short of. Like principles (in my preferred sense, the first), ideals do not require any particular acts. Ideals can be served or disserved but not obeyed or disobeyed.

I enclosed "principle" in quotes in the paragraph introducing this section to signal that I was not then choosing between these uses, though we must choose before we go much further. Consider, for example, the AMA's Principle I. Does it state a rule, a principle, or an ideal of professional practice? It must, I think, state a *rule*, not just a principle or ideal. A physician who, for example, even once provides incompetent medical care would not simply have fallen short of a medical ideal (though he certainly would have done that) or failed to give due weight to professional standards (though he might have done that, too); rather, he would have done something forbidden to physicians. He would have disobeyed the first *rule* of medical ethics. He would have provided incompetent medical care.

What about Curran and Casscells? What do they mean by "principle"? While they don't say, we must, I think, assume that they too mean "rule." They are, after all, arguing for an "unconditional condemnation" of physician participation in executions, not just for an important principle weighing against such participation and certainly not for a mere ideal of avoiding such participation. The very statements of medical ethics that they cite in support of their position are written in the preemptory language of rules. Consider, first, the World Medical Association's Declaration of Geneva (the "modern version" of the Oath of Hippocrates, adopted in 1948). It states (in part) that "even under threat, I will not use my medical knowledge contrary to the laws of humanity."[20] That statement sounds like a rule of conduct. Using one's medical knowledge contrary to the laws of humanity is wrong, even under threat. The declaration is an *oath* not to violate the laws of humanity—laws that, being subject to *violation*, must themselves be understood as rules.

What then does the declaration tell us about the permissibility of physician participation in executions? The answer is disappointing. The declaration merely tells us that, *if* the death penalty is against the laws of humanity, physicians are forbidden to use their special knowledge to help execute a sentence of death. Is the death penalty against the laws of humanity? The declaration does not say, but its history offers some guidance concerning what its authors thought. In 1948, when the declaration was adopted, Nazis were still being hanged (only a few miles from Geneva) for violation of the laws of humanity. If the declaration's authors thought the death penalty inconsistent with the laws of humanity or physician participation in enforcing them, would they not have said so? Since they did not, it seems that Curran and Casscells are not entitled to claim the declaration's authority for their argument against physician participation in executions. Indeed, if anyone is entitled to claim the declaration's authority for that, it would seem to be those who think that physician participation in executions is not a violation of medical ethics. Plainly, Curran and Casscells need to give content to "the laws of humanity."

The Declaration of Tokyo (1975) provides some of this content. Its Principle 1 forbids physicians to participate "in any practice of torture or inhumane or degrading procedure." Principle 3 similarly forbids physicians to provide "the premises, instruments, substances, or knowledge to facilitate the practice of torture or other forms of cruel, inhumane, or degrading treatment or to diminish the ability of the victim to resist such treatment."[21] Torture, or any other cruel, inhumane, or degrading practice, is plainly contrary to the laws of humanity (and so physician participation in such practices is plainly unethical because physicians are not exempt from the laws of humanity). No surprise in that.[22] But what about the death penalty? Is it also a cruel, inhumane, or degrading practice (and so prohibited)?

To their credit, Curran and Casscells (after drawing several misleading conclusions) admit that the "Declaration of Tokyo [like the Declaration of Geneva] does not deal directly with capital punishment."[23] They then appeal to the U.S. Supreme Court for help in establishing that the death penalty, even when carried out by lethal injection, is "cruel, inhumane, or degrading." Unfortunately, the best they can do is Justice Brennan's 1972 opinion in *Furman v. Georgia*, an opinion five years older than the oldest statute authorizing lethal injection as a means of execution.[24] More than two decades later, not only has the Supreme Court not declared the death penalty "cruel and unusual [or degrading]"—that is, inhumane—it has allowed the use of lethal injection and seems unlikely to change its mind any time soon.

Curran and Casscells do not draw on philosophical discussions of inhumanity. That is understandable for at least two reasons. One is that philosophers have yet to identify a good argument for the inhumanity of the death penalty. The other is that the bad arguments philosophers have identified (see chapter 3) generally stress the analogy with torture, the painfulness of execution. Even if such arguments could demonstrate the inhumanity of hanging or electrocution, they might well fail to do the same for lethal injection, the least painful form of execution in use.[25] Like everyone else, philosophers have been unable to provide a decisive argument for including participation in execution by lethal injection within the Declaration of Tokyo's prohibition of involvement in cruel, inhumane, or degrading practices.

In fact, of all the internationally recognized statements of medical ethics that Curran and Casscells cite, the only one explicitly concerned with the death penalty (or at least with causing death) is the Hippocratic Oath. The difficulty with relying on the Hippocratic Oath is that, though a commonplace of medical ethics, its only official status for at least the last two-hundred years seems to have been as a formality of graduation ceremonies. The reason it has had no other status should be evident to anyone who reads it carefully: much of it is an embarrassment. The oath requires physicians to share their earnings with any of their teachers who are in need, to give the sons of physicians free tuition in medical school, and to keep medical knowledge from anyone but would-be physicians; it also forbids physicians to give abortions or engage in surgery ("use the knife"). The question, then, is not whether the oath also forbids physicians to give "any deadly drug" but why physicians so often bring the oath up in contemporary discussions of medical ethics.[26]

A FUNDAMENTAL PRINCIPLE, "FIRST, DO NO HARM"?[27]

I may seem too picky. When physicians appeal to the Hippocratic Oath, they are (it will be said) really appealing to a "fundamental principle" of medical ethics, one actually in the Oath: "First [or above all], do no harm."[28] Let us agree.[29] What then? Curran and Casscells (or someone else) must still tell us what that "principle" means. I shall now show that, whatever it means, it cannot both be a rule of conduct for physicians and forbid physician participation in executions. It cannot even be a principle providing a weighty argument against such participation. I begin with the obvious:

Physicians do much harm without violating medical ethics, for example, to the animals they experiment on, to the society whose resources they use without counting the cost, and to the environment into which their medical waste must be dumped.

"Oh," physicians may respond, "you know what we mean: harm to *people*." But physicians do much harm to people without violating medical ethics. They fire employees who, they believe, are not doing their job. They testify in criminal trials, knowing that their expertise may help achieve a verdict of guilty, perhaps even a sentence of death. They heal soldiers so that they may again become instruments of death. Physicians have even been known to save the life of a brutal parent, knowing that he may return home to torture, maim, or even kill his child.

"Oh," the response becomes, "you know what we mean: harm to *one's patient*." But physicians do harm their patients. They give them dangerous drugs, cut off parts of their body, and not infrequently cause them considerable pain; they even turn some slow-paying patients over to a collection agency for dunning or take them to court to force payment. Danger, loss of a limb, pain, and loss of possessions are all harms (in the ordinary sense of the term). Physicians do such harm to patients knowingly (and ethically).

"Yes," physicians will say, "but we meant: harm to a patient's *health*: we would not give a dangerous drug unless needed, not remove a limb except to save a life, and so on." Though this formulation of "first, do no harm" rings true (in a way the preceding did not), it is still open to counterexamples. For example, physicians experiment on patients, doing clinical trials of drugs to test for toxicity as well as for effectiveness. Such tests, though sometimes fatal, are not unethical, provided the patient is beyond saving and gives her informed consent. By such tests, physicians sacrifice today's patients (sometimes causing discomfort or even premature death) to benefit those to come. Medicine remains an empirical enterprise in which patients occasionally serve as (voluntary research subjects. While physicians have made the patient central to medicine, they have not made the individual patient's health paramount.

I may by now seem to have whittled "First, do no harm" down to a splinter. I am, however, not done. I have left the impression that health, whether of today's patient or tomorrow's, remains the physician's pole star. Health has no such privileged status. Physicians may (ethically) risk health for other goods. A physician may, for example, undertake risky cosmetic surgery, even where the object is mere fashionableness (for example, large breasts) or some odd desire (for example, to live as a woman rather than as a man). Physicians may also practice sports medicine, where the object is helping athletes to win rather than protecting their health or curing them of disease. "Do no harm" does not rule out sacrificing health to other ends or, it seems, even weigh heavily against such sacrifice. Why then should it rule out physician participation in a lawful execution—or even provide a weighty reason against such participation? Why believe "Do no harm" should carry more weight with physicians than with anyone else?[30]

MEDICAL PRACTICE, TYPICAL AND NOT SO TYPICAL

In most jurisdictions, a physician cannot legally practice medicine without a license. But nowhere can a physician practice without a patient—that is, a human being whom she is supposed to benefit by using her knowledge of human disease, its prevention, course, and cure. Indeed, we might say that, *strictly*, one is a physician only if, in addition to the knowledge and skill of a physician, one has a patient. A physician without a patient is only a physician of sorts, a physician potentially (in the way ice is water) or historically (in the way a dead tree is still a tree). A physician without patients is retired, unemployed, or otherwise "not in practice." So, the physician who tests for toxicity using human subjects is not quite a physician, even though his tests serve medicine, and even though his test subjects are human. Insofar as the test subjects are not expected to benefit directly from the physician's knowledge or skill, he has no patients. He is acting as a (medical) scientist rather than as a physician. That status creates special problems in recognition of which the AMA has adopted special (relatively complex) standards.[31]

The medical researcher is not the only physician acting as something other than a typical physician. The physician with a dying patient is also not quite a physician (with respect to the dying patient). Health (rather than bare life) is the physician's typical objective. Once health is no longer possible, the physician can only maintain biological life and provide comfort. Using knowledge developed for prevention and cure, she may sedate the patient, tell him what to expect, or cheer him with small talk. Critics of medicine often complain that physicians are ill-prepared for the role of helpless comforter. No doubt, physicians should be better prepared for it. But given what physicians usually do, we must recognize comforting the dying as an activity lying in that shadowy country between medicine (strictly so called) and other legitimate related occupations (nursing, social work, psychology, the ministry, or the like).[32] Indeed, the "hospice movement" seems, in part, an attempt to create a new profession skilled at doing what hospitals and other medical institutions seem to do so badly: comfort the dying without pretending to do more.

Physicians who do cosmetic surgery also work in that shadowy country between medicine and other occupations. While (mere) cosmetic surgeons do have patients (or perhaps more accurately, clients), the benefit that they provide is independent of disease.[33] Much of what they know was developed in the course of treating burns, birth defects, and other pathologies, but at least some of what they know is not necessary to treat any disease, defect, or wound but simply to achieve effects not unlike those beauticians aim at. For cosmetic surgeons, health is (at best) a side-constraint, not an object in the way it is for most physicians (most of the time). Like medical scientists, cosmetic surgeons work close to the boundary of medicine.

The same is true of physicians who practice sports medicine. While much of what they do resembles ordinary medical practice—for example, setting bones or diagnosing illness—there are striking dissimilarities as well. Sports medicine is as much an extension of the trainer's art as of the physician's. Much of what sports physicians know about diet, medication, and treatment of injuries developed independently of medicine proper. For sports medicine, as for cosmetic surgery, health is at most a side-constraint.[34]

Physicians have moved almost imperceptibly into these (and other) atypical areas of practice for at least one of three reasons.

First, much of what physicians typically do carries over to such "quasimedicine." For example, the skills that develop when one treats patients are also useful when one does toxicity tests on human subjects. One can talk to a subject much as one would to a patient. There is still a human body to examine. Symptoms of toxicity are symptoms of disease. And so on.

Second, the moral structure typical of medicine will be present in these atypical areas, at least in large part. So, for example, the researcher's "subject" or the cosmetic surgeon's "client" will be there voluntarily. The cosmetic surgeon's client will, like an ordinary physician's patient, be seeking some benefit (though not a medical benefit, strictly speaking). The researcher's subject, while not there seeking a benefit for herself, will still be there in the service of medicine (much as would some healthy human donating a kidney, bone marrow, or fresh blood to a patient in need).

Third, society may have no other way to perform the function in question, or at least no other way that is nearly as satisfactory. So, for example, part of what makes it seem appropriate for physicians to become cosmetic surgeons is that we have no other obvious candidate. Who but an M.D. with a specialty in plastic surgery would we want to reshape a nose or suck fat out of a hip?

Physicians generally avoid work for which they lack the skill, but most of what I have called "the shadow country of medicine" consists of areas of potential practice where physicians seem clearly more skillful than those who might take their place. So, for example, whatever objections we have to physicians practicing cosmetic surgery or sports medicine, they seem more likely to protect health and otherwise do more good than harm than would, say, beauticians or trainers.

Returning to physician-assisted execution, we see immediately that it too lies deep in the shadow country of medicine. Many typical practices of physicians seem out of place at an execution. For example, physicians typically swab the skin with alcohol before inserting a needle. Should they swab the skin before inserting the executioner's needle (seemingly mocking standard medical practice) or instead ignore standard medical practice in this odd environment where infection is no longer a worry?

Medical knowledge, insofar as distinct from skill, also does not carry over to executions without reworking. While much that they know can be used to kill, physicians must rethink it to kill well. So, for example, to use a paralytic to kill, a physician must begin with the maximum safe dosage, extrapolate to a dosage likely to cause death, and then add a "safety factor" to get the dosage to be used in an execution (without giving a dose so large that it causes unpleasant side-effects before death). The problem of carryover is the same as in physician-assisted euthanasia (or even as in physician-*administered* euthanasia), another area where the role of physicians is controversial. Physician-assisted executions are, however, necessarily more controversial.

Physicians who oppose physician-assisted euthanasia seem to do so primarily because they do not want any physician intentionally to cause a patient's death, even when the patient not only wants death but would clearly benefit from it. The death does not serve health (though it does not disserve it, either). Those physicians can oppose today's physician-assisted executions on similar grounds (adding only that execution actually does disserve the prisoner's health). For such physicians, physician-assisted execution is hardly more controversial than physician-assisted euthanasia.

But for physicians who *defend* physician-assisted euthanasia, physician-assisted execution is necessarily more controversial. They generally defend physician-assisted euthanasia by appealing to "patient autonomy" (what the AMA's Principle I calls "respect for human dignity"), the same consideration that makes cosmetic surgery and sports medicine seem acceptable uses of medical knowledge. Appeal to "patient autonomy" seems to cut against physician-assisted execution because, ordinarily, execution is against the prisoner's will.

The last of the three reasons explaining why physicians might support Opinion 2.06 is that the skills actually needed intentionally to kill a human being by lethal injection are not clearly those of a physician. Nurses are generally better at inserting the needle. A veterinarian might actually be better at ordering the necessary equipment, determining dose, and the like, since vets *routinely* put their "patients" to death. The physician's skills do not seem to give her a clear technical advantage over others who might replace her.

These reasons are, I think, enough to explain why most physicians might oppose physician-assisted executions. There are, nonetheless, two other reasons worth mention, though neither is "medical" in the way these are.

One of these reasons is social stigma. Even when executions were far less controversial than they are in the United States today, the executioner was at best a bird of ill-omen, someone to be avoided much as one avoids the graveyard or the prison. Physicians would probably resist association with the executioner even if they had no other reason to oppose physician participation in executions.[35]

The other reason is economic. Executions, unlike cosmetic surgery or sports medicine, are likely to remain a rare part of any physician's practice. There are just not that many executions.[36] In addition, executions are likely to pay poorly. No state has ever paid prison physicians (or executioners) well; physician-executioners are unlikely to do much better.

These five reasons are, I admit, together of great weight (as the classic argument was not). Yet even these are not necessarily decisive. There are alternatives to Opinion 2.06 that, together with relatively small changes in the death-penalty statute, would make physician participation in executions enough like typical medical practice that even physicians who oppose such participation could understand why a good physician might participate and why they should not condemn him for doing so.

REWRITING THE PHYSICIAN'S ROLE
IN EXECUTIONS

Like most jurisdictions adopting execution by lethal injection, Illinois made a serious conceptual error. It assumed that physicians are necessary because lethal injection is indisputably a medical procedure. In fact, though resembling a certain medical procedure (indeed, being physically almost indistinguishable from it), lethal injection lies (at best) at the outer margin of medical practice today. Execution by lethal injection is no more necessarily a medical procedure than execution by firing squad is necessarily a military procedure.[37]

State law often contributed to this conceptual error. For example, in many states, the drugs required for execution could not be obtained for injection into a human without a physician's prescription. Laws, designed to protect the public from incompetent dispensers of drugs, turned out to be too broad, making physician participation legally necessary when the state had no interest in protecting the "patient's" health.

Yet once we admit that execution by lethal injection is not necessarily a medical practice, we face a dilemma.

On the one hand, if execution by injection is not a medical practice at all, what business can a professional society have advising its members not to participate (much less forbidding them to participate)? That an executioner (or executioner's assistant) would use knowledge gained in medical training or practice (as well, perhaps, as knowledge gained outside) seems only the weakest of reasons. Physicians use knowledge so gained in many lawful nonmedical activities, including buying stock, raising children, serving on juries, and holding public office. How many physicians would want to argue that the AMA has a right to regulate their participation in such activities because physicians use knowledge gained in medical training in those activities? Claiming that execution by lethal injection is *not* a medical procedure thus seems to undermine the AMA's right to adopt Opinion 2.06.[38]

However, once we admit that execution by lethal injection *is* a medical procedure, though an atypical one, we can at least ask how the procedure could be made more typical, how we might rearrange things so that a physician could conduct herself at an execution much more as she would anywhere else. The door to physician participation is open, if only wide enough for theory.[39] For our purposes (the purposes of theory), it will be enough to identify three (not necessarily exclusive) ways in which physician participation in execution by lethal injection could be made more like typical medical practice.

First, Opinion 2.06 might be rewritten to allow physicians to participate in executions, but only to protect the prisoner from unnecessary pain. Physicians could easily take this part.[40] A physician would, for example, have a better sense than a nurse or vet of what dose of barbiturates would be sufficient to keep a prisoner unconscious long enough for the paralytic agent to kill. Since the prisoner would not want to have the barbiturate wear off after the paralytic had begun working but before he had suffocated, such physician participation would (in that respect at least) seem consistent with Principle I's dedication to "compassion."

Second, Opinion 2.06 might be rewritten to allow a physician to serve as executioner (or executioner's assistant), but only at the prisoner's request (and provided the physician follows ordinary medical practice insofar as it is consistent with the purpose of execution). The prisoner would then be much more like an ordinary patient. The prisoner has good reason to want a physician to handle the execution. Consider again the best alternatives to a physician: a veterinarian or nurse.[41]

The veterinarian would have considerable experience killing animals by lethal injection. In that respect, vets seem preferable to physicians. In other respects, however, physicians seem preferable. There is, of course, the obvious implication of having an "animal doctor" practice on a human. Many prisoners would feel the slight. There are also more practical worries. Animals are (or at least seem to be) less sensitive to pain than humans; a vet might therefore tend to underestimate the pain a human feels in similar circumstances. Because the skin of animals is generally looser, a vet's sense of where best to place a needle might also be off enough to turn a simple procedure into an ordeal. The vet's "bedside manner" may even be rougher than a physician's would be in the same circumstances.

A nurse would probably be more comforting than either a vet or a physician and, ordinarily, better at placing the needle, too. He would, however, be less skilled at determining dosage than either a physician or vet. And in an extraordinary case, for example, where a prisoner's veins are hard to find or damaged because of drug use, a physician would have a clear advantage over a nurse. "Cut downs" (cutting into the skin to open a vein to a needle) are part of a physician's practice in a way they are not part of a nurse's.

Allowing the physician to participate, but only at the prisoner's request, would still mean that medical knowledge, whether in the hands of a physician, nurse, or veterinarian, would be used to kill a prisoner *against his will*. The prisoner would not have chosen to die by lethal injection. Physicians, unable to prevent such a use of medical knowledge, might still want to distance themselves from it. That brings me to a third possible way to make physician-assisted execution more like ordinary medical practice.

The death-penalty statute could be amended so that there is an alternative to death by lethal injection. The alternative should, of course, also be humane (and actually available should the prisoner choose it).[42] A physician would then be called upon to assist in an execution only if the prisoner chose to die by lethal injection rather than by the alternative. The statute might, in addition, allow the prisoner to choose whether to have a physician, nurse, or someone else assist in the execution.

Allowing a physician to participate in an execution only when the prisoner chose both the method of execution and the profession of the executioner, would, it seems to me, assure that the physician could participate in a way that respects the prisoner's human dignity (his status as autonomous agent). Such participation would also allow the physician to use ordinary medical skills in something like their ordinary way. The physician could be as compassionate as usual, seeking to make the prisoner as comfortable as possible. The service she provided, while not ordinary medicine, would be close enough to be judged by something like ordinary standards of competence. So, for example, she should swab the prisoner's skin with alcohol before inserting the deadly needle because execution provides no overriding reason not to follow that standard medical procedure, and the physician is there because the prisoner expects her to follow such procedures insofar as possible. (The following of such procedures is, after all, largely what distinguishes a physician from a mere executioner or "medical technician.")

But (it might be objected), there is still an important difference between these improved conditions and what would be necessary for ethical medical practice. The patient-convict would have to consent freely to having a physician poison him. The patient-convict may indeed have consented to being executed by lethal injection rather than by hanging, electrocution, or gas, and he may also have consented to having a physician be his executioner rather than to having a guard, vet, or nurse. But he has not consented to any of this freely but only because he would be executed in any case. A physician should not harm a patient without the patient's free consent. That is medical ethics if anything is.

The problem with this objection is that "free" demands either too much or too little. "Free" demands too much if it requires the patient's decision to be unconstrained. Few if any important decisions are unconstrained. A patient will, for example, normally consent to have his gangrenous leg cut off only after his physician has made it plain that death is the only likely alternative. However autonomous the decision to allow the leg to be cut off, the decision will hardly be unconstrained; nor is it likely to feel that way to either the physician or the patient.

"Free" will still demand too much if it is understood to allow only natural facts as constraints. The fact that the Federal Drug Administration has not yet approved a certain therapy would not nullify the autonomy of a patient's consent to one of the legal (but probably less effective) alternatives. Laws too can be constraints that leave the patient's autonomy intact (and so, the freedom of his consent). The laws must, however, be just (or at least arguably just).

"Free", however, will mean too little if we understand "free consent" as requiring that the consent be constrained only by natural facts and just rules. Physicians have generally tried to discuss their participation in executions *without* joining the argument concerning the justice (or the moral permissibility) of the death penalty as such. Indeed, many physicians who oppose physician participation in executions may well favor the death penalty as such. So, requiring consent to be free only in this third sense would create a dilemma for those who oppose physician participation in executions. Either they must admit that their arguments against physician participation in executions ultimately presupposes that the death penalty is unjust however executed, or they must admit that—under the revised procedures we have imagined—the patient-convict consents freely (enough) to have the physician help in his execution. While execution under such conditions would leave the physician operating far from the bright center of medical practice, it would leave her no farther, perhaps, than the physician who assists a terminally ill patient in suicide; physician-assisted suicide, while still highly controversial, is no longer explicitly forbidden by an AMA Opinion.

WHY 2.06 CAN NONETHELESS BE MORALLY BINDING

I have now shown that Opinion 2.06 is but one of several morally permissible alternatives consistent with the main body of medical ethics; it cannot be derived from general moral standards, the nature of medicine, or the dictates of society. What I shall now show is that Opinion 2.06 is nonetheless morally binding on American physicians.

Assume that Opinion 2.06 lays down a morally permissible rule of conduct (although not a rule of conduct that morality requires). Assume too that Opinion 2.06 belongs to an actual practice, medicine, in which physicians voluntarily participate and from which they derive substantial benefits not otherwise available (for example, the satisfactions of working as a physician rather than as a dentist, nurse, or chiropractor). Assume too that these benefits derive at least in part from other physicians doing what they would otherwise avoid as too burdensome (in other words, assume that medicine is a cooperative practice). Last, assume that there is a moral rule ("Don't cheat") requiring us to obey the rules governing any morally permissible cooperative practice from which we derive benefit in virtue of our voluntary participation. Then, *assuming* all that, any physician, whether a member of the AMA or not, would be morally required to obey Opinion 2.06 while she (voluntarily) remains a physician.

I have now given a (deductive) argument for the proposition that a rule of medical ethics can be morally binding without being derived by deduction, interpretation, or the like from a more general standard, whether moral, medical, or social. Of course, the argument is only as good as the four assumptions on which it rests. While space forbids me to make a full defense of any of them here, I nonetheless have room to make all four seem plausible enough for our purpose.[43] I shall discuss the four in order.

The first assumption should be uncontroversial. Whatever its faults, Opinion 2.06 does not seem to require anything immoral. It merely seeks to transform what might otherwise be a morally permissible act into one morally impermissible for physicians. In this respect, Opinion 2.06 is like a promise, the making of which changes the moral geography by requiring or forbidding what might otherwise have been optional.

The second assumption is that Opinion 2.06 belongs to an actual practice, that physicians participate in the practice voluntarily, and that they derive substantial benefits from the practice. Nothing in this assumption should be controversial. Certainly, physicians participate voluntarily in medicine. No one is forced to become or remain a physician; nor is anyone likely to starve should she give up medicine. Indeed, what makes quitting medicine hard is the certain loss of the benefits it provides: a relatively high standard of living combined with public deference and an opportunity to help people in a way most people cannot.

If anything in the second assumption should be controversial, it is the claim that Opinion 2.06 is a part of the social practice we call "medicine" (as opposed, say, to "AMA activities"). While that claim raises empirical questions too complex to be settled here, I can offer an example of the evidence supporting it. Consider the efforts the Illinois State Medical Association (ISMA) made to enforce Opinion 2.06. They are certainly evidence that Opinion 2.06 has an effect on what physicians do—an effect on both AMA members (the activists in the ISMA) and ordinary physicians (the three who had to remain anonymous to avoid investigation, criticism, and perhaps reprimand or suspension from practice). ISMA's concern that physician participation in executions would undermine the trust that exists between physician and patient also suggests that at least some physicians believe that AMA standards help to maintain an environment from which physicians, AMA members or not, benefit.[44]

The third assumption is that medicine is a cooperative practice; that is, the benefits that accrue to each participant depend primarily on what other participants do (or have done). This should not be controversial. If, for example, most physicians were "quacks," who would want to be known as a "physician"? If would-be healers want to be called "physicians" (and be licensed accordingly), is that not (at least in part) because most physicians have served people better than the faith healers, unlicensed pill-pushers, and the others who compete or could compete with them? If states today limit the practice of medicine to licensed physicians (and those working under their supervision), might that not be because experience with physicians showed that the public needed to be protected from other "medicine men" in a way that they did not need to be protected from physicians?[45]

There is, then, a sense in which no physician practices alone. All share a common profession, a code of conduct supporting public expectations of trustworthiness. Much of what physicians require of each other is, however reasonable, burdensome. Not only long years of training but even the compassion and respect for human dignity required by Principle I do not come easily. Almost every physician knows of some physician who falls short of what their common code requires. It is a measure of how hard such expectations are to maintain that the medical profession is always worried that this or that will threaten public trust. The maintenance of public trust is, then, a cooperative undertaking, a sharing of burdens in order to share the benefits.

The fourth assumption is that there is a moral rule requiring us to obey the rules governing any morally permissible cooperative practice from which we derive benefit in virtue of our voluntary participation. What makes this assumption (relatively) uncontroversial is that the moral rule in question concerns only voluntary practices—practices voluntary in the ordinary sense that one must work to get into them and work to stay in them. In fact, a physician can cease to be a physician simply by ceasing to practice (and can cease to be a physician in law simply by resigning her license). Participants in a voluntary cooperative practice are morally entitled to criticize those who cheat, to reprimand them formally, and (if all else fails) to protect the practice by withholding—in some morally permissible way—the benefits that the practice generates (for example, by denying would-be "free riders" the designation "physician").[46]

That, I hope, is enough to suggest how much might be said in defense of my four assumptions and so to suggest the strength of the preceding analysis of the ethics of physician participation in executions—including our conclusion that the objections of physicians are more or less independent of the merits of the death penalty as such.

NOTES

I should like to thank Bill Pardue for help in research for this chapter; those attending IIT's philosophy colloquium, 13 October 1993, for a spirited discussion; and three anonymous reviewers at *The Hastings Center Report* for much helpful criticism.

   1. *Illinois Criminal Law and Procedure* (St. Paul, Minn: West Publishing, 1991), chap. 38, sec. 119-5(a)(1).

   2. *Illinois Criminal Law and Procedure*, chap. 38, sec. 119-5(2)(d).

   3. Illinois's first execution was described in this way (on the morning *before*): "At 12:01 a.m., Walker, strapped to a gurney and with an intravenous tube already in his arm, will be wheeled into the death chamber, a small room with the state's $24,000 lethal-injection machine attached to one wall. Two doctors selected by the Department of Corrections will attach Walker's intravenous tube to a tube from the death machine. They also will attach a heart monitor so they and the witnesses will know when Walker's heart stops. . . . [A few minutes later] two executioners [in another room] will each push a

button. One [of the buttons] will activate the death machine. . . . When the buttons are pushed, the lethal-injection machine's green, yellow, and red lights will begin blinking, telling the executioners that it is going through its cycles and administering the lethal drugs to Walker. . . . until the heart monitor goes flat, signaling that he is dead. At that point, the doctors will approach Walker, confirm that he is dead, and turn off the machine." Rob Karwath, "Death's arrival one of precision," *Chicago Tribune*, 11 September 1990, 6.

4. American Medical Association, "Report of Council on Ethical and Judicial Affairs [A]" (December 1992), 183. Seven of these states allow a choice between lethal injection and the method of execution previously provided.

5. Rob Karwath and William Grady, "Walker becomes 1st execution in 28 years," *Chicago Tribune*, Wednesday, 12 September 1990, 1.

6. Dai Parker-Gwilliam, "M.D. fights 'execution's assistant' role," *Loyola Magazine* (Spring 1993): 82.

7. Andrew A. Skolnick, "Health Professionals Oppose Rules Mandating Participation in Executions," *Journal of the American Medical Association* 269 (10 February 1993): 721–723, at 722.

8. *Code of Medical Ethics: Current Opinions of the Council on Ethical and Judicial Affairs of the American Medical Association* (Chicago: American Medical Association, 1992), 3.

9. "Physician Participation in Capital Punishment (Resolution 5, I–91)," Report A of Council on Ethical and Judicial Affairs, Chicago: American Medical Association, December 1992, 188.

10. Determination or certification of death should be done after the execution, that is, after a nonphysician has declared the prisoner dead, the needle has been removed from the prisoner's arm, and the body has been moved from the place of execution to a room down the hall or to a coroner's office miles away. See AMA Report A (December 1992), 188.

11. It is astonishing how much the AMA's Opinions concerning these matters have changed since 1980. Not only have new opinions been added, but many of the old ones have disappeared entirely or been radically rewritten. This is another indication of the speed with which medicine is rethinking itself.

12. Opinion 2.17—on "Quality of Life"—is about as close as any other opinion comes to recognizing a duty to preserve life when there is any hope of doing so: "Life should be cherished despite disabilities and handicaps, except when the prolongation would be inhumane and unconscionable." Note that the "except" clause explicitly recognizes

that life should not be preserved soley because there is hope of doing so.

13. As far as I can tell, this proposed purpose of medicine has no historical warrant. It does not appear in the Hippocratic Oath, in Percival's classic *Medical Ethics* (1803), or in any of the AMA codes since the first in 1847. Its history deserves investigation.

14. I am, of course, assuming that assisting in a (legal) execution is legal. In fact (like almost everything else associated with the death penalty), that too can be controversial. Apparently, at least one charge that the Illinois State Medical Society wanted to investigate was whether the three interns had violated a provision of the Illinois Medical Practice Act prohibiting physicians from prescribing, administering, distributing, or giving a controlled substance or narcotic for reasons other than medically accepted therapeutic purposes. Skolnick, 722. I ignore this complication here because a) it is basically a technical legal issue of interpreting apparently conflicting laws, b) the issue can easily be resolved merely by inserting "except as otherwise provided" in the Medical Practice Act (by legislative act or judicial interpretation), and c) such a resolution would not satisfy ISMA, indeed, would probably seem only to aggravate the ethical issue.

15. See, for example, the comment of Thomas Houston, consultant to the AMA's Council on Ethics and Judicial Affairs: "[R]equiring physicians to participate in executions goes against the very nature of the practice and principles of medicine." Skolnick, 721–722. I would put most appeals to "[medical] tradition" in this category as well.

16. See, for example, Parker-Gwilliam, 82 (quoting William Gibbons, active in opposing physician participation in executions in Illinois): "'Doctors have a special social contract to act in their patients' best interest,' Gibbons explained. 'Their participation at executions is totally antithetical to that contract.'" Another writer offers what seems to be an interesting variation, appealing to a trust (in the legal sense) instead of a contract or social dictate: "Doctors hold their medical knowledge in trust for the collective well-being of mankind, and they must guard against the exploitation of that knowledge in ways that compromise the supreme aspirations of the profession." Richard J. Bonnie, "The death penalty: When doctors must say no," *British Medical Journal* 305 (15 August 1992): 381–382. Whether this is a variation of the social argument depends, of course, on who put the knowledge in trust, society or the medical profession. If society ("mankind"), then presumably society, the principal in this trust, can change the terms at will. If, however, not society but the medical profession itself created the trust, then Bonnie's position becomes a variant of the professional approach rather than the social.

17. "The Ethics of Medical Participation in Capital Punishment by Intravenous Drug Injection," *New England Journal of Medicine* 302 (24 January 1980): 226–230. The only reasoned *defenses* of physician-assisted execution I have found are two brief opinion pieces—Dennis S. Hsieh, "Physicians Should Give Injections," *Journal of the American Medical Association* 261 (6 January 1989): 132; and Howard Entman, "First Do No Harm," *Journal of the American Medical Association* 261 (6 January 1989): 134—and Jack Kevorkian's eccentric "Medicine, ethics, and execution by lethal injection," *Medicine and Law* 4 (July 1985): 307–313. (Kevorkian is, of course, now famous—or infamous—as "Dr. Death" for assisting in the suicide of more than a dozen terminally ill "patients.")

18. When, for example, a psychiatrist recently wrote on treating condemned prisoners so that they could be found sane enough for execution, he began by noting, "Direct involvement in the administration of the death penalty itself, such as by injecting a lethal dose. . . , is undoubtedly forbidden by medical ethics." His only source for this "undoubted" truth—apart from the AMA—was Curran and Casscells. Richard J. Bonnie, "Medical Ethics and the Death Penalty," *Hastings Center Report* (May/June 1990): 12–18, quote at 14. A recent report of a "working party" of the British Medical Association does the same. See *Medicine Betrayed: The Participation of Doctors in Human Rights Abuses* (London: Zed Books, 1992), 112n. The chapter on the death penalty, though full of interesting facts, neither improves any argument already in the literature nor adds any new ones. I therefore ignore it in what follows.

19. Curran and Casscells, 227.

20. Curran and Casscells, 227.

21. Curran and Casscells, 228.

22. Note that this is basically a casuistic argument in therapeutic form. Strike all reference to medical knowledge, and the argument for not participating in cruel, inhumane, or degrading practices would be the same: participation by anyone, physician or not, is a crime against humanity.

23. Curran and Casscells, 228.

24. Curran and Casscells, 228.

25. Harold Hillman, "An unnatural way to die," *New Scientist* (27 October 1983): 276–278.

26. Curran and Casscells, 227. Even the prohibition of "deadly drugs" is embarrassing. Many drugs that physicians routinely use (morphine, barbiturates, AZT, and so on) are deadly in large doses (and work by interfering with healthy bodily processes). Such drugs may well have been what the Oath originally forbad.

27. Curran and Casscells, though they use "injury" where I use "harm," must, I think, mean "harm" (a setback to an interest) rather than (as the etymology of "injury" suggests) a violation of justice or of a right (allowing execution of a just death sentence to do harm without doing any injury). Curran and Casscells do not, I think, want to have to argue that physician participation in executing a death sentence depends on whether the death sentence is just (though, of course, injustice is the chief argument against physician participation in torture). In any case, Curran and Casscells offer nothing resembling an argument for the injustice of the death penalty (apart from Brennan's comment on its inhumanity). "Harm" rather than "injury" seems to clarify what they mean or, at least, to treat their confusion charitably.

28. Physicians often quote this principle in the Latin, *"Primum non nocere,"* rather than in the Greek of Hippocrates or the English of their auditors. Why? Lawyers, it seems to me, use Latin for concepts they don't understand (for example, *mens rea*). Could it be that physicians, so unlike lawyers in most ways, are like them in this?

29. For example: "The factor that predominates, however, is that professional standards in medicine always rest on the most fundamental of concepts, 'primum non nocere', above all do no harm. It is harmful to take a life." *Report A: Judicial Council* (adopted by AMA House of Delegates, December 1980).

30. "Do no harm" is, of course, an ordinary moral *principle*. That is, while every decent person wants to avoid doing harm, all else equal, "Do no harm" lacks the preemptive force of such moral rules as "Don't kill" and "Don't disable." Harm is generally only one consideration among many. Why then do physicians appeal to that principle rather than to the morally more powerful "Don't kill" when condemning participation in capital punishment? Could it be that "Do no harm" expresses a distinctive medical ideal? Perhaps. But such an ideal will not provide much of an argument for prohibiting participation in capital punishment. After all, part of being an ideal is being subject to compromise both by competing ideals and by various practical considerations. For one writer who, though a critic of physician participation in the death penalty, seems to appreciate this difficulty, see Bonnie, "The Death Penalty," 385: "[It] is a mistake to derive a prohibition against medical participation in executions from this injunction ['first do no harm']. . . . Indeed, because suffering in the administration of punishment violates human rights it can be argued, paradoxically, that medical involvement in capital punishment actually promotes human rights."

31. See AMA Opinions 2.07–2.08.

32. See AMA Opinions 2.20–2.22.

33. The root idea of "patient" is "one who suffers"; a "client," in contrast, is merely someone who asks a service (well, actually, "inclines" in the traditional posture of submission). Since the person who asks a physician for a "nose job," "breast remake," "sex change," or other (merely) cosmetic surgery is not suffering from any disease, but only from a desire to be different, "patient" seems the wrong term (though it is, of course, the only one now used).

34. AMA Opinion 3.06, the only opinion to address sports medicine, seems wholly inadequate. If, for example, a physician were simply to be concerned "to protect the health and safety of the contestants" (as 3.06 suggests), what part could she have in, say, a professional boxing match where every blow to the head contributes to long-term disability?

35. Compare AMA Report A (December 1992), 184: "The image of physician as executioner under circumstances mimicking medical care risks the general trust of the public."

36. At the time of the Walker execution, Illinois had 125 prisoners awaiting execution, an inventory built up over a decade. Karwath, 8. By 1992, the number awaiting execution nationally was a bit more than 2,500 (giving an accumulation rate of about 200 per year). Skolnick, 722. So, a handful of physicians (perhaps, a dozen) working more or less full time would be sufficient to satisfy the nation's entire demand for executions, supposing those annually executed equaled in number those annually sentenced to death. In fact, of course, very few of those sentenced to death over the last three decades have been executed—and many of those who have been have had to fight hard for it. The actual case load nationally thus seems too small to occupy even one physician full time.

37. Compare Curran and Casscells, 228–229: "[To] call such planned killing a medically acquired skill would, we submit, be erroneous. No physicians are trained to prepare lethal 'medications' for human administration; few, if any, physicians would have experience administering poisons or medication overdoses continuously to the point of death. Thus, requiring a physician to prepare and to administer or to supervise such a procedure would not be normal medical practice; it would be a perversion of biomedical knowledge and skill for a nonmedical purpose."

38. Some might be tempted to respond to this point in some such manner as this: The AMA may properly interfere with other nonmedical activities of physicians, for example, having sex with one's patient, so why not this? My reply is that such nonmedical activities still go on within the medical context. The sex partner in question is not a stranger to one's medical practice but a patient. However con-

troversial AMA regulation of such activities may be (and they have been controversial), it must, in principle, be less controversial than regulation where (as we are now assuming) the only relation the activity has to medicine is the use of medical knowledge.

39. Note, for example, that the Illinois State Medical Society "declared unethical any role of a physician *except acting as a source of support and solace to a patient facing death.*" (Italics mine.) "Illinois Doctors Condemn Physician Participation in Capital Punishment," *News from the Illinois State Medical Association,* 14 April 1991. In effect, I am here arguing for a role as "a source of support and solace to a patient facing death." Unfortunately, since the same news release reported a declaration that "physician participation in euthanasia or physician-aided suicide" is "unethical" and "grounds for discipline," a significant gap remains between the position that I am arguing is within the realm of (morally permissible) medical ethics and the position ISMA has actually taken.

40. Compare AMA Report A (December 1992), 187: "A physician's obligation to do no harm does not require him or her to totally abandon a condemned individual or to refrain from providing comfort or medical care to a person on death row."

41. In 1983, the American Nurses Association adopted a statement similar to the AMA's, opposing all participation by nurses in capital punishment. Skolnick, 721.

42. Since both electric chairs and gas chambers seem to decay unless used frequently and are expensive to maintain, and since prisoners generally prefer the firing squad to the gallows, gas chamber, or electric chair, execution by firing squad would probably be the best alternative. At least three states, Arkansas, Idaho, and Utah now provide for the firing squad as an alternative to lethal injection. Barry Pollack, "Deserts and Death: Limits on Maximum Punishment," *Rutgers Law Review* 44 (1992): 985–1019, at 985. Several other states, including California, allow the condemned prisoner to choose between lethal injection and whatever method had previously been used.

43. For those who require more, I would suggest my "The Moral Authority of a Professional Code," *NOMOS* 29 (1987): 302–337; as well as one or more of the following: "The Use of Professions," *Business Economics* 22 (October 1987): 5–10; "Vocational Teachers, Confidentiality, and Professional Ethics," *International Journal of Applied Philosophy* 4 (Spring 1988): 11–20; "Professionalism Means Putting Your Profession First," *Georgetown Journal of Legal Ethics* 2 (Summer 1988): 352–366; "Thinking Like an Engineer: The Place of a Code of Ethics in the Practice of a Profession," *Philosophy and Public Affairs* 20 (Spring 1991): 150–167; "Do Cops Need a Code of Ethics?"

Criminal Justice Ethics 10 (Summer/Fall 1991): 14–28; and "Treating Patients with Infectious Diseases: An Essay in the Ethics of Dentistry," *Professional Ethics* 2 (Spring/Summer 1993): 51–65.

44. Still, it might be asked, who gave the AMA this power? There are two ways to answer that question, neither of which I can more than sketch here. The first answer is: "No one. The AMA made itself the solution to a coordination problem by its good deeds over a century and a half." The other way to answer the question of who gave the AMA its power is: "Physicians. It is they who have come to look to the AMA for guidance on these questions, to treat the AMA as a coordination point even when they have not been members." These two answers are, of course, consistent and, indeed, two different ways of making the same point. To have a profession, the would-be members must find means of coordinating their conduct. An organization, even one to which less than half of all members of the profession belong, may well be the best way to achieve that coordination. For more on this point, see my "The Moral Authority of a Professional Code."

45. The monopoly that state licensing of physicians is supposed to confer is harder to define than commonly supposed (and may consist of little more than the right to declare oneself "a physician"). Physicians are certainly not the only people allowed to write prescriptions for human patients or do operations: dentists and osteopaths are also licensed to do such things (for purposes within their competence). Even if we were to understand "physician" to include dentists and osteopaths (who are also licensed by the state), there would still be people (for example, shamans) who, though unlicensed, seem to have the right to give medications or do operations provided they do not claim more than they can prove.

46. Problems arise when this rule is used to defend an obligation to obey the law (or when "voluntary" is omitted). For a defense of even this stronger version of the rule against criticism made during the 1970s, see Richard J. Arneson, "The Principle of Fairness and Free-Rider Problems," *Ethics* 92 (July 1982): 616–633; and my "Nozick's Argument *for* the Legitimacy of the Welfare State," *Ethics* 97 (April 1987): 576–594.

Five

The Argument from Irrevocability

It is sometimes argued that we should abolish the death penalty (in part at least) because the death penalty is irrevocable in a way imprisonment is not. Human beings are fallible, it is said, and fallible beings should not use a penalty that in effect assumes their infallibility. Let us call this "the argument from irrevocability."

The argument from irrevocability is treated with respect by both philosophers and people with more practical concerns. Thus, Burton Leiser (who favors the death penalty) is quite willing to admit:

> The death penalty is irrevocable. Although it is true that years spent in prison can never be returned to a man who was wrongly convicted, he at least has the opportunity of starting over; with the compensation he ought to receive from those who wrongfully deprived him of those years, he should be able to enjoy whatever remains to him. But a person who has been executed cannot be brought back if he is later found to have been innocent of the crime for which he was convicted. Such mistakes cannot be rectified. Mistakes have occurred. Innocent men have been executed. Those who support the death penalty must be prepared to live with the fact. . . .[1]

U.S. Supreme Court Justice Brennan (who opposes the death penalty) made a similar point in the much-discussed *Furman v. Georgia*:

> Death is truly an awesome punishment. . . . The contrast with the plight of a person punished by imprisonment is evident. An individual in prison does not lose "the right to have rights." A prisoner retains, for example, the constitutional right . . . of access to the courts. His punishment is not irrevocable. Apart from the common charge,

95

grounded upon the recognition of human fallibility, that the punishment of death must inevitably be inflicted upon innocent men, we know that death has been the lot of men whose convictions were unconstitutionally secured in view of later, retroactively applied, holdings of this court . . . [Yet] the finality of death precludes relief.[2]

Brennan does not, of course, make exactly the same argument as Leiser does. Brennan's concern is the legal consequences of death's irrevocability (for example, loss of "the right to have rights") while Leiser's is primarily the nonlegal consequences (for example, lack of "the opportunity to start over").

The arguments are, however, sufficiently alike to be represented as a single argument from irrevocability having this form:

1. Fallible beings should not, all else equal, use a penalty not permitting correction of error if there is an alternative penalty permitting correction of error.

2. We are fallible beings.

   (So: we should not, all else equal, use a penalty not permitting correction of error if there is an alternative penalty permitting correction of error.)

3. An irrevocable penalty (and only an irrevocable penalty) does not permit correction of error.

4. The death penalty is irrevocable.

5. Imprisonment is an alternative to the death penalty.

6. Imprisonment is not irrevocable.

7. All else is equal (between imprisonment and death).

So: we should not use the death penalty.

Many people find this argument compelling. Of those who do not, most (like Leiser) argue that premise 7 is false. Imprisonment and death are (they say) not equal with respect to deterrence, incapacitation, justice, humaneness, or the like. Their arguments are not so much objections to the argument from irrevocability as to other arguments against the death penalty. We dealt with such objections in chapters 1-3. Our concern must now be with premises 3, 4, and 6. What I shall argue is that those three premises cannot, without question-begging, highly dubious assumptions, or equivocation, all be made true at once. The argument from irrevocability is not good even if all else *is* equal. This objection, if sustained, would constitute a complete refutation of the argument from irrevocability.

I proceed in this way. First, I consider those nonlegal senses of "irrevocability" that are supposed to make the premises true. Next, I do the same for the legal senses. Last, I consider several alternatives to "irrevocability" that might charitably be allowed to be what those using the argument "really" mean if they do not mean what they say. While the argument from irrevocability makes a good point, putting that point in terms of irrevocability seems to be a mistake.

NONLEGAL REVOCABILITY

There is, as Leiser points out, one obvious sense in which death certainly is an irrevocable penalty. Once a convict has been hanged, electrocuted, gassed, or otherwise put to death, he cannot be given back his life. Death is final and irreversible. A dead man cannot be returned to the condition he was in before he was put to death. When you're dead, you're dead.

Let us call the sort of revocability that would allow us to put a person subject to a penalty back in the exact condition he would have been in had he not been subject to that penalty "absolute revocability." Clearly, the death penalty is not absolutely revocable. But as Leiser readily admits, neither is imprisonment. The years in prison cannot be returned. Each day behind bars "scants our mortal lot." Absolute revocability, then, cannot be what the argument from irrevocability assumes.

Absolute revocability is one sort of nonlegal revocability. There is another, what we may call "substantial revocability." Considerations of substantial revocability yield this defense of premises 3, 4, and 6: While we cannot return a single day of imprisonment served, we can, as Leiser says, give the prisoner a chance to "start over," compensate him, or otherwise put him in a condition more or less equivalent to what he would have been in had he not been imprisoned. We can substantially undo imprisonment. But we cannot (Leiser implies) do the same for a dead man. We cannot give a dead man the chance to start life over, compensate him, or otherwise put him in a condition more or less equivalent to what he would have been in had he not been executed. The death penalty is not substantially revocable. Hence, the death penalty is irrevocable in a way imprisonment is not.

How are we to understand this defense of premises 3, 4, and 6? One way to understand it is as an argument from definition. The death penalty is, by definition, a penalty excluding all possibility of the executed starting life over (just as imprisonment is, by definition, a penalty that excludes giving the prisoner a chance to live at liberty any day served in prison). If we define "irrevocability" as (roughly) "not permitting compensation during one's lifetime," the argument from irrevocability is sound. The death penalty would not permit (substantial) revocation because (but only because) the death penalty makes compensation during one's lifetime impossible while imprisonment does not.[3] But so understood, this defense of premises 3, 4, and 6 would invite an embarrassing question. Why should revoking be limited to compensation during one's lifetime? Without an argument to show that giving the convict a chance to start life over is the *necessary* mode of correcting error, the definitional version of the argument from irrevocability would beg the question.

We cannot defend defining "irrevocability" as "not permitting compensation during one's lifetime" by pointing to the meaning of words. Ordinary usage does not require us to consider the liberty lost by a day served in prison as any less irrevocably lost than a day of life lost by execution. Any defense of that definition must give us a reason to use "irrevocable" in a narrower sense than the word's ordinary meaning allows.

There is such an argument. The argument assumes that death is the end of all. Death completes one's biography, terminates one's interests, and so makes compensation impossible by making it impossible for anything more to happen to one. The argument has some appeal. But the appeal is fatally limited. The argument requires that we identify our biography with our life. The argument should appeal only to those who make such an identification. For the rest of us—those who plant trees in the shade of which we shall never sit, who buy life insurance our children will collect, who hope to have a decent burial, or who would like to be remembered fondly after we die—death does not seem the end of all. The death that will put us beyond all joy and suffering will not put us beyond all benefit or harm. Our interests exceed bodily survival. Our biography could have a happy ending even if we died sad.

The argument for defining "irrevocability" as "not permitting compensation during one's lifetime" should, I said, appeal only to those who identify our biography with our life. But in fact, its appeal is wider. Even many who do not think their own joy and suffering are all that matters are likely to gloss "When you're dead, you're dead" as "When consciousness permanently ceases, one ceases to exist." The difference between any number of days left to live and none to live seems a qualitative difference beyond all dispute and above all price. Imprisonment takes a certain part of life. The death penalty takes it all. Taking all rather than part may (it seems) be what makes the death penalty irrevocable in a way that imprisonment is not.[4]

Is it? I think not. The death penalty may be a more severe punishment than imprisonment at least in part because the death penalty takes the whole of life rather than a part. The difference between the death penalty and even life imprisonment is indeed qualitative, not just quantitative (because—as explained in chapter 1—taking someone's life does deprive him of certain options that even life imprisonment does not). But the question here is not why the death penalty is a more severe punishment than even life imprisonment. The question is whether it is irrevocable in a way that imprisonment is not. The gloss given above on the truism, "When you're dead, you're dead," cannot, I believe, support the argument from irrevocability. It cannot both because its equation of consciousness with existence is dubious and because the connection between the death penalty and death is not quite what appeal to that gloss requires.

We do, of course, tend to equate consciousness with life (just as we tend to equate life with all we are). The permanently comatose seem to many to be "as good as dead," a haunting likeness of the person known before. Talk of afterlife without survival of memory seems no more than death by another name. The river Lethe is almost as frightening as the grave. Even sleep, if dreamless, can afterward seem outside life, a temporary death. Yet we are not consistent about such things. We seldom *treat* the permanently comatose as if already dead (for example, by burying them alive or probating their will). We recognize the rationality of traditions that find attractive the prospect of after-life without survival of memory. And so on. While we would like to have a clear border between when we are and when we are not, our practice reveals a vast region of disputed claims.[5]

The death penalty itself lies closer to the middle of that disputed region than to the dark country beyond. The irrevocability of *death* seems to be (more or less) a conceptual truth. If you're not permanently dead, you're not really dead at all. If you're also not alive, you're something for which we have no common term because we so seldom need one. ("In limbo," "undead," or "zombi" is about as good as we can do.) The irrevocability of the death *penalty* seems, in contrast, a mere matter of fact. We can easily imagine a world in which someone executed today might be revived (or perhaps, reconstituted) tomorrow (or next year or decade) if a court so ordered, his memories, personality, and talents intact even if much or all of his body had to be replaced by a copy. In such a world, we might not be willing to say that the executed person, now revived, had been dead at all. We might want to reserve the word "dead" for those whose execution has become "final." Or perhaps we might instead distinguish between the "provisionally dead" and the "finally dead."

Whatever description we eventually adopted in such a world, the death penalty there would be pretty much what it is here. The execution would look like an execution today. The physical state of the executee would be just what it is now, both before and after execution. If no one "revived" him, the effect of execution would be just what it is here. The executed would have been put to death even though describing him as dead (or at least as "really dead") might not be proper until the power to revive him had been lost too.

In such a world, the death penalty would be somewhat less objectionable than it is in this one. But the difference is not dramatic. The death penalty would be no more absolutely revocable in that world than in this one. Neither the suffering endured in waiting for execution, nor the experience of execution itself, nor even the time spent "dead" could be undone. Only the "being dead" could be interrupted. Such a death penalty would, I think, have much the same power to deter that it does now, having that power because death (while it lasts) would, in such a world, deprive the person executed of just what it deprives him of in this world.

If what I have just said seems more or less right, the qualitative difference between even life imprisonment and the death penalty cannot be attributed to the one penalty permitting compensation during one's lifetime while the other does not.

So, if the argument from irrevocability requires assuming that death is the end of all, it is an argument far harder to defend than its defenders seem to suppose. Because its defenders do not seem to be a philosophical clique organized around a special view of life (for example, the reduction of all benefit and burden to joy and suffering), we should not, I think, understand the argument from irrevocability as assuming such a controversial view.

But if we reject this understanding of the argument, we must understand the argument as indifferent to the mode of compensation. That a punishment permits compensation during one's lifetime will be a consideration but not necessarily the decisive consideration. Not the mode of compensation is important, but compensating one way or another, that is, somehow returning the person punished to a condition something like the one he would have been in had he not been imprisoned or put to death. The motivation for this way of understanding the argument is plainly moral. We should, we think, make up as best we can for any wrong we do another. If monetary compensation will do that, we can (it seems) still substantially revoke the sentence. If monetary compensation will not do it, but some other form of compensation will, all well and good. Only if there is no way to put the convict in something like the condition he would have been in had he not been punished is the punishment not substantially revocable. Only then would we owe the convict a "debt" we cannot pay. So *if* imprisonment is substantially revocable while the death penalty is not, imprisonment must (given this understanding of the argument) permit making up for the wrong done while the death penalty does not. Let us see.

Suppose we release someone from prison after he has served a sentence of just one day. Surely, if we can put someone in substantially the condition he would have been in had he not been imprisoned, we should be able to do it after one day.

How would we revoke our exprisoner's imprisonment? We could, of course, get him back his old job (without loss of status for the day missed), pay him for his day in prison, and do whatever else we can. Have we now substantially undone that day in prison? In an important respect, we have. We have done all we could to make it up to him (and what we have done is far from negligible). There is, however, also an important respect in which we may not have substantially undone that day in prison. That day remains one on which our exprisoner did not do what he would otherwise have done and did suffer much he would not otherwise have suffered—a day both he and others may never forget. He might well feel that any compensation within our power is too small for that. "Whatever you do," he might say truthfully, "you can't make up to me for that day."

Whether we agree with our exprisoner will depend in part on what we take to be the criterion of substantial revocability. Our discussion so far suggests two. If the criterion of revocability is that the convict's condition really be more or less what it was before, then even imprisonment is not always substantially revocable. The prisoner cannot "start life over." He can at best "start fresh," a dark abyss between the day he entered prison and the day he left. He has a chance to enjoy what remains of his life, nothing more. If, however, the criterion of substantial revocability is either that we do all in our power to compensate the convict (and what we do is far from negligible) or that we do enough so that he would say, "That would make it worth it," then it is sometimes in our power substantially to revoke imprisonment.

But what is true of imprisonment given such criteria of substantial revocability is also true of the death penalty. The death penalty does not prevent us from doing all in our power to compensate the person executed. While it limits what we can do more than imprisonment does, the death penalty leaves us with the power to provide compensation that is far from negligible. We cannot give the dead man back his old job, but we can pay him for what he lost in wages, benefits, and the like. Any money would, of course, have to go to his estate rather than to him personally. We cannot give him a chance to enjoy life again, but we can arrange his affairs so that they turn out much as they would have had he not been executed. He may not be able to regain his self-respect, but we can posthumously assure him the respect of others. The situation of the dead man is remarkably like that of our exprisoner. While some people might feel nothing could repay them for being put to death (just as some might feel that way about being imprisoned for even a day), certainly some amount of compensation should be great enough so that some people (in prospect, of course) would say, "Well, that would make it worth it." So, if compensation can substantially revoke imprisonment, it can, it seems, also (though perhaps not as often) substantially revoke death. Premises 4 and 6 cannot both be true if "irrevocable" means "substantially irrevocable."

LEGAL IRREVOCABILITY

But all this might miss the point. The point might be, as Brennan suggests, that the death penalty cannot be revoked in law while a sentence of imprisonment can. Once a man is hanged, his sentence is eternal. He can no longer appeal. Even new evidence cannot change the verdict. His case is closed. His legal situation is (it seems) entirely different from that of a prisoner who can still appeal. A prisoner can always be released before his sentence is complete; he can appeal even after his sentence is complete. In a sense, his case is never closed. If that is the difference between the death penalty and imprisonment, it is certainly a big one. But is that the difference?

I think not. In one way, a death *sentence* is just as revocable in law as is a sentence of imprisonment. Until the death sentence is executed, carrying out the sentence may be interrupted, and the condemned man released. He can be released after being sent to death row, after being marched to the gallows, and even after having the noose slipped around his neck. The death penalty takes time to carry out. The death sentence, like any other sentence, names a *process* as well as an *outcome*. The process of putting someone to death can be interrupted, just as the process of serving ten years in prison can.

But interruptibility may not be what those invoking the argument from irrevocability have in mind. They may be thinking of the *outcome* of the death penalty, not the process of putting someone to death. That would not be surprising. The death sentence ends so dramatically that we easily forget the process leading up to it. We even use "execution" to refer only to the last step in executing a sentence of death, as if that were all there were to a sentence of death (and as if we did not also execute sentences of imprisonment). In contrast, a sentence of imprisonment does not end dramatically. What drama it has resides in the passage of time. We tend to forget the outcome; the last day of imprisonment differs little from the first except for a handshake and the opening of a gate. So if we are to consider whether the sentence of death, once executed, is irrevocable in a way imprisonment is not, we must be careful to compare the outcome of the death penalty with the outcome of imprisonment.

What happens if we compare those two outcomes? Once a prisoner has served his full term, there is a legal sense in which his sentence is irrevocable, just as a sentence of death, once carried out, is irrevocable. A sentence of imprisonment, once carried out, cannot be legally undone. The question of imprisonment is, by itself, moot (though the related questions of compensation, clearing the record, and the like are not). *Habeas corpus* is now impossible.

There is, however, also a legal sense in which imprisonment is still revocable. The former prisoner can still be exonerated. He can still formally regain the status he had before conviction. He can still sue for compensation. In this sense, however, the death penalty is also revocable. Death does not preclude exoneration. Tim Evans was exonerated after his execution (though no doubt he took no pleasure in that). The United States still has an active movement to exonerate Sacco and Vanzetti almost a century after their execution. Execution did not close their case. Should they eventually be exonerated, they might perhaps (through a relative) sue for wrongful death. Our legal relations with a person need not end with her death. If a legal system denies the dead even "the right to have rights" (which few do), that is a failing of the particular legal system that needs correction, not a fact about the death penalty that justifies its abolition. The death penalty is no more necessarily legally irrevocable than imprisonment is.

It may still seem that I have missed the point. After all, we have only so many years to live, say, seventy. If two men are convicted of murder, and one gets the death penalty while the other gets life imprisonment, is it not obvious that the one executed will, once executed, not be a possible object of a certain form of revocation, while the one serving the life sentence will be? If, for example, both "murderers" were sentenced on the same day and at the same age, say, twenty, and both were also later exonerated twenty years later, could we not return to the lifer his last thirty years while the dead man could not have even those years returned to him? Is that not (it might be asked) an important difference—the very difference that plainly underwrites the argument from irrevocability?

This difference is, I think, what underwrites the argument from irrevocability. What I have denied is that that difference is enough to make the argument from irrevocability a good argument. Indeed, I believe I have already explained—in discussing the "nonlegal" version of the argument—why this difference cannot make it a good argument. But perhaps this is the place for a brief recapitulation.

The difference pointed to is either conceptual or practical. The *conceptual* difference would have to be that the death penalty takes a life (more or less) all at once, while life imprisonment takes a life a day at a time. The death penalty, once executed, wipes out the account from which a partial "refund" might be made. Life imprisonment preserves that account (though the balance becomes ever smaller) for the natural life of the prisoner.

Insofar as any defense of the argument from irrevocability rests on this conceptual difference, it seems to rest on a mistake. Nothing in the concept of the death penalty makes the death penalty irrevocable in this sense. As noted in the previous section, we can easily imagine "reviving" or "reconstituting" the dead should we discover a mistake. The concept of the death penalty does not preclude full refund of life (provided life is measured simply in so many days alive.) The problem with such refunds is technological, not logical.

The *practical* interpretation of the objection we are now considering would have to be that we cannot, in fact, revive the dead, although we can in fact release the living from prison. I agree that this is a significant difference. I deny only that it is enough to establish that the death penalty is irrevocable in a way life imprisonment is not. We can indeed release a prisoner before his term is up. But we cannot really refund the life he *would* have had remaining had he not gone to prison. Prison has not only taken the life he would have lived during the years of imprisonment; it has also irrevocably changed the life remaining to him. We should not make too much of the mere fact of walking about, doing day labor, or falling asleep in a dingy room just because there are no bars or guards. For some people, perhaps for most people, the chance to live the last thirty years out of prison may not (by itself) seem a substantial contribution to their welfare. The twenty years in prison, years during which friends and relatives have become strangers, skills have atrophied, and the world he knew has disappeared, may make a prisoner feel (quite rightly) that what is being "given back" is not the life that was taken from him initially, but something worth infinitely less. My criticism of the argument from irrevocability has emphasized *compensation* because I find it difficult to understand how the early release of a prisoner can make a full *refund* of even the years he has yet to serve. There is, I agree, an argument against the death penalty here. All I claim is a) that the argument cannot depend on the death penalty's being irrevocable in a sense in which imprisonment is importantly different, and b) the argument has yet to be given a convincing formulation.

ALTERNATIVES TO REVOCABILITY

There are at least three ways the death penalty differs from imprisonment that might be confused with irrevocability. Let us now consider these alternatives to see whether any can provide a way of saving the argument from irrevocability without drastically changing it.

Completeness

A punishment is complete if it takes from a person all that he has, leaving no possibility of further punishment. The death penalty is often treated as if it were a complete penalty. For example, Justice Brennan says that the death penalty deprives one even of the "the right to have rights." As I have shown, the death penalty is not a complete penalty. Even the dead can (and often do) have rights. But the death penalty is certainly a *more* complete penalty than imprisonment. The death penalty takes more than imprisonment does. That is why the death penalty is a more severe penalty than imprisonment. Does relative completeness then provide a way of saving the argument from irrevocability? I think not. We cannot substitute relative completeness for irrevocability without making premise 3 false. It is just not true that the more complete a penalty, the less it permits the correction of error.

Duration

A sentence of death is ordinarily executed more quickly than a sentence of (long) imprisonment. That difference in relative duration makes a difference in what can be done if an error is discovered within a certain period after sentence is passed. If a sentence of death is ordinarily executed within a year of sentencing, then after that year our ability to compensate for any error we make is suddenly and sharply reduced. The same is not true of a sentence of imprisonment. Whatever reduction in options for compensation goes on while a prisoner serves his term (and there certainly is some), is much more gradual and spread over a much longer period (assuming a long term of imprisonment). A prisoner serving a life sentence can be freed any time during his natural life, but the condemned man cannot be freed after his natural life is cut short by execution of sentence.

Substituting duration for irrevocability has much to commend it. Appeal to relative duration does not commit the fallacy of comparing the death penalty's outcome with imprisonment's process. The comparison is between duration of processes. The appeal rests upon a general fact about the death penalty. Even in a country like the United States where the time between sentence of death and execution can be many years, the alternative sentence of imprisonment is likely to be longer.

The substitution of duration for irrevocability is, however, not without its costs. The substitution would require a substantial rewriting of the argument from irrevocability. The distinction between the death penalty and imprisonment would not be that one permits correction of error while the other does not, but that one permits more to be done to correct error than the other does. Premise 1 would have to be rewritten to read:

1'. Fallible beings should not, all else equal, use a penalty permitting them to do less to correct error if there is an alternative penalty permitting them to do more to correct error.

The other premises would then also have to be rewritten accordingly. (For example, premise 3 would have to say that an irrevocable penalty is one that does not permit doing as much to correct
error as some alternative does.) The resulting argument would
avoid the objections made here only by giving up much of the
emotional power of the argument from irrevocability.

Contingent noncompensation

The argument of this chapter is largely "conceptual;" that is,
it depends upon certain relatively general facts about this world
(and worlds much like this one, such as the one where the dead
can be revived). This conceptualism may suggest that the "real"
argument from irrevocability is not conceptual but "statistical"
or "contingent." For example, much of what I said relied on the
relatively weak claim that we can substantially compensate some
people we put to death. That claim is consistent with the contingent claim that we can probably substantially compensate more
people for mistaken imprisonment than for mistaken execution
of a sentence of death. The "real" argument from irrevocability
may then seem to rest upon something like that contingent claim.
Premise 3 might be rewritten to read something like:

3". An irrevocable penalty (and only an irrevocable penalty) makes
substantial compensation for error less probable than imprisonment does.

Other premises would remain as they are, but the resulting argument would beg the question. In effect, premise 3" defines "irrevocability" in terms that make imprisonment the zero point.
The definition is arbitrary. Why should a mere difference of
degree (probability of compensation) be turned into the qualitative difference between revocability and irrevocability? Why is
the natural zero point not fine rather than imprisonment. The
arbitrariness can, of course, be avoided by rewriting premise 1
rather than premise 3. For example, premise 1 might be rewritten to read:

1". Fallible beings should not, all else equal, use a penalty making correction of error less probable than the alternative penalties do.

Other premises would then have to be rewritten accordingly. But the result would be, as it was for duration, an argument that is clearly not a mere restatement of the argument from irrevocability.

Other alternatives?

The death penalty is less variable than imprisonment and has more irreversible effects than imprisonment. Certainly death and imprisonment differ. Nothing I have said here should be taken to deny that. All that I have argued is that irrevocability is not one of those differences, and so no argument founded on that difference can be good. Given the number of other arguments against the death penalty, the loss of this one should not decide the controversy between abolitionists and retentionists. The loss merely simplifies the controversy a bit.

NOTES

I should like to thank my colleagues Michael Gorr, Clark Zumbach, and Mark Strasser for helpful comments on previous versions of this chapter.

1. Burton M. Leiser, *Liberty, Justice, and Morals*, 2nd ed. (New York: Macmillan, Inc., 1979), 251.

2. *Furman v. Georgia*, 408, U.S. 238, 92 S.Ct. 276 (1972), 290–291.

3. If this statement seems controversial, review chapter 1 (where I argued that death is an order of magnitude more severe than imprisonment, no matter how severe imprisonment happens to be).

4. Compare Stephen Nathanson, *An Eye for an Eye?* (Lanham, MD: Rowman & Littlefield, 1987), 106: "Death as a punishment obliterates the person and not just the citizen. . . . [The] state [should not] be empowered to inflict the total punishment, the punishment that destroys a person in his entirety." Surely Nathanson would not claim, for example, that Athens, by putting Socrates to death, destroyed him in his entirety. Yet such a claim of irrevocability seems to be crucial in Nathanson's version of the argument from inhumanity (just as it is for Brennan's).

5. For more on this, see my "The Moral Status of Dogs, Forests, and Other Persons," *Social Theory and Practice* 12 (Spring 1986): 27–59.

Six

The Argument from Proportion

Anyone interested in the death penalty is likely to have read something by H. A. Bedau.[1] Any scholar so interested should have read a good deal. For almost a third of this century, Bedau has been the most important philosopher of the death penalty. His work has deserved the attention of anyone who wanted to think clearly about that subject. His recent collection of essays, *Death is Different*, is no exception.[2] In it, Bedau refines many old arguments and puts a few new questions. He has once again raised the standard in a debate where standards tend to drift downward. He holds the high ground from which we can, if we join him, survey the death penalty debate today. What do we find?

Death is Different contains ten substantial chapters, a short "Introduction," and a longer "Conclusion." Only the first five chapters can be described as philosophy—even in the relatively expansive sense again current. The book's second half includes two chapters of legal analysis, one chapter best described as empirical sociology, and two first-person accounts of minor events in the recent history of abolition. The five nonphilosophical chapters are, however, not extrinsic to the philosophy. As Bedau moves from the abstract arguments of philosophy to the routine of death penalty litigation, many retentionist claims begin to look as out of place as a judge doing the family shopping in judicial robes. While no single argument unites *Death is Different*, its chapters slowly bring out the complex ways in which death is— or, at least, might be—not quite like any other penalty now used. Bedau does not, however, establish that the death penalty is different enough to justify its abolition.

111

RATIONAL INDETERMINACY?

Bedau's chapter 1 seeks to forge an argument against the death penalty from the moral tradition seemingly most hostile to it: the retributive tradition of right and forfeiture represented by Locke and Kant. Bedau begins by identifying the moral principles of this tradition that might plausibly be supposed to require or at least allow use of the death penalty. He then tries to show that these principles will only require or allow the death penalty if certain factual conditions are also met. Finally, he argues that these factual conditions are not likely to be met today.

Bedau's introduction makes this first chapter seem more tentative than I found it. The introduction expressly concedes that there is "[no] moral principle or ethical ideal according to which we can settle the death penalty dispute, provided only we can identify the principle, get everyone to acknowledge it, and then apply it to get the correct result."[3] We can only identify a variety of plausible moral principles that "taken together with the relevant facts of the matter, do lead to the conclusion that—on the balance of reasons—we ought to oppose capital punishment."[4]

This concession seems to me both right and surprising. Right, because politics affords few examples of longstanding controversies wth a single, rationally decisive argument against one side (hence my insistent use of "all else equal" in reconstructing arguments). Surprising, because that concession seems to commit Bedau to a form of argument both more diffuse and more difficult than the usual abolitionist approach of trying to show that imposing the death penalty is morally wrong (or the less common retentionist approach of trying to show that the death penalty is morally required). Principle must be weighed against principle, raising at least the theoretical possibility of rational disagreement concerning the weight to assign various principles. Such disagreement could mean that reason alone would not decide the question of abolition.

While such rational indeterminacy seems to me more than a theoretical possibility, indeed, a central fact about the death penalty debate, Bedau explicitly recognizes such indeterminacy at only one point in chapter 1, when considering how small a deterrent effect could be and still justify the death penalty. (Would preventing one murder be enough to justify 1,000 executions of guilty murderers? 10,000?) Otherwise, he seems to recognize no rational alternative to the weight that he assigns to various reasons (and so no rational doubt about the outcome). Indeed, he generally assigns no weights at all, proceeding instead by what seems to me an argument by exhaustion (without a proof that the list of principles is exhaustive). Each principle he identifies is shown to permit or require abolition, given certain factual assumptions. Allegiance to one principle never weighs against allegiance to another. Disputes about facts are not allowed to block the desired conclusion—that, contrary to the introduction's promise, one value, human life, is "overriding."[5] The argument of chapter 1 turns out to be a complicated version of the argument from irrevocability. (Because life is an overriding value, we should not use a penalty, like death, that does not allow for revocation of error.)

THE ARGUMENT FROM PROPORTION

Bedau makes an equally categorical (and flawed) argument in chapter 2. We might summarize it in this way: Though the state has a moral right to punish some crimes with death, exercising that right could be morally wrong under certain conditions. The state needs—in addition to a permissive right—a compelling reason to impose death. None exists. Hence, imposing the death penalty is morally wrong.

This argument plainly depends (as Bedau admits) on certain facts. If (as I argued in chapter 1) the death penalty is necessarily a better deterrent than life imprisonment, the state might have a compelling reason to impose it. If the death penalty could reduce the murder rate more than life imprisonment could, again the state might have a compelling reason to impose death. And even if the death penalty were needed only to assure that murderers get what they deserve, the state might have a compelling reason to impose it.

While chapter 2 explicitly recognizes that its conclusion rests on assumptions about the relative deterrence value, preventive effect, and retributive appropriateness of the death penalty, it says little in defense of those assumptions. It certainly gives no hint that rational people in fact disagree about each of those assumptions. This is disconcerting, especially since later chapters do acknowledge such disagreements (albeit largely in brief endnotes).

The failure to acknowledge such disagreements renders chapter 2 unpersuasive. Consider, for example, Bedau's claim that "[retribution], insofar as we think of it as a rational goal that the theory of punishment can defend, does not require the death penalty for murder."[6] This claim is, of course, true (except for the literal—and implausible—version of *lex talionis*), but it is also beside the point. Any plausible theory of punishment, retributivism included, must take into account particular circumstances. When it does, it may well yield results it would not yield when abstracted from such circumstances. So, for example, we can easily find a retributive goal of punishment that, *under certain circumstances* (those of the United States today), might seem to many, perhaps most, rational people to require the death penalty.

Suppose that a rising crime rate has led a state to try to control crime by setting penalties relatively high, for example, by making life imprisonment the statutory maximum for such crimes as armed robbery and aggravated kidnapping. Would not such a state now have good reason to make death the statutory maximum for murder committed in the course of an armed robbery or aggravated kidnapping? If murder is a crime significantly worse than armed robbery or aggravated kidnapping (and this Bedau seems to admit), then murder deserves a more severe penalty (under the principle of proportionality that Bedau also accepts).[7] If death is otherwise permissible (under the circumstances), then surely the state has a compelling reason, justice, to make murder punishable by death.

This *argument from proportion*, as I shall call it, seems just the sort of retributive argument for the death penalty that Bedau says cannot be made. No doubt, the argument is not decisive. Other considerations may weigh against retribution even when the question is statutory penalty. Nor does the argument show that death should, much less must, be imposed in each case statutorily allowed. Particular circumstances might mitigate even deserved punishment. What the argument from proportion does show is how easy it is to get around the reasoning of Bedau's chapter 2.[8]

Considering that chapter alone is unfair, even though it contains no relevant reference to the chapters following it. One way or another, most of those later chapters tacitly touch on this retributive argument (and on the nonretributive equivalents), doing so by suggesting ways in which death might not be permissible even given a need for proportion. Bedau's first two chapters set the stage for the more interesting chapters to follow.

BENTHAM'S THREE ARGUMENTS
FOR ABOLITION

The ostensible subject of Bedau's chapter 3 is a change in Bentham's arguments against the death penalty. Bentham's early attack on the death penalty (1775) failed (according to Bedau) to give a decisive utilitarian ground for abolition. While Bentham never admitted that failure explicitly, he acknowledged it when he urged what has become practice in much of the United States: "if [a legislature is] determined to preserve the punishment of death, in consideration of the effects it produces *in terrorem* [a legitimate utilitarian consideration], then it should use this penalty only for those offenses which in the highest degree shock the public feeling—for murders, accompanied with circumstances of aggravation."[9] Bentham's late writing on the death penalty (1831) shows no such ambiguity. He explicitly argues for abolition without exception. What, Bedau asks, could explain this change? Is there really a decisive utilitarian argument for abolition?

Bedau's answer is, "No—or at least not yet." Bentham's new arguments against the death penalty (his "second" and "third") turn out to be his old argument with the facts somewhat changed or with certain considerations receiving more weight than before. Bentham's second argument is that the increasing hostility to the death penalty among the accused, witnesses, prosecutors, judges, and juries undermines its preventive effect in a way having no counterpart in the other modes of punishment; his third argument is that the death penalty encourages crime by silencing a source of testimonial evidence (the executed murderer).

Such consequentialist arguments should not convince without empirical evidence. Bedau tellingly observes that Bentham offers no such evidence, that we still do not have such evidence, and that "[if] executions are to be brought to an end, as Bentham hoped they would be, it may well be without our having first carried out his utilitarian project to its proper conclusion."[10] We are left to meditate on the great utilitarian's preference for inventing facts, as opposed to unearthing them, even though he often upbraided others for disinterest in the actual effects of their policies. We are also left to wonder what about the death penalty moved Bentham to change his calculations. Here is a suggestion.

Much had happened to English criminal law between 1775 and 1831, much of it due to Bentham's reforming efforts. In 1775, death was still the normal penalty for a felony; the criminal-justice system seemed designed to incapacitate (by killing or exiling criminals) where it failed to deter (by terror); public order in the cities was precarious. By 1831, the system was moving toward Bentham's rationally calibrated deterrence as its chief purpose. Penalties for most crimes had been drastically lowered (or, at least, seemed likely to be): prisons (with programs of reform) were replacing the gallows; places to exile criminals were fast disappearing. London had a new police force. In this much-changed environment, judges, juries, and the public might well have become hostile to the death penalty in a way they were not to other penalties (and had not been in 1775). That new hostility might even have been obvious to anyone who attended a trial. The silencing of testimonial evidence would have seemed a much weightier concern as experience showed that the death penalty was not necessary for incapacitation or deterrence. In short, sometimes the social context of an argument, not its form, may explain its (justified) appeal. Does the change in social conditions in fact explain Bentham's changed attitude toward his second and third argument? That question is best left to historians. For us, the point is that it makes sense to ask.

CRUELTY

If death is different, perhaps it is different for some nonutilitarian reason. The most likely of these is that death is a "cruel and unusual punishment." What is the significance of that phrase? That is the subject of Bedau's chapter 4. Though Bedau refers to the constitutional history of the term, his focus is emphatically moral. He ultimately follows Philip Hallie in analyzing "cruelty" as "total activity smashing total passivity."[11] A penalty is "cruel *and* unusual" if it is *excessively* cruel. Cruelty can be justified (Bedau admits), but only if there is no less severe alternative. There is such an alternative to the death penalty, life imprisonment. Hence, the death penalty is excessively cruel, that is to say, unjustifiably cruel.

This conclusion depends, of course, on arguments—like those made in Bedau's chapter 2—that neither deterrent, preventive, nor retributive purposes *require* the death penalty. Only such arguments can establish that life imprisonment is a suitable alternative to death. So, Bedau's conclusion here depends (in part) on refuting the argument from proportion. To refute that argument, he must—to avoid begging the question—avoid an argument itself dependent on the premise that the death penalty is cruel and unusual. This Bedau cannot do because, for him, cruelty is "excessive" and therefore "unusual" only where it serves no deterrent, preventive, or retributive purpose not served as well by a less severe alternative. His cruel-and-unusual argument presupposes the very argument against the death penalty that it is supposed to replace. Bedau seems caught in a circle of remarkable viciousness. What now?

One option open to Bedau is to find a different conception of cruel and unusual punishment, one that would make the death penalty morally unjustified even if it serves a compelling state interest (one no other penalty serves as well). I developed such a conception in chapter 2.[12] On that conception, however, whether the death penalty is cruel and unusual is today a question about which people may rationally disagree. Though Bedau cites the article in which I first offered that conception—during a discussion of deterrence in chapter 7 of *Death is Different*—, he never refers to *its* conception of cruel and unusual punishment. Did he simply overlook it? Perhaps, but the oversight makes his alternative seem arbitrary (a point I stress in the endnotes of chapter 3).

Though Bedau ignores my suggestion, he does eventually move in a similar direction, though in considerable confusion:

> [society] has no authority to create and sustain any institution whose nature and purpose is to destroy some of its members. Cruelty, which has such a nature and purpose, matters—because our own status as moral creatures matters.[13]

While Bedau seems to be saying something obvious, the first sentence is actually controversial. If the death penalty is (morally) justified (and criminal punishment is an institution), then society certainly has (both legal and moral) authority to create and sustain an institution whose nature or purpose is (in part) to destroy the life of some members of society: those convicted of capital offenses and sentenced to death. We can save Bedau's first sentence by redefining the purpose of criminal punishment—as seeking to do justice or prevent crime by deterrence, incapacitation, or reform. But then Bedau's second sentence should not be about "cruelty" ("total activity smashing total passivity") but about "*excessive* cruelty" (cruelty lacking any retributive, deterrent, or preventive purpose). What Bedau should have written is that "society has no authority to create or sustain any institution whose nature or purpose is to be cruel." Having written this, he would, then, have had to face up to the task of understanding what about persons as such makes some hard treatment morally permissible and other treatment cruel.

Bedau's confusion here suggests that he has not yet thought through the relation between cruelty and morality. He himself acknowledges that he has reached a question about alternative theories of the person "too large. . . to try to answer here."[14] Unfortunately, *Death is Different* never reaches that question again.

DID INTELLECTUALS ALMOST IMPOSE ABOLITION?

Bedau's chapter 5, the last of the philosophical chapters, belongs to political theory rather than criminal justice. Its subject is the distinction between "imposed law" and "*self*-imposed law." Bedau's purpose is to answer the retentionist charge that the long movement toward abolition that began after World War II and ended in the late 1970s was in some invidious sense "imposed" on the country by a small elite of lawyers, academics, and judges. Bedau provides plausible criteria for distinguishing between elite imposition and the normal processes by which a society thinks and acts through intellectual minorities. He then uses those criteria to organize the sociological data.

The result is not just a refutation of the retentionist charge but a provocative indictment of the retentionist countermovement. Retentionism's success, Bedau argues, owes much to political accidents that have little to do with what we know about the death penalty. The part of society that knows most about the death penalty, thinks most clearly, and must in the long run provide the reasoning that guides policy remains as opposed to the death penalty as ever.

LEGAL, SOCIOLOGICAL, AND HISTORICAL CHAPTERS

Much less needs to be said about Bedau's remaining chapters. Chapter 6 briefly recounts how Oregon abolished the death penalty by referendum in 1964. Bedau attributes this abolitionist success to good organization and the absence of an organized opposition, a combination of factors that he does not expect to see again. In Oregon, fortune was on abolition's side.

Chapter 7 analyzes death-penalty laws adopted after *Furman*. Chapter 8 describes how the Supreme Court of Massachusetts has gone beyond the U.S. Supreme Court in prescribing the procedures by which a sentence of death must be imposed. Bedau suggests that death-penalty procedures in most states remain essentially "lawless." Chapter 9 provides a clear sense of what Bedau might mean by that paradoxical charge. (The example is from Massachusetts before the reforms, 1946-1970.)

Bedau asks what effect a mandatory death penalty would have on the rate of death-penalty sentences. This is plainly an empirical question—and, while Bentham seemed happy to invent facts, Bedau is not. Bedau not only read the relevant sociological literature but also—with the help of six undergraduate research assistants—did his own empirical study once he determined the existing literature did not answer the question. His examination of two large adjacent counties in Massachusetts reveals that the chief factor in determining whether a murderer would be sentenced to death was not whether he committed a crime with a mandatory death penalty, nor how heinous his crime was, nor even his race or that of his victim. The chief (and, apparently, the only important) factor was the county in which he happened to commit the crime. Prosecutorial and judicial discretion trumped legislative intent. The chapter includes summaries of the relevant cases. These tell far more than the abstract argument. Where is the "system" in such "criminal justice"?

Unfortunately, Bedau's research seems to have ended with death sentences. He reports no similar research concerning other crimes with mandatory sentences. As a result, his research, interesting though it certainly is, provides no evidence for the claim that death is *different*. Criminal justice may simply be extraordinarily haphazard whatever the statutory penalty—indeed, for all he tells us, substantially more haphazard in noncapital than in capital cases.

Chapter 10 describes Bedau's 1977 experience as an expert witness at a murder trial. It is a sketch for a comic novel. Little happens as Bedau expected—or as we might expect. The trial ended happily before it started. Though there seems to be no good reason why the "Dawson Five" should have been arrested, much less forced to stand trial for their lives, everybody involved seemed to be trying to do the best he could under the circumstances. Racism does not seem to have been an issue. Yet the process has an appallingly random look. But for the intervention of outsiders, the Dawson Five would probably have been convicted of murder, sentenced to death, and forced to spend many years on death row fighting execution.

Is all criminal justice like this? Or is death different? We never find out. Like chapter 9, chapter 10 fails to provide the comparative data necessary to let Bedau show that death is different.

PROPORTION REVISITED

Bedau's conclusion summarizes the main arguments against the death penalty, not those he presents in the preceding chapters. It tells us what Bedau is now *thinking* (or at least was thinking in 1986 when the conclusion first appeared in a publication of the New York State Defenders' Association). Certainly, it does not tell us what Bedau has *proved*. What now?

It seems to me that we are entitled to draw at least these four conclusions from Bedau's conclusion—or rather, from *Death is Different* as a whole:

First, retribution has plainly replaced reform, incapacitation, and even deterrence as the central concern for both abolitionists and retentionists. The statistical arguments that so dominated Bedau's early discussions now have a minor role, their place occupied by questions of desert.

The second conclusion—and the most disheartening—to draw from *Death is Different* is that the abolitionist position in the United States today is extremely weak. The arguments Bedau showed New York State's public defenders are all old. They are the very arguments with which abolition has been losing ground. Yet Bedau offers nothing more. In this practical context, his own refinements do not seem to have added noticeably to abolition's fire power.

The third conclusion to draw from *Death is Different* is that the abolitionist movement in the United States is surprisingly isolated from events outside the United States. What makes this isolation surprising is that those events should be a source of strength—more now than in the mid-1980s, but even then a source of considerable strength. Let me summarize *recent* events because my purpose now is not to criticize Bedau as much as to assess the prospects for abolition.

In 1980, the first draft of a universal treaty abolishing the death penalty was submitted to the United Nations General Assembly. A revised version was *adopted* in 1989 (though with many no's and abstentions) and began circulating to member states.[15] By that time, two-thirds of the member states of the Council of Europe had already abolished the death penalty and, except for France, the remainder had let it fall out of use.[16] The disappearance of the Soviet Union, together with the overthrow of its client states in Eastern Europe, has opened the way for that part of the world to join the European consensus. Four states of Eastern Europe have already abolished the death penalty.[17] Most of Latin America has done the same.[18]

From the perspective of the part of the world that the United States most resembles and most respects, our *increasing* use of the death penalty must seem monstrous (both in the root sense, unique, and in the popular sense, depraved)—as well as retrograde. From this perspective too, the declining fortunes of abolition in the United States seem to call for historical or sociological explanation rather than for more or better argument.

The fourth conclusion to draw from *Death is Different* is that the debate over the death penalty has been too long carried on more or less independently of debate over criminal justice in general. The argument from proportion provides one reason to pay more attention to the relation between the death penalty and criminal justice in general. The death penalty is the obvious way to maintain the distinction between, for example, robbery and murder, in a system where robbery is punishable by life imprisonment (or its practical equivalent).

Another reason to pay more attention to the relationship between the death penalty and criminal justice in general is the abolitionist strategy that the argument from proportion suggests. If higher penalties for other crimes do indeed make the death penalty more attractive to people who would otherwise reject it, then the best way to take back lost ground in the death-penalty debate is to change criminal justice in general. If crime rates, especially rates of violent crime, were much lower (as they are in Europe), perhaps Americans would be willing to lower the penalties for most crimes to the levels obtaining in Europe (or, at least, to those obtaining here thirty years ago). With most penalties lower, public opinion might no longer find the death penalty an attractive way to assure proportion between the most heinous crimes and their punishment. Life imprisonment without possibility of parole (or even a substantially less severe penalty of, say, ten years to life) might once again seem severe enough compared to the penalty for armed robbery, kidnapping, or rape. Perhaps we have more to learn from Bentham than Bedau realized.

But how are we to set about reducing the rate of crime? The answer is daunting. The underlying cause of rising crime rates—rates rising even during a period when the "criminal class," young men, has been shrinking—seems to be the business of illicit rec-

reational drugs (just as the roar of the 1920s came predominant-
ly from the business of illicit alcohol). So, if we are to reduce
the crime rate substantially, we shall have to take the money out
of illicit drugs. That means some form of legalization, whether
full legalization (as with cigarettes) or something more limited
(on the model, say, of state liquor stores or prescription medicine).[19] We might also want to consider how much crime might
be reduced through better social services, a lower rate of unemployment, or other social policies.[20] Arguing against the death
penalty must seem bizarre to those who feel themselves losing
"the war on crime."

Bedau failed to show that "death is different." Perhaps we
should be glad he did. Unique entities are hard to understand.
Understanding debate of the death penalty within the wider debate concerning how to deal with crime seems to open a new
approach. Death is not now different (or, at least, not different
enough to justify abolition); the question is, how can we make
it so? We must now explore that question. What follows is, however, only the beginning of understanding punishment within a
system of justice. Though ranging widely, we shall always keep
death in view.

NOTES

I presented a version of this paper (under the title "Rethinking the
Death Penalty") to the Philosophy Department (and others), Dartmouth
College, 27 October 1995. I should like to thank those present for a
supportive discussion.

1. See, for example, Hugo Adam Bedau, *The Courts, the Constitution, and Capital Punishment* (Lexington, Mass.: D.C. Heath, 1977);
two significant works he edited: *The Death Penalty in America: An
Anthology* (New York: Doubleday Anchor, 1964), with a 2nd ed. (1967);
3rd ed. (1982); and (with Chester M. Pierce) *Capital Punishment in
the United States* (New York: AMS Press, 1976); or more than a doz-
en articles scattered through journals (or collections) of philosophy,
law, or criminology.

2. Hugo Adam Bedau, *Death is Different: Studies in the Morality,
Law, and Politics of Capital Punishment* (Boston: Northeastern University Press, 1987). Of course, *Death is Different* is not simply an
important abolitionist work. Except for Stephen Nathanson, *An Eye*

for an Eye (Lanham, MD: Rowman & Littlefield, 1987), it is the only philosophically significant work on the death penalty published in almost two decades.

3. *Death is Different*, 5. For an only somewhat more successful attempt to carry out this balancing approach, see Hugo Adam Bedau, "How to Argue about the Death Penalty," *Israel Law Review* 25 (Summer-Autumn 1991): 466–480.

4. *Death is Different*, 5.

5. *Death is Different*, 45.

6. *Death is Different*, 60.

7. *Death is Different*, 60–61.

8. Compare Nathanson, 69–82. The argument from proportion is, however, important in its own right, as I shall explain later in this chapter.

9. *Death is Different*, 66.

10. *Death is Different*, 91.

11. See chapter 3, endnotes. Unlike Bedau, Nathanson, 96–102, more or less avoids the topic, preferring to focus on what "morality permits" rather than on trying to analyze what might make a penalty "barbaric" or "cruel and unusual" as such.

12. Which, of course, Bedau cites in its original form, "Death, Deterrence, and the Method of Common Sense," *Social Theory and Practice* 7 (Summer 1981): 145–78, at 173 n. 7 (269) and in his bibliography. Nathanson seems to have missed the article (though he cites works in which it is cited). His long discussion of deterrence suffers as a result.

13. *Death is Different*, 127.

14. *Death is Different*, 127.

15. William A. Schabas, *The Abolition of the Death Penalty in International Law* (Cambridge: Grotius Publications Limited, 1993), 162–177. So far, only a small number of states have actually signed the treaty.

16. Schabas, 235.

17. Schabas, 288.

18. Schabas, 249–283.

19. See, for example, Douglas Husak, *Drugs and Rights* (New York: Cambridge University Press, 1992).

20. See, for example, Ralph D. Ellis and Carol S. Ellis, *Theories of Criminal Justice* (Wolfeboro, New Hampshire: Longwood Academic, 1989), chapter 5.

Seven

Preventive Detention, Quarantine, and the Right to Punishment

Fifteen years ago, Ferdinand Schoeman published a paper, much reprinted since, arguing that detention of potential criminals to prevent crime is morally no more problematic than quarantining the contagious to protect public health. The paper was *not* a defense of preventive detention against practical criticisms such as Andrew von Hirsch's "problem of false positives."[1] Schoeman assumed such problems away. The paper defended preventive detention against a deeper criticism, one relying on a conception of the person then associated with Herbert Morris (but going back at least as far as Kant): preventive detention violated a person's (a rational agent's) right to punishment. Schoeman's argument seemed to show that, if such a right existed, it counted for little.

Schoeman's argument assumed certain unlikely developments, both technological (for example, perfection of a relatively reliable test for dangerousness) and legal (for example, *civil* detention for dangerousness).[2] Even on those assumptions, though, the argument had the weakness, as well as the strengths, of an argument from analogy. As Schoeman himself observed, the argument provides a defense of preventive detention only insofar as quarantine is not itself morally problematic.[3] In 1979, that was not much of a weakness because quarantine did not seem morally problematic. Today, however, it does.[4] Its changed status gives us an opportunity to reexamine Schoeman's argument.

Reexamination leads, I think, to four conclusions. *First*, quarantine is morally unproblematic only in a narrow range of cases (cases of "reckless endangerment"). *Second*, preventive detention of the dangerous is morally unproblematic only for analogous cases (cases where the dangerous are reckless). *Third*, both are

125

morally unproblematic for the same reason; that is, because they respect the right to punishment. And *fourth*, quarantine nonetheless poses a problem of medical ethics, a problem of defining the role of physicians within a system of involuntary treatment. The rights of Morris's person structure the medical relationship as they do the penal.

THE WHITE DEATH

Few in 1979 had any personal experience of quarantine. Most of those who had, having undergone only a week's "house arrest" for measles, mumps, or other childhood disease, may not have considered that loss of liberty significant. The alternative had been school.[5]

Today, however, children are not the most likely subjects of quarantine, nor is "house arrest" the quarantine most likely to be imposed. The disease now most likely to invoke quarantine, tuberculosis, strikes adults far more often than children. Once common and deadly enough to bear comparison with bubonic plague, "the black death," tuberculosis had, until the mid-1980s, been in decline in the United States and Europe for almost two hundred years. The cause of that decline was not reduced virulence. Tuberculosis is at least as virulent as ever. Those in whom it is active and untreated are as likely to cough themselves to death as they were two hundred years ago. Indeed, tuberculosis is still the most common cause of death in much of the poorest part of the world. Death rates for tuberculosis declined in part because of better nutrition, housing, and sanitation. Medical science and public health services helped as well. We have a cheap and reliable test for tuberculosis, a vaccine of sorts against it, and a cure. Since we understand how tuberculosis spreads, we are better able to prevent its spread. We know how to keep an outbreak from becoming an epidemic.[6]

Tuberculosis nonetheless remains a difficult disease. Its cure is not a matter of a week or month but, even with the best medical care, of months—and, occasionally, of years. During the first stage of treatment, contagion can be prevented only by removing the patient to a hospital, sanitorium, or other medically controlled environment. Only in the second stage may the patient live with healthy friends or family without immediate risk to them. And, even then, there is risk. The treatment is too complicated for many patients to manage on their own, too likely to fail by mistake. Mistake opens the way for the disease to return with its resistance to treatment much enhanced. Mistake also opens the way for the disease to spread to others in that harder-to-treat form.

Tuberculosis is at least as contagious as AIDS; but, unlike AIDS, it can be contracted through casual contact, even by sitting next to someone on a bus or in an office and breathing in what he breathes out. Though now primarily a disease of the poor, often a byproduct of AIDS or drug addiction, tuberculosis can infect anyone, becoming active and contagious when something else, accident or disease, weakens the immune system. Nothing we know guarantees that "the white death" will not return to plague us as it once did. Tuberculosis is a threat to public health *par excellence*.[7]

CIVIL CONFINEMENT FOR TREATMENT

As cases of tuberculosis became more common in the United States during the late 1980s, public-health workers, civil libertarians, and legislators reexamined quarantine regulations. So far, however, only New York City seems to have done anything in consequence. Its new regulations approach the legal and technical standards Schoeman set for preventive detention of the dangerous. The city's Department of Public Health may order a person removed to a hospital or detained for treatment there only if two conditions are met. First, the department must have found the tuberculosis to be active and, without treatment, likely to be transmitted to others. The finding must be based on epidemiological or clinical evidence, X-rays, or laboratory tests and on recognized infection-control principles. Second, the department must have found the subject of the order unable or unwilling to undergo less restrictive treatment. This finding must rest on past or present conduct (for example, refusal to take medication for tuberculosis or failure to keep appointments for treatment of tuberculosis). The department must be able to show all this at a court hearing similar to those now routine for commitment for mental illness. The department's case must be clear and convincing. Once issued, the confinement order may be contested at set intervals thereafter, the department bearing the same burden of proof as in the original hearing.[8]

Our word "quarantine" derives from the Italian word for forty. The term seems to have first been used in the relevant sense in a Venetian statute of 1484 setting the number of days a suspected plague ship could be kept anchored offshore before being allowed to dock. If plague did not appear aboard the ship within forty days, it would (it was thought) not appear at all. In the meantime, the ship's company lived under conditions much like those at sea. They were as free as a ship's crew or passengers en route ever are to go about their business.[9]

"Quarantine" seems to carry this history with it. The term suggests that any confinement in the interests of public health will be neither long nor out of one's usual habitat. But tuberculosis can require an arrest more burdensome than that, confinement in a public facility for at least six months, with successful completion of a course of medical treatment the condition of release. This loss of liberty is both longer and more complete than mere quarantine. Hence, I shall hereafter break with Schoeman's usage, substituting "civil confinement for treatment," a term less comforting but more accurate.

Like quarantine, civil confinement for treatment does not imply that the person so confined has violated any law; and, again like quarantine, its purpose is not to benefit the person confined. The treatment undertaken in civil confinement, though benefiting the person treated (that is, curing him of a deadly disease), is undertaken to benefit the public at large. Whether the confined benefits or not, the confinement is a means of preventing contagion. But unlike quarantine, civil confinement implies something more than mere isolation; it implies *removal* to a secure place and *treatment* there.[10]

Civil confinement, like ordinary quarantine, seems to be justified by "the state's police power." What is this power, and how can it justify civil confinement for treatment? The police power is (at least) the government's right to protect its subjects from harm they would otherwise unjustifiably suffer. The harm that civil confinement seeks to prevent is plain enough for our purpose: tuberculosis, an infection that, if it becomes active, may cause death and will certainly require long and burdensome treatment to cure. To harm someone in that way is ordinarily unjustifiable. Any moral theory that did not grant government the power to protect against such harm would seem impoverished, perhaps unredeemably so.

The police power seems to derive legitimacy, at least in part, from the moral right of each person, individually or in combination with others, to use reasonable means to protect herself and those she cares about from those who may otherwise unjustifiably harm them. That right (or rather the requirement that the means be "reasonable") suggests at least three constraints on the police power. I shall now state them without argument, in the hope that they are obvious enough to make argument unnecessary:

1. *Necessity*: The exercise of police power should be the least burdensome necessary to achieve the end in view. Civil confinement for treatment should, for example, be used only where voluntary treatment has failed or is likely to fail.

2. *Significant Benefit*: The (net) benefit in view should be significant. A marginal decrease in tuberculosis would, for example, not be enough to justify a practice of civil confinement for treatment.[11]

3. *Effectiveness*: The exercise of the police power should itself have a good chance of success. Civil confinement for treatment should not, for example, be almost certain to fail to prevent the spread of tuberculosis.

New York's new tuberculosis regulation seems designed to satisfy these three constraints. Civil confinement can only be imposed where less restrictive arrangements have failed or, at least, seem likely to fail to provide adequate protection against contagion (constraint 1). Civil confinement is, we believe, much better than nothing (constraint 2). The treatment offered will, in most cases, extinguish the contagion within six months, as well as completely cure the patient; and, in the meantime, it will protect the public from infection (constraint 3).

New York's regulation does not, however, set a standard as

high as Schoeman does for preventive detention. In particular, it does not compensate the confined person for income lost during confinement, for injury to his social life, or for any other loss normal upon long confinement.[12] Since *civil* confinement like New York's seems not to presuppose that the person confined has done anything wrong, this absence of compensation is troubling: The government is taking someone's liberty for at least six months to benefit others—or, more exactly, to prevent harm to them.[13] Surely (it may be thought), such a taking should be compensated where it cannot reasonably be avoided (and, we may suppose, just being cured of tuberculosis is not sufficient to compensate). Is something like New York's regulation nonetheless justified? I believe it is, but for reasons that will not suit Schoeman.

I take the question of justification to have two parts. The first concerns the moral permissibility of the regulation and confinement carried out under it. The second concerns its contribution to public welfare. To be (fully) morally justified, a regulation (or act under it) should be both morally permissible and a (significant, net) contribution to the public welfare. Since the regulation's contribution to public welfare is obvious (or, at least, seems so given the present state of knowledge), I shall focus hereafter on the question of how such an uncompensated taking can be morally permissible.

THE MORAL PERMISSIBILITY OF CIVIL CONFINEMENT FOR TREATMENT

What I shall now try to show is that civil confinement for treatment is morally permissible, when it is, because the only alternative is allowing the person confined to engage in "reckless endangerment," an act deserving criminal punishment.

For the purposes of the criminal law, you act *recklessly* when you consciously risk harm to others in a way that grossly deviates from standards to which a reasonable person, in such circumstances, would ordinarily adhere.[14] You commit reckless *endangerment* by doing recklessly any act, whether otherwise lawful or not, when it causes another bodily harm or endangers her bodily safety.[15] Making reckless endangerment a crime seems well within the police power. (Consider, for example, the crime of reckless driving.)

Suppose that someone with active tuberculosis, having been told of his condition and of the risk it poses to himself and others, is asked to enter a program of voluntary treatment, one involving confinement because his circumstances make successful treatment without confinement highly unlikely. Suppose, too, that he nonetheless refuses to be confined for treatment because he does not like confinement, because his affairs might suffer, or because of some other significant but not unusual reason. From the moment he refuses confinement, he would be engaged in reckless endangerment. He would, that is, know that he is putting others in great danger and yet do it for reasons that a reasonable person, that is, people like us in our cooler moments, would regard as very inadequate.

Why should we regard his refusal of confinement as relying on very inadequate reasons, as a gross departure from ordinary standards of care? If everyone, or even if many, with our potential confined's reasons did as he proposes to do, tuberculosis might soon become epidemic. Not only would our potential confined probably fail to cure himself on his own but, even if he did not fail, his chances of reinfection would be much higher than they are now (and much higher than they are likely to remain so long as most people with his reasons do not do as he is proposing to do), because he would encounter the contagion much more often than he does now. His conduct departs from a standard of conduct that he has good reason to endorse as a general rule out of both self-interest and concern for others. Whatever advantage he may gain by departing from that standard comes (at least in part) from relying on the compliance of others similarly situated. In other words, his conduct is reasonable only as a form of cheating. Since his cheating has a good chance of doing many others considerable harm, it is not merely technical or civil recklessness but gross and, therefore, criminal recklessness.

So, if the potential confined refuses civil confinement, we could justifiably jail him for a significant term for reckless endangerment.[16] If he has not successfully completed treatment by the end of his jail term, we could justifiably rearrest him as soon as he walks out, recharge him, and perhaps even deny him bail (since he cannot leave jail without again breaking the law). The same threat to public health that would justify civil confinement for treatment would, it seems, justify jailing him (as criminal punishment) for refusing to accept civil confinement. Civil-confinement-for-treatment and criminal-punishment-for-reckless-endangerment seem to be conceptual twins.

Of course, civil confinement is not the same as criminal punishment, even when the punishment is incarceration in an appropriate treatment facility. There are at least four differences. *First,* the government's burden of proof in a criminal case is (normally) heavier, "beyond a reasonable doubt," rather than the civil law's "clear and convincing evidence," "preponderance of the evidence," or the like. *Second,* in a criminal case, the government has to prove more, not just a threat to public health (as in civil confinement) but also conscious wrongdoing (acting with knowledge of an unjustified risk). *Third,* confinement for criminal wrongdoing carries a moral condemnation that civil confinement for treatment does not; a criminal is a wrongdoer, not a mere sufferer. And *fourth,* the length of criminal confinement depends upon the statutory penalty, the judge's sentence, and the parole board's willingness to be clement (though persistence of infection would justify rearrest, another conviction, and another sentence to serve). The length of civil confinement depends entirely on how quickly the medication eliminates the infection.

Are these four differences together enough to make it morally permissible for a government to force civil confinement for treatment on someone willing to accept punishment instead? No.[17] The government's right to confine must rest on need (constraint 1). The government has no right to choose the more burdensome means when a less burdensome one will serve as well. Since the "criminal" can be isolated at the same public facility to which the civilly confined are sent for treatment, criminal confinement will serve the public health just as well as civil does. If government nonetheless has the right (under the police power) to force civil confinement, it must have that right because civil confinement is less burdensome for the person confined than criminal punishment would be.

But is civil confinement less burdensome? The civilly confined can avoid the moral condemnation inherent in criminal conviction only by making the government's case for confinement easier to win; can escape punishment only by accepting unwanted medical treatment; and can trade a series of determinate sentences only for medical treatment of indefinite duration. Given this balance of considerations, many rational persons might, it seems, find criminal punishment less burdensome (while others find civil confinement so).[18]

Both criminal punishment for reckless endangerment and civil confinement for treatment seem—all else equal—morally permissible as exercises of the police power. If (as I have just argued) the police power provides no decisive reason for government to prefer civil confinement to criminal punishment, the choice between them should be left to the contagious person herself. She can, in other words, justifiably be confined for treatment only if she accepts such confinement. The contagious person can be confined for treatment only if she waives her right to be punished for reckless endangerment.[19] The justification of civil confinement for treatment thus seems to leave the right to punishment intact, indeed, to require it.[20]

This connection between (just) punishment and (just) civil confinement explains why compensation for civil confinement is unnecessary (assuming the right to punishment is respected). Civil confinement is not an injury for which compensation is appropriate but a net benefit to the person confined (or, at least, must be so treated if voluntarily accepted).[21]

THE LIMITS OF SCHOEMAN'S DEFENSE
OF PREVENTIVE DETENTION

If we now examine the "technical" conditions that Schoeman set for a "morally legitimate system of preventive detention," we find his argument consistent with our defense of civil confinement for treatment. Schoeman's "dangerousness" is a species of reckless endangerment.

Schoeman assumes a relatively reliable test for dangerousness, one giving "moral certainty" that certain acts will occur.[22] These acts must be dangerous; that is, they must involve "serious threat to life or bodily integrity."[23] The test for dangerousness must be administered in such a way as to allow substantial reduction in the crime rate.[24] Preventive detention must be the least restrictive means of achieving this reduction in crime.

We are, then, to think of the person to be preventively detained as a "bomb" whose violence we can predict with at least the assurance with which we can diagnose contagious tuberculosis and predict its spread, and of detention as the most cost-effective means of preventing harmful "explosions." An explosion would (almost certainly) cause great bodily harm if the dangerous person remained free but should not occur or, occurring, not cause much harm, if he were detained in some secure place.[25]

A dangerous person who, being informed of his condition, refused (civil) detention would, all else equal, fail to exercise the care that a reasonable person would exercise in the circumstances. He would be deviating from the standard of reasonable care at least as grossly as would someone with contagious tuberculosis who refused (civil) confinement for treatment when nothing else would protect the public. So, of course, Schoeman can defend preventive detention under these conditions. The alternative to detention is the moral equivalent of letting someone, without adequate justification, walk crowded streets with a large bomb that could go off at any moment.

Imprisonment for reckless endangerment is a way of preventing the harmful conduct that mere gross recklessness risks. It is, in effect, (criminal) preventive detention. But it is more than that; it is just punishment.[26] Schoeman's offer to make preventive detention *civil* is confused.

Schoeman makes the offer in response to the criticism that mere dangerousness does not deserve the stigma of criminality that *criminal* detention imposes. The stigma is undeserved, according to Schoeman, because the wrongful act is in the future. But the wrongdoing that justifies preventive detention is not in the future. Insofar as dangerousness is a form of reckless endangerment, dangerousness is itself wrong*doing*. Criminal detention for dangerousness is punishment for wrongdoing already done. The stigma is deserved. The criticism rests on a mistake.

But even if the criticism did not rest on a mistake, Schoeman's response would. The term "civil" normally implies procedural safeguards less demanding than those of a criminal proceeding—for example, proof by clear and convincing evidence rather than proof beyond a reasonable doubt. Schoeman's effort to avoid moral stigma might then bear a price—easing the government's burden—that many seeking to avoid preventive detention would decline to pay. A reasonable person might well prefer the less likely stigma of punishment to a more likely detention without stigma.

That, of course, is not the choice. Civil detention cannot eliminate the moral stigma in question. To be found dangerous—for example, to be found to be unjustifiably putting others in great danger of serious bodily harm—is to stand morally condemned. In this respect, dangerousness is morally different from contagiousness. Dangerousness is a moral category.

Since any civil proceeding would still have to find the person to be detained dangerous, the only advantage in stigma that a civil proceeding could have over a criminal proceeding would derive from the reduction in certainty that the laxer procedures of civil law allow. Since Schoeman's procedures are supposed to assure the *same* moral certainty as the criminal law does, he has precluded even that reduction in stigma.

The argument for the moral permissibility of civil preventive detention is, then, exactly the same as that for civil confinement for treatment. A government could not justifiably establish civil preventive detention unless it allowed the intended detainee the alternative of (just) criminal punishment.[27] That is, the government must recognize a wrongdoer's right to punishment whether or not it provides a civil alternative. Schoeman's argument from analogy between quarantine and preventive detention fails to diminish "the right to punishment" because it ignores what makes both quarantine and preventive detention morally permissible.

PUBLIC HEALTH AND MEDICAL ETHICS

We have reached the problem of medical ethics with which I promised to conclude. So far, we have seen that government may sometimes justifiably confine for treatment people with tuberculosis to prevent its spread to others. Physicians have a role at several stages leading to such confinement. A physician must diagnose the tuberculosis as contagious, report the diagnosis to the public health department, and testify to its contagiousness at a hearing.[28] Medical ethics has long permitted such breaches of confidentiality for the sake of public health.[29] When the law so requires, the physician may betray her patient's trust. Such betrayal does, I think, raise a problem of medical ethics deserving more attention than it has received. But that is not the problem I want to raise here.

The problem I want to raise here concerns what happens during confinement. Presumably, any treatment during confinement would be under the supervision of a physician. Physicians are supposed to provide "competent medical service with . . . respect for human dignity."[30] Part of respect for human dignity is, it seems, allowing the (competent) patient "to accept or refuse any recommended medical treatment."[31] What, then, is a physician to do when, as an agent of a state hospital or other treatment facility, she is ordered to treat for tuberculosis a patient who, though mentally competent (or at least not yet declared incompetent), refuses treatment (saying, for example, "I will not be treated while I am a prisoner here")? The answer, it seems to me, is that the physician can do nothing except try to convince the patient to change his mind. For physicians, the competent patient's bodily integrity takes precedence over the health of both public and patient.[32]

What, however, if the patient is willing to submit to treatment only because successful treatment is the only route to freedom? The physician then faces a different problem of voluntariness. In one sense, the patient's submission to treatment is now voluntary; it is a rational response to necessity. But in another sense, the submission is *not* voluntary. If the patient were free, he would not allow this physician to treat him. He would reject all treatment or, at least, seek treatment from another physician. His willingness to submit to treatment depends entirely on the government's threat to hold him until this physician has treated him successfully. His submission to treatment seems no more voluntary than the transfer of property following the traditional robber's offer, "Your money or your life."

Most physicians will, I think, reject this claim. They find little difficulty in going ahead with treatment where a patient has decided to submit to legal necessity. Not having to use force or otherwise conduct treatment in an unusual way, the physician may even view herself as conspiring with the patient to free the patient (legally) as soon as possible.[33] But recent discussion of medical research on prisoners seems to have concluded that, because prisoners are in the government's power, their consent is not voluntary enough to satisfy the requirement of informed *consent*.

They require special protection even when they consent.[34] The corollary for forced treatment seems clear: any pressure involved in winning the consent of prisoners to participate in research is both less direct and less certain than that involved in telling someone, "You cannot leave here unless you undergo treatment." Hence, any consent to legally forced treatment is even more suspect.

My question of medical ethics, then, is: Under what conditions should a physician treat a patient whose submission to treatment is merely submission to legal necessity? I would suggest at least two conditions:

> 1. *Justice*. The treatment should be morally justified as well as legally required. In particular, it should meet the three constraints on the police power identified earlier.
> 2. *Little Harm*. The treatment should benefit the patient or, at least, be unlikely to do substantial harm.[35]

I believe that treating a (competent) tuberculosis patient who was submitting to New York City's health regulations would ordinarily meet both these conditions.

To say only that is, of course, not so much to answer the medical-ethics question as to refine it, but it is nonetheless all I shall do here. Our purpose was to eliminate a challenge to the claim that the criminal has a right to punishment, not to answer a question of medical ethics. We have achieved our purpose. We must move on.

NOTES

I presented the first version of this chapter to the Philosophy Colloquium, Illinois Institute of Technology, 14 September 1994. I thank those few present, especially Warren Schmaus, for several helpful comments. I read a later version to a symposium jointly sponsored by the American Philosophical Association's Committee on Philosophy and Medicine and its Committee on Philosophy and Law, in Boston, 27 December 1995. I should like to thank those present, especially my fellow panelists John Arras, Michael Corrado, and Bernard Gert,

for an informed and informative discussion. Last, I should thank Ellen
Fox for much help with the research for this chapter.

1. Andrew von Hirsch, "Prediction of Criminal Conduct and Preventative Confinement of Convicted Persons," *Buffalo Law Review* 21
(Spring 1972): 717-758.

2. Ferdinand D. Schoeman, "On Incapacitating the Dangerous,"
American Philosophical Quarterly 16 (January 1979): 27-35.

3. "Those undisposed to think quarantine legitimate will find little in this paper to persuade them that preventive detention has virtues which outweigh its costs, even assuming the modifications in
technology and law described above." Schoeman, 35.

4. For evidence, see literature cited below.

5. House arrest may seem more like exclusion than imprisonment.
Perhaps quarantine-as-exclusion is morally less problematic than quarantine-as-confinement. Yet in what follows, I shall ignore the distinction. Quarantine-as-confinement seems better suited both to Schoeman's
purposes and mine.

6. For the facts contained in this paragraph and the one above, I
have relied on M. F. Perutz, "The White Plague," *New York Review
of Books* 41 (26 May 1994): 35-39.

7. Victor W. Sidel, Ernest Drucker, and Steven C. Martin, "The
Resurgence of Tuberculosis in the United States: Societal Origins and
Societal Responses," *Journal of Law, Medicine and Ethics* 21 (Fall-
Winter 1993): 303-316 (as well as other articles in that special issue
devoted to "The Dual Epidemics of Tuberculosis and AIDS").

8. The question is to be reconsidered after the first sixty days of
confinement and thereafter every ninety days. New York City Health
Code (3-31-93), chap. 11.47 (RCNY: 10309-10312). For the history of
this chapter, see Susan L. Jacobs, "Legal Advocacy in a Time of
Plague," *Journal of Law, Medicine, and Ethics* 21 (Fall-Winter 1993):
383-389.

9. *Black's Law Dictionary*, 4th ed. (St. Paul, Minn.: West Publishing Co., 1968), 1408.

10. I should like to thank Kenneth Kipnis for pointing out that there
are really two issues here: first, removal to a safe place, and, second,
treatment there. Arguments adequate to justify (medically-secure) confinement (for example, public health) probably would not be adequate
to justify legally enforced treatment. To justify legally enforced treatment, the government would have to show a) that staff cannot be
adequately protected against infection or at least, b) that staff cannot
be adequately protected at reasonable cost. I shall ignore this refine-
ment of the argument in what follows (except in the last section). If

legally enforced treatment cannot be justified, then my argument should be rewritten striking all references to "for treatment" after "confinement."

11. There should, of course, be some principle of distributive justice in any complete list of constraints on the police power. I have not included one in my list because it seemed to me that: (a) any version I chose would probably be controversial, and (b) no plausible version would make a difference in what follows.

12. Schoeman, 31.

13. For comparison, consider military conscription, where the government takes the liberty of young men in order to protect the country; or jury duty, where the government takes the liberty of citizens in order to guarantee others a fair trial. In both these cases, doesn't paying compensation seem appropriate?

14. Compare the risk posed by the typical "drunken driver" (that is, a driver who would fail a breathalizer test). The risk posed by someone with active tuberculosis sitting in a restaurant, taking an elevator, or even just coughing on a crowded street is probably substantially greater. Douglas N. Husak, "Is Drunk Driving A Serious Offense?" *Philosophy and Public Affairs* 23 (Winter 1994): 52-73.

15. *Illinois Criminal Law and Procedure* (St. Paul, Minn.: West Publishing, 1991) chap. 38, secs. 4-6 and 12-5 (Reckless Conduct). The corresponding statute for New York City seems to be NY Penal Law 120.25: "A person is guilty of reckless endangerment in the first degree when, under circumstances evincing a depraved indifference to human life, he recklessly engages in conduct which creates a grave risk of death to another person." This crime, a class D felony, may set a standard higher than I have in mind (depending on how much gets read into "depraved indifference"). Please note that my argument does not depend on the exact wording of reckless endangerment statutes but rather on the propriety of such statutes in general.

16. This assumes that we have the appropriate statute or common-law rule. In Illinois, for example, reckless conduct is a class A misdemeanor punishable by up to one year in jail. *Illinois Criminal Law and Procedure*, chap. 38, sec. 12-5(b) and sec. 1005-8-3(1).

17. It is perhaps worth noting that our answer here might well be different did the question concern commitment for mental illness; we now commit the mentally ill for treatment even if they would prefer punishment. But even where the person in question is mentally ill, there may be reason to work within the criminal rather than civil law. For more on this, see chapter 8.

18. A rational person might even prefer criminal punishment if, as

Schoeman assumes for preventive detention, the government had to bear the same burden of proof as in a criminal case. Hospitals can be more confining than prisons (and are not necessarily healthier).

19. This is, I'm afraid, not quite accurate. What the contagious would be punished for in most jurisdictions would be (indirect) criminal contempt—for disobeying the court's order (out of the court's sight). This is, however, sufficient for my purposes, since the procedures for contempt would, in this case, differ little from ordinary criminal procedures, and the maximum penalty would fall only somewhat below the typical penalty for reckless endangerment. For a general discussion of contempt, see Wayne R. LaFave and Austin W. Scott Jr., *Criminal Law* (St. Paul, Minn.: West Publishing Co., 1972), 39-44.

20. Governments keep this option open by providing criminal punishment for disobeying the relevant court or health-department order.

21. This argument is decisive against compensation only as a "property right" or "tort right." When I presented this chapter in Boston, Alan Wertheimer argued in favor of compensation as a matter of distributive justice, a way of compensating for a natural defect (whether lack of immunity to tuberculosis as such or economic or social disabilities leading to a life increasing the likelihood of infection). Michael Corrado argued in favor of compensation (in part) as a way of making sure costs to the confined figured in the social calculus, that is, as an economic incentive to use confinement only when it was indeed the most cost-effective means available (after internalizing all externalities). My argument here does not address either of these arguments for compensation. I should, however, say two things about them: First, it seems to me that the idea of compensation is going to present conceptual problems where the burden, being cured of tuberculosis, already returns a primary good (health). Second, it seems to me that most of what Wertheimer (and perhaps Corrado) would do in compensation might be easier to justify as necessary to maintain medical standards, to prevent unnecessary harm, or to treat people decently. I nonetheless agree that such questions of compensation deserve more thought.

22. Schoeman, 28-29.

23. Schoeman, 30.

24. Schoeman, 30.

25. Schoeman, 33-34.

26. We are, of course, assuming that the term of imprisonment (or other punishment) is proportional to the seriousness of the crime and that any imprisonment beyond that will require a separate crime (for example, trying to walk out of the prison uncured).

27. We are, of course, at this point assuming a) that the person to be detained is mentally competent, b) that the government has a compelling interest supporting its exercise of police power, c) that confinement (whether civil or criminal) is the least restrictive means likely to protect that interest, and d) that there are no merely practical problems about placing the contagious or dangerous person in criminal rather than civil confinement. What, then, if the prisons cannot handle the contagious or dangerous person properly, and there is no legal procedure for transfer (under penal supervision) to an appropriate facility? The answer, I think, is that involuntary civil confinement or involuntary civil detention might be *excused* as a temporary expedient until the facilities or law could be changed—much as seizure of property can sometimes be excused in an emergency. The argument from necessity cannot be resisted. But such a temporary expedient would not be justified, and those who suffered in consequence, even if only in their right to punishment, would be due apology and compensation not for loss of freedom or for the harm that loss causes, not necessarily even for the stigma, but just for breach of the right to be treated with the respect due a rational agent.

28. Consider, for example, NYCHC 11.47(a): "A physician who attends a case of active tuberculosis . . . shall report to the Department at such times as the Department requires . . . the address of the case, the stage, clinical status and treatment of the disease, and the dates and results of sputum and X-ray examinations and other information required . . ."

29. See, for example, the AMA's Principles of Medical Ethics IV: "A physician shall . . . safeguard patient confidences within the constraints of the law." *Code of Medical Ethics: Current Opinions* (Chicago: American Medical Association, 1992), x.

30. Principle I, *AMA Code*, x.

31. "Fundamental Elements of the Patient-Physician Relationship 2," *AMA Code*, xi.

32. Compare Kenneth Kipnis, "Heath Care Ethics: Establishing Standards of Professional Conduct," *Corrections Today* 54 (October 1992): 92-95.

33. This psychology may explain why there has only been muted discussion of the medical ethics of carrying out a Caesarian on a competent adult undergoing the operation only because a court ordered it, and the patient's only alternative seems to be imprisonment, fine, or other punishment. For details of one such case, see Daniel B. Kennedy, "A Public Guardian Represents a Fetus: Court refuses request for a C-section and boy is born apparently healthy," *American Bar Association Journal* (March 1994): 27.

Eight

Guilty but Insane?

The verdict in the Hinckley case (1982), "not guilty by reason of insanity," seems to have substantially strengthened an already reviving interest in the Victorian verdict of "guilty but insane" (as well as spurring less temperate calls for outright abolition of the insanity defense or for its circumvention by addition of "guilty but mentally ill" for those cases where the mental illness of the accused might otherwise tempt a jury to acquit).[1] That interest is understandable. The verdict of not-guilty-by-reason-of-insanity means that Hinckley is subject only to civil commitment, though he was proved to have deliberately shot Reagan and two others with the intent to kill. The outcome would (or at least should) have been the same had he actually killed Reagan. Hinckley could have been set free a few weeks or months after his trial because a *civil* magistrate found that there was then insufficient evidence that Hinckley was still dangerous to himself or others. Guilty-but-insane would, it is said, assure instead that the decision to release someone like Hinckley would remain with the criminal-justice system for many years. Only after such a person had "served" his sentence could the procedures of civil commitment and release take over. The "new" verdict would not require someone like Hinckley to serve even one day in *prison* (or, at least, not unless he recovered his sanity before he had served out his sentence). Those supporting the new verdict seem to propose it as a useful practical measure without moral complications. Those opposed, in contrast, have reacted as if the new verdict were a moral monstrosity akin to "punishing the innocent."[2] A thoughtful observer is bound to wonder whether some deep misunderstanding divides supporters from opponents, a misunderstanding about the moral basis of the insanity defense in particular or about criminal desert in general. Let us see.

REFORM, DETERRENCE, AND RETRIBUTION

One explanation of the division between supporters and opponents of guilty-but-insane is that it mirrors the standard division over the aim justifying punishment as an institution, with various consequentialists favoring the new verdict and retributivists opposing it. Such a division would make perfect sense. For reform theorists, the change would appear minor. The new verdict would substitute one form of incarceration (criminal commitment) for another form (civil commitment). Either way, the law could still incapacitate the dangerous, force rehabilitation of offenders, and otherwise serve public order. For deterrence theorists, the new verdict might seem to do even more, by making it clearer to potential offenders that they cannot escape conviction simply by pleading insanity. Clarity about that might help to discourage some potential offenders who, though sane (or only marginally insane), suppose they can win the protection of the insanity defense. Consequentialism seems to provide no principled objection to the new verdict (except perhaps at the cost of introducing exogenous considerations like "humaneness" into the argument).

In contrast, the verdict of guilty-but-insane appears to violate a basic principle of retribution: The guilty, and only the guilty, should be punished. To find someone guilty is, it seems to many retributivists, to say that the person is blameworthy and *so* deserves punishment. To deserve punishment, one must *both* have knowingly (or perhaps only recklessly or negligently) done the wrong *and* be the sort of person capable of doing otherwise (that is, not doing that wrong). For the retributivist, to punish someone is to recognize him as a free agent, a being capable of rational choice. But, *by definition*, the insane are those who cannot know the nature of their act, or cannot know that the act is wrong, or cannot control what they do.[3] The insane lack precisely those capacities necessary for rational choice that retributivists generally consider preconditions of guilt. For retributivists, then, the verdict of guilty-but-insane may seem a contradiction in terms. Insofar as someone really is insane, he cannot be guilty. And insofar as he really is guilty, he cannot be insane. For the purposes of the criminal law, then, Hinckley must be guilty or insane. He cannot be both. The new verdict would, it seems, be a moral monstrosity because it would make an "innocent" like Hinckley liable for punishment he does not deserve.

This explanation of the division between supporters and opponents of the new verdict would be quite convincing were it not that many *supporters* of the new verdict talk like retributivists. Hinckley is, they say, guilty even though he is insane. He deserves conviction even though he "needs help," too. The supporters of the new verdict may not want to punish Hinckley, but they do not want him to get off scot-free, either. Finding him not-guilty offends their sense of justice at least as much as it makes them fear for their safety. Finding him guilty-but-insane is, they seem to say, just what he *deserves*.

Such opinions might result from simple confusion, something common enough in political debate. Certainly the absence of scholarly support for the new verdict suggests exactly that. Still, there may be something more interesting in what the supporters of the new verdict are saying. How much more I am not sure. What I shall argue here is that, however confused the supporters may be, they are not committed to a contradiction even if they *are* retributivists (provided they hold a now-common version of retributivism). A retributivist may, I shall show, usefully distinguish between the implications of conviction and the implications of punishment. The retributivist may admit that the insane can be guilty and yet deny that they deserve punishment. Conviction and guilt are not as tightly connected to deserving punishment as traditionally supposed. The retributivist must, however, admit that the insane are not *by right* under the criminal law.

INSANITY AND THE CRIMINAL LAW

Under American law today, insanity can prevent a criminal conviction in one of three ways: (a) by preventing trial, (b) by making it impossible to prove criminal intent (or the equivalent), or (c) by providing an "affirmative defense" of insanity. The verdict of guilty-but-insane would eliminate only the last of these. It is important to see why.

If the accused is so mentally deranged that he cannot "meaningfully participate" in his own defense, he cannot be tried. He must be held until he is fit to stand trial. He cannot be tried, it is said, because *fairness* requires that the accused be able to understand what is happening to him at trial, be able to testify in his own behalf, and otherwise be able to aid in his own defense. Even if the accused had been sane at the time he committed the crime, his insanity (while it lasts) protects him from trial, conviction, and punishment. He may, in a sense, be guilty but insane, but only in a sense of no interest here. The new verdict would not rush such a person to trial before he is ready.

Even if the accused is capable of participating meaningfully in his own defense, his insanity at the time of the "crime" may make proof of wrongdoing impossible. Most crimes require an intent to commit a prohibited act (for example, the intent to kill a living person). If the accused lacked the appropriate intent, he cannot have committed the crime (for example, murder) even though he caused the harm the law seeks to prevent (for example, unjustified killing). Thus, a woman suffering from the delusion that her husband is a log would not be guilty of murder for giving him forty mortal whacks with a wood ax. She would not even be guilty of reckless homicide. She would not be guilty of murder because she lacked the intent to kill (and there can be no murder without that intent or something like it). She would not be guilty even of reckless homicide because there is nothing reckless about chopping what (on the evidence of one's senses) is obviously a log. Because she was insane, such an accused would not be guilty. But she would *not* be not-guilty-by-reason-of-insanity. She would be not guilty for the same reason a man who killed his son because he (reasonably) mistook him for a wolf is not guilty. She would not have had the appropriate intent. That she *could* not have had the appropriate intent *because* she suffered from insane delusions would be relevant only indirectly, that is, only insofar as it helped to make the lack of intent plausible.

The new verdict is not intended to change any of that. It is supposed to be a minor reform, not a revolution. Its purpose is not to subject the insane to liability stricter than that the rest of us are subject to, but to end a *special* protection from liability that the insane now enjoy. The insane can now (successfully) plead not-guilty-by-reason-of-insanity. The rest of us cannot. The supporters of the new verdict seem to make a distinction between "the evil" and "the merely dangerous." For them, the deluded woman of our example is merely dangerous. Hinckley, though perhaps equally insane and equally dangerous, is evil, too. He did what he did intending to kill. He is, they would say, guilty of attempted murder in a way our deluded woman is not guilty of murder. Hinckley had the "mind of a murderer." Our deluded woman did not.

The verdict of guilty-but-insane would become important, then, only once the prosecution had proved the "basic case." Hinckley need not, for example, invoke the defense of insanity until the prosecution proved that he shot Reagan, intending to kill him and using means appropriate to that end. Once the prosecution proved that, the only question would be whether there is *nevertheless* reason to find for the defense. The defense of insanity now provides such a reason. The defense is "affirmative," that is, counsel for defendant cannot make this defense merely by showing that the prosecution *failed* to prove this or that element of the basic case. Counsel for defendant must actually show that there is some reason to believe Hinckley to be insane (and that his insanity stands in the appropriate relation to his crime). In most jurisdictions, such a minimal showing imposes a new burden of proof upon the prosecution. Sanity becomes an element of an enlarged case that the prosecution must prove. The insanity defense thus recognizes that, in a sense, the accused is guilty. He did what the law forbids (and did it with the intent the law dreads). The question is whether he should nonetheless be excused from conviction. The new verdict would rule out insanity as an excuse usable *before* conviction.[4]

THE PROBLEM FOR RETRIBUTIVISTS

Opponents of the new verdict must be understood to oppose doing away with the affirmative defense of insanity. They oppose relegating the excuse of insanity to consideration (if at all) only after conviction. We must now turn to the reasons for that opposition. We have two courses open to us. We could try to examine the opposition in all its variations, each determined in part by the idiosyncrasies of the particular jurisdiction's provision for minimum sentences, probation, early release, and the like. Or we could examine the opposition concerning only a special

case, one chosen to make the opposition's objections as strong
as possible in a way consistent with the actual range of provisions in force. Because the show of legal scholarship required
for the first course would be difficult, tiresome, and unnecessary, I shall take the second.

Let us assume that the verdict of guilty-but-insane would
be instituted within a legal system (a) mandating minimum
and maximum penalties with little room for judicial discretion,
(b) prohibiting probation for persons convicted of serious crimes,
(c) providing that sentence may, as appropriate, be served in
prison or in a state mental hospital (but in any case under lock
and key), and (d) making no provisions for discretionary parole,
early release, or the like (except the usual provision for *executive* pardon, commutation, and so on). Given these assumptions,
we may conclude that someone like Hinckley would, upon a
verdict of guilty-but-insane, receive a long sentence to be served
(at least initially) in a state mental hospital. If he recovered his
sanity before the end of his term, he would have to serve the
remainder in an ordinary prison (unless the executive granted
clemency—an option I shall hereafter ignore). If there is something a retributivist would find objectionable about the verdict
of guilty-but-insane, it should, I think, be evident in a legal system like this.

Retributivism (as commonly understood) holds that punishment is for wrongdoing, that the wrongdoer and only the wrongdoer should be punished, and that the severity of punishment
should not exceed the seriousness of the wrongdoing to be punished. "Wrongdoing" is simply doing what the law forbids, provided the law is part of a reasonably just legal system. What the
law forbids usually includes a "mental element" such as intent,
recklessness, or negligence (which is part of the "basic case").
Retributivism rules out punishment for acts that are not crimes,
punishment for crimes that one did not commit, and punishment
in excess of what the crime deserves. But retributivism (strictly
so-called) neither rules out nor requires punishment *less* than the
crime deserves. Retributivism is a theory of what the criminal
deserves for her *act* (what she should be given back for *that*).
What lesser punishment she deserves for other reasons is a matter of "clemency." Retribution is the maximum the criminal
"owes" on the "debt" her crime creates. Clemency forgives that

"debt" in whole or in part (and so assumes the possibility of retribution instead). The theory of clemency is an appendix to the theory of retribution.[5] Convenience will nonetheless excuse our speaking of retributivists hereafter as if they accepted both retribution strictly so-called and clemency.

Retributivists might then be supposed to raise two objections to the verdict of guilty-but-insane (as we have assumed the verdict to operate). One concerns retribution strictly so called. Hinckley, it might be said, did not "do" the crime of which he is accused. Punishing him for it would not be punishing for *his* wrongdoing. The other objection concerns clemency. Hinckley, it might be said, did the act (and it was wrong), but it would not be fair to punish *him* for it. His insanity constitutes a complete excuse for what he did. Let us consider these objections in order.

WAS THE ACT HIS?

An event in which I am somehow involved can fail to be my act in many ways. It can, for example, fail to be an act at all. The epileptic does not kill someone during a seizure just because his hand uncontrollably strikes the fatal blow. There is an event, the blow, but no act, only a bodily movement; and so, no question of anyone having killed anyone. The death just happened. The same would be true if the blow resulted from a reflex or from automatism.

But even if an event is an act, it may fail to be mine. It may fail to be mine because it is someone else's. For example, if by brute force you make my finger squeeze the trigger of a gun, you squeeze the trigger, not me. My finger is your instrument, not mine. You act. I do not (though my body moves). Perhaps the same would be true if you got me to pull the trigger by posthypnotic suggestion or will-destroying drugs.

An act may also fail to be mine because it "misfired." I may, for example, have killed someone by accident. I shot at a stump, but the bullet unaccountably ricocheted, hitting a passerby. Or I may have killed by mistake. What I shot at turned out to be my son rather than a wolf. Here the act I "did" is not the "act" as it turned out. We have an agent, an act, and the sort of harm that the law seeks to prevent. But the connection between them is not quite right for wrongdoing. The harm done is (we are supposing) not what I intended (or risked by reckless or negligent conduct). My act does not include the harm. The harm consequent upon my act is not a wrong, only something bad that happened.

Hinckley's attempt at murder does not fail to be his act in any of these ways. Hinckley's act was not at all like an epileptic seizure. He had full control of what he did (though not "self-control"). Hinckley's act was his rather than someone else's. He was not someone else's instrument. There was no accident or mistake about the attempt. Hinckley did what he intended to do, as he intended, and because he intended to do that. Accident interceded only to save Hinckley from actually committing murder. If we are to refuse to attribute the attempted murder to Hinckley, we must do so because, though what Hinckley did would ordinarily be an act, it is not an act because Hinckley is the sort of person to whom such acts cannot be attributed.

Why not attribute such acts to someone like Hinckley? Whether we think of an act as the "union of bodily movement and will" or as "behaving intentionally," Hinckley certainly acted. Or rather, he certainly acted unless we disqualify him *in advance*. To disqualify him in advance from acting requires supposing that the insane *cannot* act even though they can (in the ordinary sense) unite bodily movement with will and behave intentionally. How could such a supposition be defended? We might, I think, be tempted to argue that rationality is necessary for agency. We cannot, it might be said, make sense of the concept of an agent to whom acts are to be attributed without the concept of rationality.

That temptation is not hard to resist. The conceptual claim is either too weak to support disqualifying Hinckley as an agent or is subject to counterexample. We regularly attribute acts to children, the senile, and even our pets without supposing any more rationality than we would have to attribute to Hinckley. Our *civil* courts regularly hold children, the feebleminded, and the insane liable for *their* torts (provided they *did* something). These practices do not seem to suffer from any conceptual problem about attributing acts to such persons. So why not Hinckley?

Hinckley was more capable of laying plans and shaping his acts accordingly than are many children, senile, or feebleminded.

It might be argued, however, that an act is not mine unless I acted "voluntarily"; Hinckley did not act voluntarily; so we cannot attribute the attempted murder to him. What of this argument? We must, I think, begin by noting the ambiguity of "voluntarily." The epileptic's spasm is not voluntary. Neither is the movement of my finger when produced by another's brute force. Neither is what I do by accident or mistake. But each is not voluntary in a somewhat different way. Hinckley's act might well not be voluntary too and yet be so in a way irrelevant to whether the act is his. Some acts that it would be true to say I did not do voluntarily are still mine. For example, in a chess game I might attack your queen because I had no other choice. It was attack your queen or lose the game. The attack was not voluntary. You forced me into it. Yet it was my attack, and if it succeeds, I deserve the praise.

Hinckley's act, although quite different from my attack on your queen, still does not seem to fail to be voluntary in a way that would bar its attribution to him. Hinckley's act is not voluntary (we may suppose) because he suffered from a mental disease that destroyed his self-control. But for that loss of self-control, he would not have attempted murder. Loss of self-control is quite unlike spasm, being another's instrument, or doing something by accident or mistake. These latter failures of voluntariness count against intent, recklessness, or negligence. Loss of self-control (whatever it is) does not. Hinckley remained in control of what he did (that is, he did what he wanted to do). He lacked self-control because his wants were themselves a product of disease rather than reason (and, it seems, we suppose the "true self" to be reasonable).[6] Because Hinckley remained in control of what he did, there seems to be no problem about attributing what he did to him (though there is, as we shall see, some problem about *who* "he" is). The problem now is what to do with him, given the way he did what he did. Hinckley, it might be said, should not be punished because he could not help doing what he did ("could not help it" even though he knew enough to know he should not do what he did and could have done otherwise had he chosen to).

This point might be made another way. Many retributivists hold that breaking the law deserves punishment (in part, at least) because breaking the law is taking unfair advantage of those who obey the law (especially if the law is part of a relatively just legal system and those who obey the law might benefit from breaking it provided most others did not break it). Punishment takes back (or at least, does away with) the wrongdoer's unfair advantage, leaving him no better off than he would have been had he obeyed the law. The advantage one gets by breaking the law is, it is said, the advantage of doing what one wants while others do as the law requires even when they do not want to. The various failures of voluntariness that count against intent all have this in common: In the ordinary case of each, the "agent" does not do what he wants to do. The epileptic, someone who is made by brute force to pull a trigger, or someone who kills by accident or mistake, does not *take* any advantage. What advantage he might receive just happens to him. Someone like Hinckley, on the other hand, does what he wants to do (in a perfectly straightforward sense of "wants"). He *takes* advantage. If there is a reason not to punish him even so, that reason is clemency, not retribution (strictly so called). The "debt" is certainly his.

There is, of course, a set of considerations that, though retributive (in the strict sense), do not defeat intent. They include self-defense, lawful execution of sentence, act of war, defense of innocents, apprehension of a felon, and defense of habitation. They are "justifications." Justifications resemble insanity in providing an "affirmative defense." They are nonetheless strikingly different from insanity. Justifications concern the act itself, not the agent or extraneous circumstances. A successful justification fills out the description of the act in question. Justification defeats the presumption of wrongdoing established in the basic case by dissolving the apparent wrong. Justification shows there to be no *unfair* advantage for punishment to take back. The agent did what everyone is generally willing to permit everyone else to do. For example, self-defense makes an intentional killing that is *prima facie* murder an upright act. We think it a good thing (or at least not a bad thing) for people to defend themselves against unlawful attack (within certain limits, of course). Because no one supposes insanity to work in this way, I shall say no more of justification. Hinckley's disease cannot make what he did an upright act even if it provides reason enough not to punish him for what he did. Excuse, not justification, seems to be his only escape from punishment.

KINDS OF EXCUSES

That brings me to the second objection that a retributivist might make to the verdict of guilty-but-insane. Someone like Hinckley, though he did wrong, should be excused (it might be said) because he deserves neither conviction nor punishment. His act may accuse, but his condition excuses. Considerations beyond mere retribution forbid his conviction or punishment. Insanity provides a full excuse.

The claim that insanity like Hinckley's provides a full excuse might be defended in one of two ways. One way focuses on conviction, the other, on punishment. The first, though it would bar the verdict of guilty-but-insane, seems to be indefensible. The second, though defensible, would *not* bar the verdict of guilty-but-insane but would substantially limit its effect. Let us begin with the first way.

Conviction, it might be said, imports "culpability," "responsibility," or "blameworthiness" and imparts a "stigma," "the condemnation of society," or "blame." The criminal is made to answer for his crime. But (this objection runs) the insane are not culpable, responsible, or blameworthy. They cannot "really" answer for their crime, because "really" nobody is there to answer. They are pitiable victims of disease, persons who could not know that they did wrong or, even if they did know, could not keep themselves from doing it. To convict someone like Hinckley is to blame him for what he suffered, not for something he "truly" did. Such a person (it is said) deserves our pity, not our blame, help, not conviction of a crime.

This objection to the new verdict seems to depend on either a conceptual or a moral claim. The *conceptual* claim is that a criminal's inability to know what he should do or inability to do as he should (owing to a "disease of the mind") makes it "logically" improper to inculpate him, hold him responsible, or blame him. One might as well blame the wind. The *moral* claim is that, while logically proper, stigmatizing, condemning, or blaming is nevertheless unfair (or otherwise morally objectionable). Because we cannot fairly expect the insane to behave other than they do, stigmatizing, condemning, or blaming them for what they do is likewise unfair.

THE CONCEPTUAL POSSIBILITY
OF BLAMING HINCKLEY

The conceptual claim seems to be that we can sensibly blame (inculpate or hold responsible) only agents of a certain kind, perhaps only rational self-conscious agents with the full array of intellectual powers. "Liability-responsibility" (it might be said) logically presupposes "capacity-responsibility." That claim is certainly suspect. Convicting someone of a crime may be thought to include third-person blaming ("He is guilty") and second-person blaming ("I find you guilty") along with the making-liable-for-punishment itself. No conceptual difficulty arises from blaming someone like Hinckley either in the third person or in the second. Let us begin with third-person blaming.

Some third-person blaming seems to have little use outside legal contexts. "He is culpable" is (unlike "culpable act") rare even in legal contexts. "Culpability" seems a technical term, the meaning of which depends on words like "responsibility" and "blame." Such remarks as "The wind was responsible for the destruction" or "Blame the weather" are, unlike "The wind was culpable," too common to be dismissed as ungrammatical, semantically odd, or otherwise logically improper. Some of these remarks may be metaphorical; that is, they may be so distant from the central concept that the usage (though proper) depends upon some striking similarity amid differences too vast to permit a morally convincing argument. While drawing the line between the literal and the metaphorical is not that easy, we may suppose that, in general, the nearer a usage is to a word's original meaning, the more likely it is that the usage is literal. Given that supposition, we cannot conclude that saying the wind was (or is) responsible or to blame is much more or less metaphorical than saying a criminal was (or is) responsible or to blame.

The root idea of "responsibility" is being able to perform one's part in a solemn agreement.[7] To respond is literally to perform as agreed. The wind cannot literally do that, because the wind has no solemn agreements to perform. But a criminal (as such) cannot literally do that either; the harm for which he is responsible is not literally a solemn agreement, a "debt," to which he could respond. The language of "responsibility," if metaphorical in expressions like "X was responsible for the destruction," seems to be metaphorical whether "X" is the wind, Hinckley, or an ordinary criminal. Interestingly, "liable" and "answerable," though not substitutable in the context of concern here, have analogous ideas of bond or swearing at their root. "Blaming," on the other hand, does not. The root idea of "blaming" is speaking ill of. Literally "blaming" Hinckley is quite proper. One can literally speak ill even of the wind.[8]

One might try to get around all this talk of "root ideas" without giving up the claim that there is something logically improper about blaming Hinckley. Our concern, we might say, is only with the logic of *one* sense of "blame," "responsible," or the like, with a particular "conception" of blaming, not with the whole linguistic concept. What is logically improper is applying the words in *that* sense to Hinckley or the wind.

Because we want to report usage, not merely legislate it, we need some way to identify the sense in question without begging the question. The standard way to do that is to translate the relevant statements into a neutral "language" sensitive to the sense in question. We provide a definition of the crucial words that picks out the usage without destroying the point of the statements we are interested in translating. The sense in which we are concerned with "blame," "responsible," or the like includes more than causing something to happen ("causing" being the sense in which both the wind and Hinckley are admittedly responsible or to blame). "The wind caused the destruction" is equivalent to, "The wind was responsible for the destruction," but, "The criminal caused the death" says less than, "The criminal was responsible for the death." The wind was *only* causally responsible; the criminal, something more.

Such translation has a problem often noted. The language of "cause" is not especially appropriate for literal (or at least neutral) discussion of what *things* do. The root idea of "cause" is closer to that of "responsibility" than to the blind forces of physics. "Cause" originally meant (and still does mean in one sense) a lawsuit or what would move one to sue, that is to say, a "cause of action." That root meaning seems to infect all others. To cause is still to provide a cause of action (more or less). If the wind caused the destruction, then there is no one to sue but the wind. Tough luck. To say the wind "caused" the destruction is, then, hardly less metaphorical than to say that the wind is responsible for the destruction. The idea of being a cause of action includes assumptions about liability (the basis of the cause) that "natural causation" is supposed to exclude.

The technical language of "causal factor" would, of course, allow us to separate the wind (and perhaps Hinckley) from the ordinary criminal. Rationality was not, we might say, a causal factor in what the wind or Hinckley did; in what the ordinary criminal did, it was. Hence, the ordinary criminal is blameworthy in the appropriate sense, but the wind and Hinckley are not. "Capacity-responsibility" is implied by a certain sort of causal responsibility.

This will not do. The move from talk of "cause" to talk of "causal factor" either assumes an independent criterion of blaming or loses much of the meaning of the remarks about responsibility to be translated. Either way the move would fail. The language of causal factor does not place blame (or responsibility) except insofar as being a causal factor is necessary for blame. The presence of air or "destructibles" is, for example, as much a causal factor in the destruction for which the wind was responsible as the wind itself. The destruction could not have happened without them all. Because the language of causal factor does not do what the language of blaming does, there is something arbitrary (from the perspective of the language of causal factor) about making rationality (or anything else) a necessary condition of blaming. Knowing what the causal factors are, we must still ask which are relevant to blaming. We cannot answer that question by another appeal to the language of causal factor, as we might by appeal to the language of cause. So, there seems to be no reason to believe that blaming someone like Hinckley in the third person is logically improper. Hinckley seems to be culpable, responsible, and to blame in a perfectly straightforward sense of these terms.

That brings us to second-person blaming. Blaming someone "to his face" is governed by somewhat different rules than blaming someone in the third person. Addressing blame *to* the wind is odd (even if blaming the wind in conversation with someone is not). But that oddity does not seem important here. Addressing blame to the wind is odd because we believe addressing anything to the wind is odd. Poets can address their words to the wind, but they must "personify" the wind to do it sensibly. And even poets seem not to take such personification literally. The rest of us certainly do not. So if there is a problem with addressing blame to someone like Hinckley, the problem would have to be that Hinckley, like the wind, is not literally a person.

To claim that some of the insane are, like the wind, not literally persons, is shocking, yet the claim is not without truth. Some of the insane are so deranged that trying to communicate with them is like trying to communicate with the wind. Such persons are, however, also likely to be so deranged that we cannot sensibly attribute intention to them. They would not need the affirmative defense of insanity. Someone like Hinckley, in contrast, can communicate. Indeed, such persons seem to be able to converse intelligently, to obey orders, to do such complex tasks as traveling from one city to another without calling attention to themselves, and otherwise to behave as relatively sophisticated agents. Addressing blame to such persons does not seem at all odd. Attendants at mental hospitals do it frequently (though many therapists do not). If there is something wrong with blaming someone like Hinckley for a crime, the wrong is moral, not conceptual.

THE MORAL PROPRIETY OF
BLAMING HINCKLEY

To convict someone is, we are assuming, both to blame him and to make him liable for punishment, but not necessarily to punish him (provided "punish" means more than "blame," "find guilty," or "convict"). Convicting someone is consistent with sending him to a mental hospital rather than to a prison (provided his commitment remains under the jurisdiction of criminal courts). The question now is what moral objection could a retributivist have, given this assumption, to finding an insane person guilty. We postpone to the next section the question of *punishing* a person for what he did while insane.

The moral objection to convicting someone for what he did because of his insanity seems to be that treating someone who could not obey the law as if he could obey is unfair. Being unable to stop doing some act should excuse one from all blame (or at least from such blame as would be involved in a verdict of guilty). This objection seems to rest on three claims, each surprisingly controversial: (a) that one should not visit any evil (or at least an evil like conviction) upon someone for what he did if he could not help doing it; (b) that the insane cannot (in an appropriate sense) help doing what they do; and (c) that being convicted is, on balance, an evil for the insane. Let us consider these claims in order.

At first, the claim that we should not visit evil upon someone for doing what he could not help doing sounds safe enough. Yet, a little reflection reveals danger. Consider, for example, someone hired for a job he cannot do. Once his inability is discovered, his employer would, presumably, have a right to fire him for not being able to do the job. Firing him would return him to the misery of unemployment. That would certainly be an evil visited upon him for doing badly what he could not do well.

The claim that we should not visit evil upon someone who cannot help doing what he did must then at least be narrowed to visiting evil upon someone for violating a rule of conduct rather than a standard of competence. But even so narrowed, the claim is risky. We may, it seems, properly visit evil (for example, a slap) upon a young child to teach what the rule is. We sometimes have no other way to teach rules than to "punish" for their violation. The "punishment" is justified by pedagogy, though not deserved as retribution.

The claim might be further narrowed. We should not, it might be said, visit an evil upon someone for violating a rule of conduct if he could not obey the rule and he cannot learn obedience from suffering the evil that follows disobedience. This last claim seems much safer. But safety may have been bought at the cost of relevance. What reason is there to believe that someone like Hinckley might not learn from his conviction? (Hinckley seems to be considerably more sensitive to what others think of him than many of the insane and even some we do not classify as insane.) What reason is there to believe that such a conviction might not help a person who recovered his sanity to be more law-abiding than he would have been if he had been found not-guilty-by-reason-of-insanity? What place do such considerations of *reform* have in a discussion of retributivist objections to the verdict of guilty-but-insane?

Discussion of visiting evil upon those who cannot help doing what they do presupposes a certain sense of "could not help doing what they did." Finding a satisfactory interpretation of that term is not easy. Besides insanity, the category of could-not-help-doing-what-he-did excuses includes duress, coercion, necessity, mistakes of law, mistakes of fact not affecting the basic crime, extreme provocation, extreme youth, diminished responsibility, and intoxication.

For some members of that category, "could not help doing what he did" means could not have done otherwise without showing *more* courage, self-control, diligence, or the like than most of us possess. If, for example, someone points a gun at your child's head and demands that you embezzle a large sum from your employer this afternoon as a ransom for your child's life, you could refuse. But if you did, you would demonstrate a strength of character beyond that of most of us (supposing you are no less indifferent to your child's welfare than most of us would be to ours). If you yield to the gunman's threat instead, you nevertheless do something wrong. You break the law and wrong your employer to escape a greater wrong to yourself. You take advantage of your employer. What you do is "reasonable" ("the lesser evil"), but it is not right. We would like a world in which no one ever gave in to such threats, in part because such threats would then very seldom be made, but we know this is not such a world. If we cannot bring ourselves to punish you, it is because we hesitate to punish others for what we would, in similar circumstances, have done as well. We hesitate to punish, but we are also unwilling to license such acts (as we do license self-defense). The situation excuses the act without justifying it.

Such excuses are, we might say, "situational" because the focus is not the agent but the situation in which she finds herself. A situational excuse can be a full excuse if the situation is sufficiently extreme. Usually situational excuses provide only a partial excuse. But even where they provide full excuse, what moral objection is there to saying of the person so excused "guilty but excused"? Such a verdict seems more accurate than our present "not guilty," which does not distinguish between "disproved," "not proved," "proved but justified," and "proved but excused." (I shall come back to this point later.)

For other members of that category of excuse (for example, extreme youth, diminished responsibility, and intoxication), "could not help doing what he did" means "could have helped doing what he did had he not lacked the courage, self-control, or similar virtue that most of us possess." Such excuses are "personal." They focus on some weakness in the person, not some fact about the situation. For example, extreme youth, if it is to be an excuse in a particular situation, must actually explain why the person did what he did when an ordinary person would not have.

There is, I think, no single way to handle personal excuses. Extreme youth does not so much excuse as lead to a transfer of jurisdiction before there can be a trial. But insofar as it excuses at all, extreme youth is a full excuse. The youth will be sent to juvenile court, where youth is no defense at all. In contrast, diminished responsibility provides at most a partial excuse, for example, an excuse permitting murder to be punished as manslaughter. Intoxication is seldom admitted as an excuse (at least as long as the intoxication is "voluntary").

Insanity is a personal excuse. So, the claim that insanity is a full excuse (in part) because the insane cannot help doing what they do must explain both why insanity differs from those personal excuses that are not full excuses and why the difference is relevant to making insanity a full excuse. How much difference is there between insanity and the examples of personal excuse listed above?

We do, of course, picture the insane as "stark raving mad." But someone like Hinckley is not like that. He is no more disconcerted, heedless of consequences, or out of control than many a drunk. True, drunkenness is (ordinarily) a voluntary state while insanity is not. Extreme youth and diminished responsibility are, however, like insanity in (ordinarily) being involuntary. Those extremely young or of diminished responsibility could, it seems, be at least as disconcerted, heedless of consequences, or out of control as Hinckley was "through no fault of their own." Yet we do not treat their condition as a full excuse.

Even if someone like Hinckley were far more disconcerted,

heedless of consequences, or out of control than someone extremely young or of diminished responsibility, the question would remain why the difference of degree (supposing it to exist) should bar conviction altogether while those other excuses do not. After all, someone like Hinckley has taken advantage of his fellow citizens in much the same way the extremely young or those suffering diminished responsibility or intoxication take advantage when they break the law. Hinckley did what he wanted to do, something we did not want him to do, and something people even much like him may very well not have done though tempted. Why, then, may we not say guilty-but-insane (on the model of guilty-but-excused)?

The likely answer to that question is that convicting the insane is visiting an evil on them, and that is unfair, inhumane, or otherwise morally objectionable. The answer fails. There is, of course, the problem already discussed. It is not clear why visiting an evil on the insane is unfair, inhumane, or otherwise morally objectionable. But another problem lies beyond that. The answer presupposes that convicting the insane is, all things considered, visiting an evil upon them. That presupposition is itself doubtful.

Being blamed is something most people would want to avoid, *all else equal*. In this respect, blame is certainly an evil. But, from its being an evil in that respect, it does not follow that all blame is equally an evil or that other considerations may not make some blame, *all things considered*, a good. To treat someone as if he were a dog is a greater evil than to blame him as if he were a sly devil. Given that those were the only options in a particular situation, blaming him would not, all things considered, be an evil.

Finding someone guilty is a special kind of blaming. The criminal law treats those fully under its jurisdiction with a respect not accorded them by elementary schools, mental hospitals, juvenile courts, and other helping institutions. The criminal is treated as a full person, a being capable of knowing the rules and acting accordingly, a being who acted with reasonable foresight of the consequences (including conviction and punishment). The average criminal may, in fact, not deserve that respect. He may be rather dull, living in the present, without thought for tomorrow. He may have stumbled into his crime, not really thinking what he was doing and perhaps not even realizing that he was doing something wrong. He may (as we say) "have done something stupid." He will nevertheless be treated (at least until conviction) as if he were everything he is supposed to be. And even he may, given the alternatives, prefer to be treated that way.

The importance of treating a person as a person has received careful statement.[9] I need not repeat that statement here. I need only draw out one consequence: The less like the ideal a particular criminal is, the greater the compliment conviction pays him. For someone close to the ideal, "blameworthy" means little more than "to blame." Such a criminal gets no more than he deserves. But for those falling far below the ideal, "blameworthy" means something closer to "*worthy* of blame." Such criminals are permitted a range of rights, procedural safeguards, and the like that others much like them (for example, the very young) are not. They are (in this respect, at least) treated better than they deserve. Treating them that way is a good that might well overbalance the evil inherent in conviction itself.

Let me put this point another way. If the insane were not presumed to be blameworthy (while, of course, also being presumed not to blame), there would be no point to trying them like full persons. There would in any case have to be a *civil* hearing to decide insanity. The *criminal* trial does not do that. The criminal trial decides whether someone is to blame for the act in question (presuming the accused to be capable of blameworthy action). We need not presume the insane to be capable of blameworthy action. We might simply excuse them from criminal trial as some other legal systems (for example, the French) do now and as we now excuse the very young. Their condition, not their acts, would then be all that determined disposition of their case. The prosecutor would not have to prove the basic case *before* insanity became a relevant consideration. The prosecutor would not have to prove anything beyond a reasonable doubt. The prosecutor would only have to show that the evidence favored a finding of insanity, crime or no crime. Making the insane undergo criminal trial admits them (if only "by courtesy") into the class of persons who could be convicted and so treats them (however provisionally) as blameworthy.

Those defending the verdict of not-guilty-by-reason-of-insanity against guilty-but-insane thus face a dilemma. They must either admit that the insane are under the criminal law only "by courtesy" (and so must also admit that no important principle would be violated by a verdict of guilty-but-insane) or argue instead that the insane are under the criminal law "by right" (in which case, again, no important principle seems to bar their conviction even if one requires them to be excused from punishment). With respect to trial and conviction, the insane are either like very young children or like you and me. They cannot be both.

PUNISHING HINCKLEY

For a retributivist then, the hard question is not whether convicting the insane is morally permissible. Because the insane can be guilty, convicting them is morally permissible. The hard question is what is morally permissible *after* conviction. The arguments against (mere) conviction are weak because convicting is *only* blaming. But the same arguments may, when used against punishing, be stronger because punishing is more than blaming. The objection to the verdict of guilty-but-insane that we must now consider is that convicting the insane makes an insane person liable for punishment, a punishment that he does not deserve even if he deserves blame for his act. Punishment is perhaps a continuation of blaming by other means, but those means are not morally indifferent. We blame almost all moral failures (as well as many that are not moral), but we think it proper to punish only the more serious.

The question of whether to punish someone for what he did while insane may be divided into two parts. The first concerns punishing him while he remains insane; the second, punishing him after he has recovered. Provided we do not think of hospitalization as punishment, it seems plain that those favoring the verdict of guilty-but-insane do *not* favor punishing the insane. The insane should, they seem to say, be helped once convicted so long as helping goes on under the criminal law. To punish a person while he is insane is, at least, inhumane. To punish such a person shocks our sense of decency whether he committed his crime while insane or before. We would not, for example, execute a murderer who went insane on death row until he recovered his sanity, no matter how sane he was at the time of his crime and no matter how heinous the crime. What moral sense this makes is a question for another time.[10] The point here is that such treatment is not controversial (or at least does not now appear to be). Excusing the insane from punishment while they remain insane is common ground between those favoring the new verdict and those opposing it.

The only question left, then, is whether an insane person may, once recovered, be sent to prison for any part of his sentence not served in a mental hospital. This question has not been much discussed. Yet given the system of criminal law assumed earlier, we cannot simply dismiss it. The question marks the only potentially important difference left between not-guilty-by-reason-of-insanity and guilty-but-insane.

What might be the retributivist argument *for* punishing the insane after he has recovered for what he did while insane (and because of that insanity)? The argument would, I think, have to be much the same as that for convicting him in the first place. He deserves the punishment for what he *did*. His excuse is based on what he *was*. If we do not recognize that excuse, we treat him as if he were a rational agent, a full person, when in fact, at the time of the crime, he was not. We treat him with a respect greater than he deserves. We treat him exactly as we would if he had gone insane only after he committed the crime.

Whatever the appeal of this argument for conviction soon after the crime, its appeal is nil when punishment has been delayed for many years. Why? There is, of course, the fact that punishing someone is much rougher treatment than blaming him. But for a retributivist, the mere fact of rougher treatment is irrelevant if the punishment is deserved. The difficulty with punishment long delayed is that, even if the criminal has been sane all along and simply changed much over the years, we are inclined to excuse (or at least forgive). The less the person today resembles the criminal of yesterday (or yesteryear), the less comfortable we are about attributing the crime to him and exacting retribution. Time itself seems to dissolve the taker of unfair advantage. Retributivism itself includes a "statute of limitations" (as a side constraint).

The effect of time is likely to be most dramatic if it includes the change from insanity to sanity. Part of recovering one's sanity is coming to see the world differently, coming to see one's insane self as a different person, and coming to be seen in that way by others, too. We do not (once our sanity returns) take moral responsibility for what we did while insane any more than (once grown up) we take responsibility for what we did while very young. We could, of course, but we do not (except for certain types of civil liability themselves governed by a statute of limitations). Insanity is a kind of moral bankruptcy. The insane may have to pay his "debts" as best he can with what few resources he has (for example, by suffering conviction), but we do not ordinarily carry over the remaining "debts" to be collected after he has been "reorganized." Something similar is true of children. If a youth is convicted as a juvenile, his "punishment" (generally) ends with his coming of age.

Why this should be is another question beyond the scope of this chapter. That it is so (for us at least) is enough for our purposes. If the verdict of guilty-but-insane *required* (as we have assumed) punishing the sane for crimes they committed while insane, adopting the new verdict would be more than a minor "reform." The new verdict would require a major change in how we view the relationship between the insane person and his recovered self. Insofar as defenders of the new verdict have seen this consequence at all, they have tried to fend it off by calling the fact of insanity into question ("There's really no such thing!"), by making insanity seem far too easy to prove ("If you killed someone, there's a psychiatrist who'll testify you had to be insane to do it."), or by otherwise dissolving the terms in which a discussion of the verdict of guilty-but-*insane* must be carried on.

Though consistent with a major change in how we view the relationship between the insane and his recovered self, the new verdict does not itself require such a change. Even under a system of criminal law like the one that we have been supposing, the new verdict need not require a convict, once recovered, to suffer punishment for what he did while insane. The verdict need not require that because, even under such a system, "insane" could be read as "excused (upon recovery of sanity)."

Because the new verdict need not require the sane to be punished for crimes committed while insane, the new verdict can be a minor reform even for retributivists. The verdict can serve to distinguish more sharply than is now done between justification and excuse (as well as keeping the criminally insane under jurisdiction of the criminal law). Far from being self-contradictory, the new verdict might help to clear up our thinking about the criminal law.

CONCLUDING RECOMMENDATION

We now have three distinctions worth recalling. First is the distinction between conviction as such and punishment. That distinction is, as we have seen, important because the argument against punishing the insane is far stronger than the argument against convicting them (even though the arguments are otherwise quite similar). Second is the distinction between those personal conditions that bar conviction because they block proof of some element of the basic crime and those other personal conditions that excuse from punishment. (Both these must, of course, be distinguished from those other personal conditions—for example, ill-health, pregnancy, or the dependence of one's family—that would justify clemency without requiring it.) These distinctions are important, as we have seen, because someone like Hinckley is not innocent in the sense of being someone who did not do an act satisfying the definition of the basic crime. To convict him is not exactly to convict the innocent. The third distinction is between "situational excuses" that recognize the difficult circumstances of a person with the capacities the criminal law takes for granted and "personal excuses" that recognize that some people fall short of the capacities the criminal law takes for granted. People with personal excuses represent a problem for any legal system. There is more than one solution. While innocent-by-reason-of-insanity is one solution, guilty-but-insane is another. The choice between these solutions, while intellectually significant, need not be morally important.

These three distinctions suggest that those supporting the new verdict might strengthen their position by making it part of a wider reform. A general verdict of guilty-but-excused would make clear the point of guilty-but-insane. Guilty-but-insane is a special case of guilty-but-excused. There is nothing odd about someone being guilty but excused. To be guilty is to have done what one should not have done and to deserve blame for it, to deserve conviction but not necessarily to deserve punishment. "Convict" does not mean "punish." Blaming and punishing do not have the same logic.[11] Punishment without blameworthiness is a moral outrage (hence our outrage at punishing those who are "innocent" in the strict sense—that is, free from all blameworthy connection with the crime). But blameworthiness without liability for punishment is no more morally objectionable than forgiving in advance those who trespass against us as we would have them forgive our trespasses.

NOTES

I should like to thank Michael Gorr and Mark Strasser for helpful criticism of the first draft of this chapter.

1. The best critique of the insanity defense probably remains Norval Morris, *Madness and the Criminal Law* (Chicago: University of Chicago Press, 1982).

2. For example: "[It] would be a moral error and a grave injustice to abolish the insanity defense." Stephen J. Morse, "Excusing the Crazy: The Insanity Defense Reconsidered," *Southern California Law Review* 58 (March 1985): 777–836, at 806.

3. "'Insanity' means the lack of a substantial capacity either to appreciate the criminality of one's conduct or to conform one's conduct to the requirements of the law as a result of mental disorder or mental defect." *Illinois Criminal Law and Procedure* (St. Paul, Minn.: West Publishing Company, 1991), chap. 38, sec. 1005-1-11.

4. Compare Morris, 83–87.

5. For a good recent work on clemency, see: Kathleen Moore, *Pardons* (New York: Oxford University Press, 1989).

6. For a defense of this claim (for those who think it needs one), see Michael Davis, "Brandt on Autonomy," in *Rationality and Rule-Utilitarianism*, ed. Brad Hooker (Boulder, CO: Westview Press, 1993), pp. 51–65.

7. Eric Partridge, *Origins: A Short Etymological Dictionary of Modern English* (New York: Macmillan, 1958), 149.

8. Partridge, 48–49.

9. Herbert Morris, "Persons and Punishment," *Monist* 52 (October 1968): 475–501.

Nine

Punishment as Language

Much has been written over the last two decades on behalf of one form or another of the "expressive theory of punishment." R. A. Duff, Jean Hampton, Sanford Kadish, Herbert Morris, and Andrew von Hirsch are among the theorists who have explicitly endorsed the view that punishment is primarily a form of communication rather than a mere deprivation or penalty.[1] Though their views differ in many respects, all hold that punishment is justified (when it is) not because (or not primarily because) the penalty as such deters, reforms, restores a just balance of benefits and burdens, or otherwise satisfies some traditional theory of punishment, but primarily because punishment is a moral lesson, an appropriate rebuke to the criminal, a sufficiently emphatic denunciation of the crime. So, for example, one of these writers might argue (though none has) that a mass murderer, like John Wayne Gacey or Klaus Barbie, should be put to death because society cannot adequately condemn the criminal for his crimes using any lesser penalty.

Igor Primoratz's recent "Punishment as Language"[2] is an important contribution to our understanding of these expressive theories. Primoratz enriches our vocabulary by distinguishing two forms of "normative expressionism"—"extrinsic" and "intrinsic." He also advances the substantive debate by showing that extrinsic expressionism (or at least one form of it) suffers from most of the serious disabilities that traditional utilitarian theories of punishment do.

Yet "Punishment as Language" does not go far enough. Having provided the necessary vocabulary, Primoratz should have drawn a similar conclusion concerning the relationship between traditional retributivism and *intrinsic* expressionism. Instead, he suggests that intrinsic expressionism may offer an *independent* justification of punishment. For example, he explains the justice of punishing criminals in this way: "[If] society's condemnation of their misdeeds is really to reach them, if they are really to understand how wrong their actions are, [the condemnation] will have to be translated into the one language they are sure to understand: the language of self-interest. This translation is accomplished by punishment."[3] For Primoratz, it is not enough to point out that punishing criminals is just because it gives them what they deserve. The punishment must vindicate the laws that they broke, reaffirm the rights of their victims, and demonstrate to any and all that their deeds were indeed crimes. Punishment cannot do this unless it is conceived as language ("condemnation") and then shown to satisfy the requirements of honest communication: "Society may legitimately express moral condemnation by punishment only when its conscience speaks strongly and unequivocally, with one voice."[4] For Primoratz, language is primary, punishment is derivative.

What I shall argue here is that intrinsic expressionism adds nothing of value to (traditional) retributivism. Whenever we can sensibly speak, as Primoratz does, of legitimately expressing moral condemnation by punishment, we can speak more simply of legitimate punishment. Intrinsic expressionism can only justify punishment, either as an institution or case by case, if a (nonexpressive) retributive theory can also justify it. Intrinsic expressionism adds nothing to retributivism apart from a misleading formulation of its central thesis. Intrinsic expressionism is, if anything, less appealing than extrinsic expressionism.

WHAT IS EXTRINSIC EXPRESSIONISM?

Since my argument will presuppose Primoratz's, I must begin with a brief summary of his. Primoratz first distinguishes between (a) "descriptive expressionism," which offers a definition of punishment or a description of punishment's function, and (b) "normative expressionism," which offers a rationale for or justification of punishment. Though obvious once made, this distinction has the noteworthy effect of denying normative expressionists like Hampton and von Hirsch the authority they seemed to derive from Feinberg's early elaboration of descriptive expressionism. Punishment may in fact have the function that Feinberg attributes to it. Nothing follows concerning its justification. No particular function of punishment *necessarily* has a role in its justification. That a certain function has such a role must be shown by separate argument. Normative expressionism must provide such an argument.

Having distinguished between descriptive and normative expressionism, Primoratz examines extrinsic expressionism. He argues that this normative theory is fundamentally utilitarian. It understands punishment as a neutral fact (or positive evil) that, owing to a convention, can be made to carry a message in much the way a word or other token can be made to stand for something more or less arbitrarily connected with it. The message expressed is something grafted on, something extrinsic to, the punishment that expresses it, even if there is something appropriate in responding to harmful acts by doing harm in return. The bond between crime and punishment is conventional, much as is the bond between our word for a child too young to speak ("baby") and the sounds such a child makes.[5]

For extrinsic expressionism, then, punishment must be valuable as a means of expressing blame, condemnation, or the like. Punishment must also be valuable primarily because of its effect on society, not because of what punishment is "in itself"—since "in itself" punishment is a neutral fact (or positive evil). The effect on society of what punishment expresses, not its truth, will be what makes punishment valuable. Like ordinary utilitarian theories of punishment, extrinsic expressionism is, as such, a theory of efficient rather than just punishment.

That is Primoratz's analysis. I think that matters are a bit more complicated. Extrinsic expressionism requires both a convention and a purpose the convention is to serve. The alleged utilitarianism of extrinsic expressionism requires that the purpose served be something *causally* connected to the expression itself, for example, some effect on the criminal or society. Primoratz seems to have overlooked another possibility, a nonutilitarian purpose for the convention, for example, disavowing the crime (whatever contingent effect that disavowal has on the criminal or society). Punishment would still gain its value by being a means to something else, only now that "something else" is, thanks to the convention, accomplished by the very act of punishing (much as promising is accomplished by saying "I promise" in appropriate circumstances). "Nonutilitarian extrinsic expressionism" must also rely on a convention, rather than considerations of criminal desert as such, to connect the act of punishment and the purpose that the act is to achieve; in consequence, nonutilitarian extrinsic expressionism is, like its utilitarian twin, open to the objection that it leaves justice extrinsic to punishment and so leaves itself open to counterexamples in which communicative purposes are achieved but justice is not.

While I shall say no more about nonutilitarian forms of extrinsic expressionism here, I think it worth keeping in mind. It may in fact be the view that many supposed intrinsic expressionists actually hold; it is certainly capable of generating arguments for punishment easily mistaken for retributive ones.[6]

Utilitarian extrinsic expressionism is subject to most of the common criticisms made of traditional utilitarian theories of punishment; for example, it can exclude punishing the innocent only by appeal to some contingent fact or side-constraint. Indeed, (utilitarian) extrinsic expressionism differs from other utilitarian theories only in the preferred means of achieving its effect. What, then, is its appeal?

Primoratz does not say, but the answer is already obvious in Feinberg. Utilitarian theories of punishment tend to rely heavily on the deterrent effect of punishment. Relying on deterrence tends to make punishment look like a tariff on conduct ("a mere penalty," as Feinberg says).[7] Punishment seems to imply more than that, both moral condemnation of the act and moral rebuke of the agent. How explain this additional fact without committing oneself to some form of retributivism? Feinberg's suggestion is that punishment be defined to include condemnation. Any theory of punishment, even a deterrent theory, would then automatically distinguish punishment from mere penalty. The only question would be the empirical one of whether the society in question had the appropriate convention. For utilitarians, extrinsic expressionism has a distinct advantage over other forms that their theorizing about punishment take. It can explain, within utilitarian categories, the difference between punishment and mere penalty. That, I think, is enough to explain its appeal to utilitarians.

WHAT IS INTRINSIC EXPRESSIONISM?

If extrinsic expressionism has the forward-looking vices of traditional utilitarian theories (as well as some virtues they lack), intrinsic expressionism has the backward-looking virtues of traditional retributivism. That is no accident. Like traditional retributivism, intrinsic expressionism requires an "internal" connection between the crime to be punished and the punitive response.[8] An internal connection is, of course, nonconventional, but it is more. The connection between dark clouds and rain is non-conventional without being internal. Dark clouds are merely a natural sign of rain, made that by the frequency with which rain follows the appearance of dark clouds. Something similar is true of the connection between genes and the information embedded in them. Contingent physical laws determine the "message" that a particular gene expresses (or can be made to express by the appropriate chemical environment). What means what is a matter of fact that cannot be learned without observation and experiment.[9]

In contrast, the connection between the "message" intrinsic expressionism says punishment expresses and punishment as such is *conceptual*. A particular punishment cannot really vindicate the law that has been broken, reaffirm the right that has been violated, or demonstrate that a certain deed was a crime unless the punishment is a just response to what was in fact done. The message must be intrinsic to the punishment. Neither convention nor physical law but the concept of justice must, according to intrinsic expressionism, connect punishment with crime: "Intrinsic expressionism," says Primoratz, "does not construe the expression of moral condemnation that is punishment as a means to an end external to it, but as intrinsically right and proper."[10]

THE INFORMATIVE POWER OF
JUST PUNISHMENT

Since intrinsic expressionism requires a conceptual connection between punishment and crime, the expressiveness that intrinsic expressionism requires of punishment is strikingly unlike that of language. Languages are systems of conventional symbols—or with a bit of stretching, systems of natural signs as well. Except for a few self-referential uses, the relation of language to what it expresses is *never* conceptual. Languages do, of course, allow us to express conceptual relations. But to speak of punishment as language in the sense that intrinsic expressionism does (as involving a conceptual relation between particular crimes and their punishments) demands more; it demands that we think of a certain conceptual relation on the model of a nonconceptual relation. We must, for example, think of the relation between the just execution of a certain criminal and the moral condemnation of his murder in the way we think of the looser (conventional) relation existing between the cry of "Fire!" and the fear it expresses. Intrinsic expressionism's analogy between punishment and language is therefore not a mere variation of extrinsic expressionism's. It demands more of the relation between crime and punishment than extrinsic expressionism does. And it is precisely that demand that assures that it will have a weakness that extrinsic expressionism does not.

Here, perhaps, is the place to distinguish between two senses of "express": the *communicative*, which is concerned with transmitting a message (strictly so-called); and the *informative*, which is concerned instead with the mere carrying of information.

Communication requires that someone intends to share some information with someone (or something) whom he expects (or hopes) will accept it, understand it, and respond appropriately. ("Communication" shares its root with "commune.") Communication is not a uniquely human activity. (Many of us have pets of whose ability to communicate we do not doubt.) Still, in an obvious sense, communicating is both intentional and social. For example, when Feinberg talks about the expressive function of punishment, he clearly supposes that someone, "society," intends to send a message to someone else—to the criminal, to the law-abiding, or to everyone individually.

Carrying information is not like that. Even lifeless rocks carry information. Most of the history of the planet is embedded in them. We need only interpret what the rocks are "saying." Intention and society have nothing to do with the information rocks carry (though, of course, intention and society have much to do with how we interpret the information).

Not only lifeless rocks carry information. Human speech, that paradigm of communication, can (and usually does) carry information (whether it also communicates or not). Brave words can betray fear just as effectively as a scream. The tight-lipped "no comment" in response to a reporter can (as we say) "speak volumes." We do not have the same control over the information we give out that we have over what we communicate. Communication is a special case of carrying information.

Conceptual relations assure that much of what we say and do can carry information whether or not we intend to communicate (and even if we try not to communicate it). The information is implicit—to be learned, for example, by working out the logical consequences of what we do say. You need not tell me that you have four children to inform me of that. You need only tell me of two now and of two others later. I can (as we say) "put two and two together."

Legal punishment certainly carries information in this (nonconventional) way. To be legal punishment, punishment must execute a judicial sentence. A judicial sentence is supposed to be just; an unjust sentence is, as such, one that should be revoked. A sentence can be just only if imposed after the criminal has been shown to have done something that deserves the punishment. The desert must be moral as well as legal. So, for example, punishment deserved only according to an unjust law could not be just punishment. Not only must the sentence be imposed after a showing of guilt but also upon a formal finding. The judge (or jury) must *declare* the criminal guilty of the appropriate crime. (Unless the judge has so declared—and under the appropriate circumstances—the punishment cannot be legal and so cannot do criminal justice.) The sentence is also supposed to impose a penalty proportioned to the wrong done. (A penalty greater than deserved would be unjust.)

A just penalty, then, quite literally entails the moral, as well as legal, condemnation of both criminal and crime.[11] The judge must "condemn" the crime (that is, state the penalty it deserves) and "condemn" the criminal (that is, state that the criminal deserves the penalty). Legal punishment can never be a "mere penalty" (so long as it is just). Theories of just punishment necessarily resolve Feinberg's problem before it can arise.

Those imposing just punishment may intend to communicate this condemnation, to send a message to actual criminals, potential criminals, or the law-abiding generally. But even if they do not, just punishment entails this (nonexpressive) condemnation. The "message" will go out anyway, necessarily embedded as information in the just punishment itself.

THE REDUNDANCY OF
INTRINSIC EXPRESSIONISM

If retributivist theories are already theories of just punishment, what can intrinsic expressionism add by making expression of moral condemnation central to punishment? The answer is, I think, nothing good. Consider these two possibilities.

First, suppose that a punishment is justified (or at least shown to be just) under some (nonexpressive) retributive theory and that the theory is true. If the punishment is so justified, imposing it must vindicate the law (that is, show that justice is still a presence in the world), reaffirm the victim's right (for example, by making the criminal "pay" for violating that right), and demonstrate that the deed in question is a crime (by treating it like one, that is, by punishing it). How will just punishment do that? *Simply by doing justice* (whatever else it does). How else could punishment really vindicate the law, reaffirm the victim's right, and demonstate that the deed in question is a crime? Since retributivism is, as such, a theory of just punishment, any retributive punishment should, as such, do justice and so necessarily vindicate the law, reaffirm the victim's right, and so on.

Second, suppose instead that no (nonexpressive) retributive theory is true. Supposing that implies, among other things, that a criminal could not be shown to deserve punishment simply by citing justified nonlinguistic principles connecting her punishment with what she did. But on this supposition, expressing condemnation by imposing punishment could not be shown to be just, either. The connection between the crime and the punishment would depend on language (conventional or natural) rather than on (nonlinguistic) desert. It becomes conceptually possible that the punishment is not deserved and so not just.

Nonexpressive retributivism is simply intrinsic expressionism without the linguistic apparatus. So, as Primoratz says, "the adherent of intrinsic expressionism commits himself to just those considerations of justice and desert on which retributivism insists."[12] Since intrinsic expressionism must generate the same conclusion about desert and condemnation as retribution does, intrinsic expressionism would itself contain a false element if no (nonexpressive) retributivism were true. Intrinsic expressionism cannot be true if an essential element is false.

Intrinsic expressionism thus appears redundant. That redundancy is itself a consequence of intrinsic expressionism's being a theory of *intrinsic* expression. Unlike extrinsic expressionism, intrinsic expressionism requires a conceptual connection between penalty and crime (that is, a connection fixed by principles of justice already accepted). The penalty must be proportioned to what the crime deserves (or at least not exceed what it deserves). The penalty is justified only if it is so proportioned. This proportion is precisely what any (nonexpressive) retributive theory would require. (Nonexpressive) retributivism differs from intrinsic expressionism only in offering formulations of that (conceptual) connection that omit reference to punishment's expressive function. Retributive punishments, as such, necessarily carry the same information as intrinsically expressive punishments, so long as the punishments of intrinsic expressionism contain nothing external to the concept of justice.

I hope I will not be misunderstood. I am not denying that the justification of punishment as an institution may lie (in part) in the information punishment might carry or transmit. Neither am I making any claim about what judges should seek to communicate by the sentences they impose. I am simply explaining how moral condemnation could be deducible from (nonexpressive) retributivism and why, in consequence, intrinsic expressionism cannot be true unless some form of (nonexpressive) retributivism is. I am explaining why intrinsic expressionism is redundant.

THE DISADVANTAGE OF INTRINSIC EXPRESSIONISM

While retributivism makes intrinsic expression redundant, they are not simply equally attractive formulations of one theory. Intrinsic expressionism is misleading in at least two ways that retributivism is not.

First, in *extrinsic* expressionism, the analogy between punishment and language is both accurate and suggestive. Punishment can indeed be used like language if one has the appropriate intention. For extrinsic expressionism, what punishment communicates need have little or no connection with what the punishment is "in itself" or what else it does. What punishment will communicate is as extrinsic to the punishment itself as a statement is to the state of affairs it expresses. In intrinsic expressionism, however, the analogy between punishment and language is less happy. It necessarily understates the closeness of the bond between punishment and condemnation. Rather than merely *communicating* moral condemnation, just punishment *entails* it (and unjust punishment is, presumably, unjustified whatever it communicates). To talk here of merely expressing (or communicating) condemnation, then, is to suggest something false: that just punishment could have been used to express something else instead. Just punishment can, of course, be used to express something in addition (extrinsically) but not instead (intrinsically).

But can intrinsic expressionism really mislead in this way? The answer, I think, is that it not only can, but has. Consider some remarks that Primoratz makes near the end of his generally careful paper. Having noted that contemporary society is typically as pluralistic and conflict-ridden in the field of morals as in any other, he asks, "Which of [the various opposed moral views espoused by significant sections of society] is to be expressed in law and in punishments for offending against it?"[13] The law, of course, (quite literally) communicates what society allows or forbids. The law is language. Punishment does not communicate in that way, though it can carry the same information. Primoratz's use of "express"—"*expressed* in law *and* in punishments"—is therefore starkly ambiguous.

But it is more than ambiguous. It suggests that we have something like the same freedom in choosing how much to punish a certain act (or class of acts) as we have in choosing whether to make the act (or class) punishable. Yet for desert theorists, whether retributivist or intrinsic expressionist, that cannot be. A pluralistic society may force us to tolerate much that we would prefer to outlaw. Neither retributivism nor intrinsic expressionism requires that all morally condemnable acts be made legally condemnable. But both sorts of theory do oblige us to punish justly (whatever we take just punishment to be). The punishments cannot, for example, exceed what justice (as we see it) allows, whatever could be communicated if we did. The moral condemnation that just punishment necessarily expresses is a mere byproduct of desert (not a factor shaping punishment independently). Primoratz's fixation on language seems to have led him to think in extrinsic terms—quite against his intention.

Nonexpressive retributivist theories of punishment thus differ from ordinary utilitarian theories in an important way that is seldom noted. Ordinary utilitarian theories cannot explain why the punishment they would impose must carry moral condemnation. Extrinsic expressionism compensates for that weakness of utilitarian theories. Retributive theories have no such weakness. As theories of just punishment, they necessarily explain why the punishment they would impose must carry moral condemnation. Retributivism does not need an expressionist supplement, even though utilitarian theories do. This, then, is the second way in which intrinsic expressionism is misleading. It suggests a weakness in retributivism that isn't there.[14]

NOTES

I should like to thank Anthony Duff, Igor Primoratz, and Don Scheid for helpful comments on one or another early draft of this chapter. I should also like to thank those who discussed a later draft at a session of the Midwestern Division Meeting, American Philosophical Association, 27 April 1991, especially Jacob Adler, my official commentator, for helping to give the chapter its final polish (without polishing it off).

1. See, for example, R. A. Duff, *Trials and Punishments* (Cambridge: Cambridge University Press, 1985); Jean Hampton, "The Moral Education Theory of Punishment," *Philosophy and Public Affairs* 13 (Summer 1984): 208–38; Sanford Kadish, "Complicity, Clause, and Blame: A Study in the Interpretation of Doctrine," *California Law Review* 73 (March 1985): 323–410; Herbert Morris, "A Paternalistic Theory of Punishment," *American Philosophical Review* 18 (October 1981): 263–71; and Andrew von Hirsch, *Past or Future Crimes* (New Brunswick, NJ: Rutgers University Press, 1985).

2. Igor Primoratz, "Punishment as Language," *Philosophy* 64 (April 1989): 187–205.

3. Primoratz, 200.

4. Primoratz, 205.

5. Note that, as I am using "convention," conventions need not be altogether arbitrary. For example, the English word "baby" means baby by convention (in my sense) though there is a certain onomatopoeic fit between babies (their babble) and "baby" (as there is not, for example, between babies and "infant"). Conventions are arbitrary only in the sense that reason does not require them. The French are not unreasonable for calling their babies "les infants." What Bentham called charactisticalness in punishment corresponds to onomatopoeia in language. Like onomatopoeia, it is something rational people will consider when formulating a convention. But, like onomatopoeia, it is only one factor among many, not an overriding consideration in the way justice, deterrence, or cost would be.

6. I owe this distinction to Jacob Adler (though he originally labeled this nonutilitarian form of *ex*trinsic expressionism "weak *in*trinsic expressionism").

7. J. Feinberg, "The Expressive Function of Punishment," *Doing and Deserving* (Princeton University Press, 1970): 100.

8. Primoratz, 196 ("intrinsic"), 198 ("inherent"), and 201 ("determined solely by the nature of").

9. Compare A. J. Skillen, "How to Say Things with Walls," *Philosophy* 55 (October 1980): 509–523, "Whereas black is arguably neutral in itself and only contextually and conventionally constituted as mourning wear . . . it is pretty clear that losing money, years of liberty, or parts of one's body is hardly neutral in that way. [. . .] Feinberg vastly underrates the natural appropriateness, the nonarbitrariness, of certain forms of hard treatment to be the expression or communication of moralistic and punitive attitudes. Such practices *embody* punitive hostility, they do not merely 'symbolize' it." (Quoted in Primoratz, 199.)

10. Primoratz, 201.

11. By "entail," I mean that relationship between statements that permits us to deduce one from another by standard logic. I should perhaps point out the nontrivial assumption on which such talk rests. It assumes that we can translate "the language" of punishment into statements of the sort logic can operate with (for example, by identifying the presuppositions of particular acts), indeed, that reason requires just that translation. This assumption is required if I am to take any form of expressionism seriously. Without it, the expressionist's analogy with language would dissolve into uninteresting metaphor. But I do not endorse that assumption. Indeed, I wonder at its daring.

12. Primoratz, 202.

13. Primoratz, 204.

14. Deciding who is and who is not an intrinsic expressionistis not as easy as it might seem. Some writers are easy to classify. For example, citing Primoratz, von Hirsch recently declared allegiance to intrinsic expressionism. "Proportionality in the Philosophy of Punishment: From 'Why Punish?' to 'How Much?'" *Criminal Law Forum* 1 (Winter 1990): 259–90. So for now at least, we can classify von Hirsch as an intrinsic expressionist. Others are not so easily classified. For example, Primoratz classifies Hampton as a (utilitarian) extrinsic expressionist (Primoratz, 194–95) because of her emphasis on crime prevention as the object of a system of punishment. I, however, am inclined to assign her to the intrinsic expressionists because of her emphasis on the logical connection between punishment ("the disruption of the [criminal's] pleasure") and the conclusion that the criminal should draw from the punishment ("you did something wrong"). Hampton, "Moral Education," 226–227. Some theorists—Kadish, for example—may need to make up their mind. Since von Hirsch has suggested that I have softened my view on condemnation (von Hirsch, "Proportionality," 271), perhaps this is the place to make clear that I have not. I continue to deny that "moral condemnation" (that is, moral condemnation *all things considered*) is a measure of deserved punishment. What I have always thought, though I have not always said it clearly, is that legal punishment presupposes a form of moral condemnation (moral condemnation considering *only* legally relevant factors). The measure of (maximum) just legal punishment is legal desert, not moral desert, all things considered (and certainly not moral blameworthiness). Compare *To Make the Punishment Fit the Crime*, chapters 2 and 10, and "Postscript: In Fairness to Condemnation," *Israel Law Review* 25 (Summer–Autumn 1991): 581–594.

Ten

What Does Rape Deserve?

In 1978, California raised the penalty for rape from "three, four, or five years imprisonment" to "three, six, or eight years." Because California sharply restricts judicial discretion in sentencing, that change meant that a conviction for rape without mitigating or aggravating circumstances would require a sentence of six years imprisonment rather than four. If we call a crime without mitigating or aggravating circumstances "simple," then the change amounted to a declaration that simple rape was about as serious a crime as simple aggravated arson rather than simple assault with a deadly weapon.[1]

One might suppose that feminists applauded the change. They have, after all, for years talked about how rape supports the oppression of women, how fear of rape darkens much that a woman does, how actual rape can shatter its victim. But, in fact, some California feminists opposed the change. They feared stiffer penalties would mean fewer convictions, less deterrence, and more rapists looking for victims. They may have had good reason to fear such consequences. Even so, they found themselves with an awkward argument. They had to argue that, while rape is a very serious crime, it should not be punished that way in California. Ideally (they had to say), the penalty should be very severe, but such severity is impractical in a society as sexist as our own. Better a light punishment than none at all.[2] Those feminists lost the argument. The importance that they assigned rape in theory helped to defeat their efforts to protect women in practice.

Those feminists were, I think, right in their conclusion. The penalty for rape should be relatively low. They were wrong only in their premise. Rape is *not* a very serious crime. Rape should be treated as a variety of ordinary (simple or aggravated) battery because that is what rape is. Treating rape in that way is theo-

183

retically sound. That, anyway, is what I shall argue in this chapter.

I do not, however, reject the feminist analysis of rape. Rape *is* a serious crime. The question is, *how serious?* The question is emphatically comparative. It is a question to which feminists have not given much thought. They have not, I think, because the question is important only in the context of setting penalties. Even in that context, it has not been important for long. The question becomes important only when the accepted theory of punishment is retribution or deterrence rather than reform or incapacitation. Until the 1970s, reform (and incapacitation) dominated both practice and theory. Today that is no longer so. The "principle of just desert" (a.k.a. retribution) has replaced reform as the dominant theory. Legislatures now calibrate crimes with a specificity not seen in generations. Statutes regularly carry maximum and minimum sentences with little room for judicial discretion. (The California statute cited above illustrates how little room may be left for judicial discretion.) The courts are laying down new doctrines about proportioning penalty to crime. Theorists have begun to discuss an array of intriguing problems that, until a few years ago, hardly seemed problems at all: How do we justify recidivist statutes if the criminal already gets what he deserves by being punished for each crime? How do we justify punishing attempts less severely than completed crimes if the criminal's desert is the measure of proper punishment? What makes a victimless crime deserve any punishment at all? And so on.

The feminists' argument from conviction-rate could not succeed where everyone else was concerned with "just deserts." To argue that a statutory penalty should be lower than the crime deserves is to take on a heavy burden. Except in the most extreme circumstances, mitigation is for sentencing (if it is proper at all). The feminists could not *demonstrate* such extreme circumstances. Even allowing for underreporting, rape is a relatively rare event, not at all as common as burglary or assault.[3] Feminist concern with conviction rates must therefore have sounded to California's legislators like a sad echo of the days when statutory penalties were still reached through the "serpent windings of utilitarianism." You cannot play Bentham to a legislator's Kant. What I do here is provide an argument to make trying that unnecessary.

I proceed in this way. First, I describe the place of rape in a typical statutory scheme; I use Illinois's rather than California's because Illinois's is more familiar to me, simpler, and somewhat more typical than California's. Second, I consider justifications that have been or might be offered for giving rape the status that it has in Illinois's statutes. I conclude that all fail. Third, I analyze rape as battery and provide a justification for treating rape as ordinary battery. Last, I catalogue some practical advantages of treating rape as battery (for example, simplifying proof of the crime). Throughout this chapter, I take the principle of just desert as a given. I do that in part because much practical discussion of punishment now takes the principle as a given, but also because the principle seems to me to yield the only adequate justification of punishment. And, of course, I am entitled to take the principle as a given here because I have defended it at great length elsewhere (in *To Make the Punishment Fit the Crime*). This chapter will be long enough without repeating what I have done elsewhere.

The chapter's argument is often philosophical in a way likely to irritate social scientists and embarrass some philosophers. There is a good deal of armchair social science and deductions from plausible but unproved empirical assumptions. In particular, I regularly make claims about what "we," "men," or "women" would choose. I make no apologies. Theory must begin somewhere. Theorists cannot always wait until social scientists do their job (in part because theory helps social scientists to know what their job is). Often my only evidence is what I know about myself or those few people whom I have asked. Such evidence fills a vacuum left by social science, a vacuum filled till now by tradition's unexamined residue. Feminists have, it seems to me, unconsciously taken over much of the traditional view of rape while supposing themselves to have rejected it all. My method, however irritating or embarrassing, at least corrects for that.

I intend this chapter to suggest rather than to prove, to provoke rather than to silence, to be the first word rather than the last. So when I say "we" would do such-and-such, ask yourself whether you, at least, would do that. When I say "men" would choose thus-and-so, ask yourself (if you are a man) whether you would so choose or (if you are a woman) ask men you know how they would choose. Treat my claims about how "women" would act in the same way. We must begin with what we know. When we think about rape, we must be careful not to go beyond what we know. We must not suppose that we know what women-in-the-abstract or men-in-the-abstract would do, feel, or prefer. Such abstractions take a long time to coalesce out of the bits and pieces people know (or think they know) about one another. So much both of how we think about rape and of how we respond to it have changed so quickly that such abstractions are almost certainly misleading. My evidence, though anecdotal, is at least empirical. My sample, however skewed, is at least contemporary. The conclusion I draw, however startling, is still quite weak: What evidence we have (or can easily get) supports treating rape as battery. We need to know more, to think harder, and to be wary of much that passes for common sense about rape. We need to compare rape with other serious crimes.

RAPE IN THE STATUTORY SCHEME

How serious a crime is rape? Until 1977, sixteen American states still provided death as a penalty for rape.[4] Apparently, those states thought rape could be as serious a crime as murder. The Supreme Court thought otherwise, and in 1977 it declared the penalty of death for rape unconstitutional because it was out of proportion to the crime. Nonetheless, both majority and minority agreed with the Georgia Supreme Court that "short of homicide, [rape] is the ultimate violation of self."[5] Today, most American jurisdictions treat rape as only somewhat less serious than murder. At least thirty states provide for up to life imprisonment for rape. Many others provide for sentences of up to thirty, forty, or fifty years.[6]

Illinois' treatment of rape is more or less typical. Illinois recognizes two forms of rape:

1. where a "male person of the age of 14 years and upwards . . . has sexual intercourse with a female, not his wife, by force and against her will" (rape strictly so-called); and

2. where a "person of the age of 14 years and upwards . . . by force or threat of force, compels any other person to perform or submit to any act of sexual gratification involving the sex organs of one person and the mouth or anus of another" (so-called "deviate sexual assault").[7]

"Sexual intercourse" as used in the "rape" statute means male penetration of the female organs with or without emission. "Intercourse by force and against her will" includes intercourse with a female who is unconscious or so mentally deranged or deficient that she cannot give effective consent to intercourse—but not sexual intercourse with a willing child (which can usually be treated *either* as "indecent liberties with a child," a class-1 felony, or as "contributing to the sexual delinquency of a child," a class-A misdemeanor).[8]

Both forms of rape are class-X felonies. The penalty for a class-X felony is 6-30 years imprisonment. Only murder can be punished more severely. Crimes one might suppose to be more serious than rape (because they are more life-threatening) are punished no more severely than rape. Some are punished much less severely. Aggravated kidnapping (for example, kidnapping in which the victim suffers physical injury), armed robbery, and aggravated arson (that is, arson of an occupied building) are also only class-X felonies. Voluntary manslaughter is, in contrast, only a class-2 felony (3-7 years imprisonment); involuntary manslaughter, a class-3 felony (2-5 years imprisonment).[9]

Many crimes that one might suppose to be more or less analogous to rape are punished much less severely. For example: Simple kidnapping resembles (simple) rape insofar as both crimes temporarily deprive a person of control of his own life, by force or threat, but without serious injury. Simple kidnapping is (like voluntary manslaughter) only a class-2 felony. Aggravated battery resembles rape insofar as both involve cruel and unlawful touching, though aggravated battery requires maiming, use of a deadly weapon, or some other special aggravating factor. Aggravated battery is (like involuntary manslaughter) only a class-3 felony. And aggravated assault (for example, threatening someone with a deadly weapon) is only a class-A misdemeanor (maximum of one-year imprisonment). Only when a battery is committed with caustic chemicals or a "Category I" weapon (such as a handgun) is the crime a class-X felony.[10]

Clearly, Illinois takes rape very seriously. The question is, why? The answer cannot be some Victorian horror of sex in general. Illinois punishes pandering (including *compelling* someone to become a prostitute) as only a class-4 felony (1-5 years imprisonment). "Adultery" and "fornication" are punishable only when "open and notorious" and then only as a class-A or class-B *misdemeanor*.[11] Consensual sex in private, whatever the marital status of the parties and whatever its dissimilarity to the normal, is perfectly legal. Illinois understands rape as a crime against persons rather than as an affront to common standards of sexual conduct.

Nor can the answer to our question be some simple equivalence between crime and punishment. Whatever the appeal of the slogan "rape the rapist," it is hard to explain why (literally) raping the rapist should be equivalent to 6-30 years imprisonment instead of to, say, 2-5 years or even 2-5 months. Most rapists would, I suspect, prefer literal "penal rape" to even one year of imprisonment (supposing, of course, we can make a precise penalty out of that poetic notion). If anything, the slogan "rape the rapist" suggests penalties much lower than Illinois now imposes.

Nor can the answer to our question be that Illinois has neglected its rape laws. Illinois, like most other states, made substantial changes in its rape laws in the late 1970s and again during the early 1980s. Among those changes was the addition of deviate sexual assault (and elimination of the old and less serious "crime against nature"). Those changes were part of a national movement to reform rape laws. "Reform" meant making it easier to convict rapists, broadening the definition of rape, and extending to men the same protection against rape women have long had. In Illinois, as elsewhere, the changes gave men protection they had not had before (if raising statutory penalties gives added protection). The penalty for rape of a woman was not reduced. Instead, the penalty for the analogous offense against men ballooned.

We must then look upon the rape laws described here as the work of contemporary legislators who were more or less aware of what they were doing. To look upon those laws in that way is to see how difficult it will be to justify Illinois's view that rape should be a class-X felony. The statutory scheme contains many oddities that suggest a deep confusion rather than some underlying justification. Let me point out six of those oddities to make clear what I mean. I shall limit myself to what is evident from the statutes themselves. (The case law offers another collection of oddities, but enough is enough.)

First: under the statutes quoted above, a husband cannot "rape" his wife (though he can commit deviate sexual assault upon her). If he forces her to have sexual intercourse with him, he commits only the class-A misdemeanor of simple battery (or if he uses an unregulated weapon such as a scout knife the class-3 felony of aggravated battery). The *maximum* penalty that a husband can receive for doing what would net any other man 6-30 years imprisonment is one year if no weapon is used (or five years if an unregulated weapon is used). Only by using a regulated weapon such as a handgun can a husband commit a class-X felony, "armed violence."

Second: no woman can "rape" a man even if she overpowers him to get him to have sexual intercourse with her (though she can commit deviate sexual assault upon him if she overpowers him in the same way to get him to engage in "deviate" sexual acts). Her forcing him in that way to have ordinary sexual intercourse with her is simple battery.

Third: if a man gets a woman to have sexual intercourse merely by threatening to overpower her, he too commits no more than simple battery. He must (according to the statute) actually *use force* to commit rape (and what he does then is rape, weapon or no weapon). Because rape requires (by definition) force (not just the "mere" threat of force), prosecutors like to have rape victims with bruises or other physical evidence of applied force (though by case law, the force need not actually be applied, only imminent).

Fourth: no one under the age of 14, whatever the sex and however sexually mature, can commit rape or deviate sexual assault (though a 13-year-old is legally capable of murder, robbery, arson, battery, and most other crimes).

Fifth: a male who has sexual intercourse with a mentally deranged or deficient woman is guilty of rape, however willing she may be (provided, of course, the circumstances are such that he is taking an unjustified risk that she is too mentally deranged to give consent, and his conduct constitutes a substantial deviation from the standard of care that a reasonable person would observe). If, however, he engages in deviate sexual conduct with the same willing woman or with an equally willing and equally deranged or deficient man, he does not commit deviate sexual assault. Indeed, he probably does not commit any crime at all. (Battery requires a "harmful," "insulting," or "provoking" physical contact, and his sexual conduct is none of these.) There are (in Illinois) no laws protecting adult wards like those protecting children.

Sixth: neither rape statute distinguishes between "simple" and "aggravated" offenses, though the distinction is made for all other class-X felonies and for many other crimes. The law seems to assume either that rape generally involves great bodily harm or that rape itself is so bad that suffering great bodily harm cannot make it much worse.

Such oddities might be of little interest if they were confined to Illinois. They might then be explained as the eccentricities of an otherwise admirable legislature. But such oddities, while not found everywhere else in the same profusion, are not limited to Illinois. They permeate much of American law. Like the severity with which we punish rape, the disanalogies between "rape" and "deviate sexual assault," between the treatment of men and women, between the status of agents above and below a certain age, and between rape statutes and other criminal statutes, appear regularly in American law, are well known, and cry out for explanation and (insofar as possible) for justification.

Illinois's rape statutes have undergone major revisions twice since I first wrote these words (1983 and 1989). Most of the oddities identified here are gone, but others have taken their place, rape law remains unchanged in its fundamentals, and the reforms defended here have yet to become law.[12]

POSSIBLE JUSTIFICATIONS OF
THE STATUTORY SCHEME

Rape has become a popular topic among social scientists, legal writers, and philosophers only within the last two decades or so.

Social science has found out much about rape, rapist, and victim. Because much discussion of rape seems to ignore what the social sciences have found out, especially about how rape compares with other violent crimes, it may be useful to summarize those findings here. Rape does not much resemble other sex crimes. Rapists are less likely than other sex offenders to have a previous record of sex offenses and more likely than other sex offenders to have a record of nonsexual offenses. Rapists are seldom sex-starved. They tend to treat sex as a useful weapon to degrade their victim, to vent their aggression, or to demonstrate their power. Rape is like other violent crimes in age, race, marital status, and socioeconomic status of the victim; in variation of incidence by locale, time of day, day of week, and season; in proportion of interracial events; in level of reporting to police; and in proportion of false reports. Rape is usually premeditated. Rapist and victim are more likely than not to know each other before the crime. Rape usually does not involve great bodily harm to the victim. Even threatening with a deadly weapon is not that common. In the typical rape, a man overpowers a weaker woman or makes it clear that he will do so if she does not do what he wants. The woman quickly gives in to avoid the mess, pain, and danger of a useless fight against superior force. The victim becomes passive, putting distance between herself and her body much as a patient might while being examined for hemorrhoids. The victim does not automatically become hysterical after the rape. Few suffer serious long-term psychic injury. Just as there is no typical response to most crimes, there is none to rape. Rape differs from other violent crime in only two ways: The rape victim is less likely to have precipitated the offense than most victims of violent crime, and she is more likely than most to have her word doubted.[13]

Legal writers have had much to say in criticism and defense of rape laws, though the criticism now seems to have crushed the defense. We may draw three conclusions from the legal writing. First, there is general agreement that oddities like those noted above should be reduced. Second, there is general agreement that the penalties for rape are not too high for the crime (now that death has been eliminated). But, third, there is no agreement about how to justify the penalties we now have (or even any agreement that there is a problem of justification).[14]

Philosophers have taken more than a passing interest in rape only since the late 1970s. Their concern has not been to justify any particular punishment of rape but to fit rape into the scheme of *moral* wrongs. Their work, together with that of some sociologists, legal writers, and feminists, provides disconcertingly many analyses of what makes rape a crime deserving very severe punishment. We may conveniently divide these into four (more or less) distinct categories: *sociology-based, loss-based, fear-based,* and *miscellaneous.* Each category could contain any number of specific analyses. But I shall only examine ten here, limiting myself to those analyses different enough or popular enough to warrant separate treatment. Examining these discloses enough about the difficulties of justifying present penalties for rape to make such justification seem unlikely.

For our purposes, a justification consists of (a) a set of (putative) facts, (b) a set of principles, and (c) an argument showing that the facts and principles together require (or at least permit) the acts the justification of which are in question. "Facts" may include both plain facts such as conviction rate, and complex "facts" such as a social theory. I shall refer to a social theory—along with supporting evidence—as an "explanation" when it purports to show that our current penalties for rape were to be expected given certain other general facts about our society. "Principles" may include principles of rationality, prudence, benevolence, or anything else we find appealing, *provided* their recommendations are consistent with the principle of just desert. ("Principle" may, as chapter 4 explained, include "considerations" as well as relatively abstract rules.) The principle of just desert has a privileged status here because it now has (and, as I believe, should have) a privileged status in the practice of setting penalties. A justification is good if, and only if, its facts are correct, its principles appealing, and the argument connecting them to its conclusion valid. Our concern is to find a good justification, not any justification at all. A justification that is not good is only a justification in a sense, that is, an attempted or failed justification. I shall hereafter use "justification" (and "justify") to mean "good justification" ("really justify"). What I shall now argue is that none of the ten analyses provides a (good) justification for punishing (simple) rape more severely than such lesser felonies as aggravated battery.

Sociology-based Analyses

A sociology-based analysis begins with general facts about how we behave, "our culture." The analysis then shows that such facts lead to a certain perception of rape, which in turn leads to something like our present statutory scheme. Sociology-based analyses were originally designed to predict behavior, not to justify it. Because the most interesting predictions are those that explain behavior insofar as it is not obviously rational, sociology-based analyses tend to explain behavior in ways that make it look unjustifiable. It is not surprising, then, that when we try to convert such analyses into justifications, they fail. What *is* surprising is that most seem to fail even as explanations of why we punish rape as severely as we do. Let us consider the three chief examples of such analyses: *Marxist*, *feminist*, and *radical feminist*. (These three names are meant to suggest who might accept the analysis in question, not necessarily who in fact does.)

Marxist analysis. According to this analysis, our culture puts women in the category of some man's property. The act of rape is wrong because it violates the property rights of the owner— some man (father, brother, or husband). A woman is among the most valuable property a man can have. What makes rape so serious is, according to this analysis, that rape violates a man's control over his most valuable property.[15]

The Marxist analysis has several weaknesses. First, it does not fit the facts. Rules governing women and rules governing property do not, in this society, bear much analogy. Second, even if there were a close analogy, the Marxist analysis would still not explain why we consider rape such a serious crime. Under the Marxist analysis, rape would be a trespass or robbery. Criminal trespass is only a misdemeanor in Illinois; simple robbery, only a class-2 felony (though *armed* robbery *is* a class-X felony, like rape). Third, even if the law worked as the Marxist analysis suggests, the analysis would still need to explain what makes a husband's or father's sexual control of a wife or daughter his most important property right. Explaining that looks suspiciously like explaining what the Marxist analysis was supposed to explain in the first place. The explanation is also unlikely to be given. In societies where women are much more analogous to property than in our society, they do not seem to fetch more on the market than a few good horses or swords, even though they are treated as much more valuable. The property analogy, even in such societies, seems to be misleading.

Feminist analysis. According to this analysis, our culture puts women in the category of mere sexual beings; only men occupy the category of full moral agent. The act of rape reveals to women that they are not viewed as full moral agents but as the helpless objects of men's sexual agency. What makes rape so serious is, according to this analysis, that it humiliates women in a way no other act can (since no other act can remind them so effectively of their peculiar status).[16]

The feminist analysis may well be right about what makes rape so humiliating for women. Even so, it does not explain why *this* society punishes rape as severely as it does. The feminist analysis might explain why a society dominated by women would punish rape severely. Those who run society do not like to be humiliated and are likely to respond cruelly even to those who only try to humiliate them. The feminist analysis cannot, however, explain why a society dominated by *men* who think women mere sexual beings would punish rape at all. What harm would such men see in treating women as they suppose women to be?

Our society, of course, fits neither the Marxist nor the feminist analysis, though it fits the second far better than the first. Men here view women as sexual beings, but, it seems, neither as mere sexual beings nor as the only sexual beings. Men dominate without entirely excluding women from power. Rape laws have recently been reformed to protect men as much as women. Rape in our society is undoubtedly humiliating. And humiliation is undoubtedly a bad thing. But the question now is, how bad *compared* to battery, kidnapping, or robbery? The feminist analysis does not say. It thus fails even to explain the place of rape in our law.

Radical feminist analysis. According to this analysis, our culture categorizes women as mere sexual beings much as the feminist analysis says. Since women are in fact not mere sexual beings, our culture must have some means of keeping women in that

category. The radical feminists call this strategy "the male protection racket." The strategy is, like many other social mecha-
nisms, largely unconscious but otherwise very much like a male
conspiracy. It works like this. Some men rape. Most men en-
courage rape by behaving as if rape were no more than ordinary
sexual conduct carried a little too far. Men thereby make life for
women more dangerous than it would otherwise be. Women must
fear doing what men do because women must fear rape while
men need not. Men then offer women protection, for example,
an escort so that a woman can feel safe entering a bar or a husband so that other men will not be too forward at work. Such
protection makes women more dependent on men than they would
otherwise be. They need a man to go safely where they want to
go and to do safely what they want to do. Rape laws are, according to this analysis, just part of the racket. The law appears
to offer protection to all women but in fact protects only those
women who keep their dependent place. Often, a rapist who picks
on a woman going out alone will not be convicted because he
will have the defense, "She was asking for it." The high penalty
protects *men* by making judge and jury resolve every doubt in
favor of the accused.[17]

The radical feminist analysis does at least address the question of rape's place in the statutory scheme. The penalty is high
(it says) to *decrease* convictions. The analysis thus assumes that
most men believe (at least "deep down") that the penalty for rape
is so high that reducing it might substantially increase convictions. The analysis assumes widespread self-deception among
men. Though legislators claim to want high penalties to protect
women, really they want high penalties to protect men. The analysis may appear as grotesque an explanation to some as it appears attractive to others. The radical analysis does not, however,
fail to fit the facts in the same obvious way the Marxist and
feminist analyses do. Even recent reforms in rape law may be
squeezed in as clever devices for keeping the racket going while
seeming to give it up. An analysis based on unconscious conspiracy is very flexible. Still, for all its strengths, the radical
feminist analysis will not justify our rape laws. If the analysis is
correct, our rape laws must be *un*justified. Even *men* must de-
ceive themselves to support the current high penalty. They would
not (according to the analysis) support that penalty if they did

not *consciously* believe that it protected women more than a lower penalty would.

Loss-based Analyses

A loss-based analysis identifies something the victim actually suffers if raped. The analysis then compares that loss with other losses, showing the rape victim to suffer a loss greater than victims of other crimes suffer. A loss-based analysis must assume that the seriousness of the crime is determined (in part at least) by what the *victim* suffers. The feminist analysis is a loss-based analysis as well as a sociology-based one. The victim's humiliation is supposed to explain why we punish rape as we do. Other loss-based analyses fail to justify for the same reason the feminist analysis does. They do not explain the difference between rape and those other serious crimes that we punish much less severely. Let us now consider three loss-based analyses: *personal integrity*, *objectification*, and *traditional*.

Personal-integrity analysis. According to this analysis, any act that violates a person's sense of self is seriously wrong. Sex lies close to the center of the self. So, according to this analysis, rape (and deviate sexual assault) are particularly serious because they are particularly serious violations of the self.[18]

The personal-integrity analysis might justify punishing rape severely. But it cannot justify punishing rape *more* severely than, say, aggravated battery (and justifying that is what is needed to justify the current penalties for rape). Sex is not the only attribute close to the center of the self. The rest of our physical integrity lies there too, as may some of our property. Even coming home to find one's house vandalized can be a personal affront so unnerving that for years afterward any strange noise around the house will arouse dread. The reaction of a man who has been badly beaten for no particular reason does not seem all that different from that of a woman who has been raped. Both will feel humiliated, frightened, violated. Perhaps there are differences in reaction. There are no *comparative* studies I know of, and even comparative anecdotal evidence is hard to find. What little I have gathered is inconclusive (no one I talked to having experienced *both* a simple rape *and* an independent severe beating under otherwise similar circumstances). We must not be too quick to decide. Still, it is hard to see that the difference between a beaten man (or woman) and a raped woman (or man) can be all that great. Most women would, I think, prefer to be raped if forced to choose between simply being raped and being very badly beaten (but not raped).[19] On the personal-integrity analysis, then, simple rape cannot, it seems, even be as severe an invasion of personal integrity as aggravated battery is. The personal-integrity analysis does not justify punishing rape more severely than we punish aggravated battery. The personal-integrity analysis also suffers from another weakness. The analysis makes it hard to explain why, until recently, we did not punish deviate sexual assault (whether of men or women) as severely as we do now, or why even now most men view the statute prohibiting such assault as there for the protection of *women*.

Objectification analysis. According to this analysis, a person is his or her own body. To rape (or commit deviate sexual assault upon) a person is to treat his or her body as if it did not belong to the victim, to use it as if it were a mere object one owned or controlled. According to this analysis, what makes rape so serious a crime is that treating a person as a mere possession is seriously wrong.[20]

The objectification analysis differs from the personal-integrity analysis only in that it emphasizes what the attacker does to the victim rather than what the victim suffers. The objectification analysis therefore suffers from the same problem as the personal-integrity analysis. All crimes of violence are seriously wrong for the same reason the objectification analysis says rape is (*if* that is the reason rape is wrong). All treat the victim as an object in much the same way as rape does. The victim's body becomes an inconvenience that the attacker treats in any way he thinks may serve his own ends.

The objectification analysis also has a problem that the personal-integrity analysis does not. The objectification analysis makes it hard to explain why many rapists bother to rape. The objectification analysis works well enough for those rapists who rape to vent aggression. One can vent aggression on an object.

The analysis does not, however, work so well for rapists who rape to degrade or demonstrate power over a victim. If the rapist's victim becomes an object in his eyes as soon as the crime begins, what then is the point of continuing the crime? One cannot degrade an object. If the point of continuing the crime is to keep the object from becoming a person again, then the crime must end in murder or the victim's victory. Similarly, demonstrating power over an object seems to make sense only if someone else owns the object. Are we to suppose "power rapists" are always demonstrating their power to someone thought to "own" the victim? For many rapists, it is probably important that the victim remain a person in their eyes throughout the rape. If so, the objectification analysis seems to give us a misleading picture of rape as well as failing even to explain why we take rape as seriously as we seem to.

Traditional analysis. According to this analysis, the crime of rape consists in forcibly (and perhaps irreversibly) depriving a woman of what is (or should be) dearer to her than life itself, that is, her chastity. Rape is a serious crime because depriving a woman of chastity is very serious.

The traditional analysis does pretty well as an explanation of much of the law described earlier. It readily "explains" many oddities that no other analysis seems to. For example: *Why should there be a requirement of force for rape* (strictly so-called)? Why should the mere threat of force not be enough? Answer: Because to yield to the mere threat of force would be to show one's chastity less dear than life and hence not deserving the special protection the rape law offers. *Why should a husband be legally incapable of raping his wife*? Answer: Because his having sexual intercourse with her leaves her chastity untouched. *Why is the law so late and so half-hearted in punishing deviate sexual assault as severely as rape*? Answer: Because deviate sexual assault does not violate what has traditionally been considered the *sine qua non* of chastity.

The traditional analysis also readily "explains" why rape may be a very serious crime (though at the cost of showing rape to be *at least* as serious as murder). A woman's chastity is, under this analysis, more valuable to her than her property, her body, even her life. If beating or mutilating someone is bad because of what the person suffers, then (according to this analysis) rape must be worse (if it is worse) because what is suffered is worse. The traditional analysis is, nevertheless, quite unsatisfactory today even as explanation. The analysis presupposes a knightly society in which everyone is willing to die for his or her honor and in which a woman's honor is (in part at least) her chastity. This is not such a society. Few people today actually choose death over dishonor. We seldom kill over an insult. Most of us think many things dearer than chastity (for example, life, limb, or health). We no longer even speak of a woman who has lost her chastity as "undone" or "fallen" (except perhaps as a joke). Police, rape counsellors, and most feminists regularly advise against resisting rape if resistance would be at all risky (basically, the same advice police give to potential victims of robbery, kidnapping, and other violent crimes).

The traditional analysis certainly cannot explain why we should keep the laws we have (though it may help to explain how we came to have them). The traditional analysis is at best a dead justification.

Fear-based Analyses

Fear-based analyses are quite different from loss-based analyses. Fear-based analyses assume that we are justified in prohibiting an act if we fear its occurrence. Our fear need not be a function of loss (though it may be). We fear an act insofar as we want to avoid having it occur. Fear-based analyses also assume that we are justified in punishing most severely the crimes we fear most. The most serious crimes should be punished most severely because their being feared most makes committing them deserve the most punishment (perhaps because they are the ones we most want to discourage or because committing them gives a criminal the greatest unfair advantage). Fear-based analyses differ only in procedure for determining which crimes are most feared. We may distinguish two fear-based analyses: *prospect* and *forced-choice*.

Prospect analysis. According to this analysis, the fear that decides how serious a crime is, is fear of that crime *in prospect*—that is, how much we actually fear, all things considered, that we or someone for whom we care will be a victim. Our prospective fear is a function of both the supposed harm the crime would do and the supposed probability of the crime occurring. Our (prospective) fear of rape is in fact greater than our fear of any other crime except murder. We fear rape that much in part because of what rape itself is, in part because rape seems to be relatively common, and perhaps in part too because we have been taught to worry about rape more than most other crimes. Our reasons do not matter. The fear itself does. So, according to this analysis, rape is only somewhat less serious a crime than murder because we fear it only somewhat less.[21]

The prospect analysis provides a powerful explanation of why we punish rape (and deviate sexual assault) of *women* as severely as we do. If women are asked, "Which crimes do you fear most?" rape will no doubt rank very high. If we asked men, "Which crime do you most fear happening to your wife, mother, daughter, or some other woman for whom you care?" rape will no doubt again rank very high. That high ranking would explain why legislators are willing to make penalties for rape of women so severe. Great and widespread fear would generate enormous pressure for toughness. The easiest way for a legislator to show toughness is to support severe penalties.

The prospect analysis provides no such explanations of why we now punish rape of *men* as severely as rape of women. A man who is asked, "Which crimes do you most fear?" is, I think, unlikely to include rape (unless he is in prison). Women asked the corresponding question ("Which crimes do you most fear happening to a male for whom you care?") would be unlikely to answer differently. Few women think of men as potential rape *victims*. This failure of the prospect analysis is, however, not necessarily a fault. Perhaps the only explanation of why we now provide severe penalties for rape of men is a public policy of *equal* protection. The prospect analysis is no less good just because it provides only a partial explanation of rape penalties (though it is good for less).

Our concern, however, is justification, not mere explanation. So since the prospect analysis seems to explain at least part of the statutory scheme, we must consider whether it justifies even that. It does not. Prospect analysis allows seemingly extraneous facts to decide what a crime *deserves* in punishment. The analysis confuses the seriousness of a crime *problem* with the seriousness of the *crime* itself, panic with desert. A particular crime would, according to this analysis, deserve less punishment just because most people did not know how common it was or because it was in fact not very common. Legislators could justify a statutory penalty in some such way as this: "The crime deserves 30 years imprisonment, 15 for what it is and 15 because people worry about it so much." While utilitarianism may allow such justifications, the principle of just desert does not. If a certain crime deserves a certain punishment, it deserves it (according to retributive theory) for what it is, not because it is common and certainly not just because people happen to worry about it a lot. Panic may be a good reason not to set the statutory penalty lower than a particular crime deserves, but it does not seem to be a good reason for treating the crime as if it deserves a penalty higher than it would otherwise deserve. Prospect analysis seems to be a prescription for injustice.

Forced-choice analysis. According to this analysis, the fear relevant to how serious a crime is, is fear of the crime itself, not of the crime in prospect. Fear is measured by describing crimes in reasonable detail and then forcing a choice between suffering one and suffering another. We are to put questions like this: "Which would you prefer to avoid suffering yourself (or having someone for whom you care suffer) if it is not possible to avoid both?" To claim we fear rape more than any other crime except murder is to claim that we would rank rape only a little below murder if forced to choose between suffering rape and suffering other serious crimes. Forced-choice analysis can give results quite different from those of prospect analysis. It does for rape.

Let us begin with men. Do they fear rape more than any other crime? Men, of course, do not act as if they themselves fear suffering rape more than suffering other serious crimes. The old crime-against-nature statute did not treat rape of a male as much more serious than battery. Indeed, that statute did not even treat force or absence of consent as an element of the crime. Only a few decades ago, a crime against nature was a minor "sex crime," violent or not. Only considerations of equal protection seem to have gotten male-dominated legislatures to protect men with the same penalties long used to protect women. If men are asked to choose between suffering rape and suffering a severe beating or maiming, most will, I believe, choose to be raped.

Do men fear rape of a woman much more than rape of a man? It seems not. A husband hearing that his wife has been raped is, I think, more likely to ask whether she has also been injured than a husband hearing that his wife has been badly beaten is likely to ask whether she has also been raped. It is clear which he fears more and which he would choose to have her suffer if she had to suffer one.

Men and women are different, of course. But they do not seem to differ when forced to choose between suffering rape and suffering other serious crimes. If asked to choose between being badly beaten and being raped (without being beaten), most women will, I think, choose to be raped. That, anyway, has been my experience.[22] It seems, then, that the forced-choice analysis will not justify treating rape as more serious than aggravated battery.

Miscellaneous Analyses

Miscellaneous analyses (as the name suggests) have little in common except not fitting neatly into another category. I have collected two: the *pragmatic* and the *affirmative-action* analyses.

Pragmatic analysis. According to this analysis, rape is a charge easily made, a charge that (even if not proved) may ruin the accused's reputation, a charge hard to disprove if the accused has engaged in the sexual conduct in question with the consent of his accuser. Treating rape as among the most serious crimes makes unjustified charges of rape far less likely than if rape were treated as no more serious than battery; makes it less likely that the accused will be convicted without strong evidence; and does this without reducing the protection of potential victims (the decreased likelihood of conviction being compensated for by the increased severity of the possible penalty). Society benefits overall by discouraging in this way both rape and unfounded charges of rape. So, according to this analysis, the severe penalty is justified even if rape itself is not all that serious a crime.[23]

The pragmatic analysis fails as justification for two reasons. First, the analysis presupposes that it is just to punish a person more severely than his crime deserves—if the result will be some social good. The pragmatic analysis (like the prospect analysis) thus requires us to reject the principle of just desert and accept instead a utilitarian theory of punishment.

But second, even if the utilitarian theory of punishment were not itself inconsistent with the principle of just desert, the pragmatic analysis would fail. The analysis must presuppose a highly sophisticated calculus of deterrence permitting us to know that, by raising a penalty to x, we prevent the increased incidence of crime that would otherwise follow decreasing the likelihood of punishment to p. I know of no such calculus.[24] The clearest cases of this terrorist application of deterrence—for example, to theft in eighteenth-century England or to marijuana use in 1960s America—are notorious failures. To set the penalty substantially above what the crime deserves seems to be the surest way to make punishment for the crime something only misfits, social outcasts, and the unlucky need fear. Indeed, one way to understand many of the oddities of rape law identified here is as escapes for people we cannot bring ourselves to punish as class-X felons no matter how grievous the rape they commit. In this class, I think, belong husbands, any minor under 14, and a woman who forces a man to have sexual intercourse with her.[25]

Affirmative-action analysis. According to this analysis, rape should be punished very severely because such severe punishment is one way that the law can compensate for the special vulnerability of women to rape and the special temptation of raping a woman. Such laws compensate for a preexisting disadvantage. Rape laws are thus analogous to typical affirmative-action laws (hence the name of this analysis). If, for example, beatings were suffered largely by blacks, we would (according to this analysis) be justified in making beating a black person an especially serious battery. We would be so justified even if blacks did not fear being beaten any more than whites feared it. According to this analysis, then, the severe penalties for rape are justified because they provide women the degree of safety they would have in a nonsexist society without such penalties and that they lack in this society because it is sexist.[26]

The affirmative-action analysis seems to be the conservative's response to the radical feminist analysis discussed earlier. The affirmative-action analysis provides a feminist defense of the high penalty that radical feminists attribute to the "male protection racket." The analysis is certainly correct in pointing out that we sometimes define crimes to give special protection to classes of people thought especially vulnerable or tempting targets of certain crimes. Murder of a police officer is (in many states) a more serious crime than murder of an ordinary citizen (all else equal). The extreme youth, age, or infirmity of a victim is (in many states) an aggravating factor for robbery, kidnapping, battery, and some other violent crimes. The affirmative-action analysis thus seems to be correct insofar as it claims only that vulnerability and temptation are relevant to deciding how serious a crime is.

The affirmative-action analysis must, however, claim more than that. It must claim either that the more severe penalty is deserved or that affirmative action is an exception to the principle of just desert. The affirmative-action analysis should claim that the severe penalty is deserved because the severe penalties for analogous crimes seem to be deserved. For example, if forced to choose between the murder of a police officer and the murder of an ordinary citizen, we would (all else equal) prefer the murder of an ordinary citizen. While recognizing that police put themselves in danger that ordinary citizens avoid, we must also recognize that our safety depends in part on police being safe in a way it does not depend on the safety of ordinary citizens. If, however, the affirmative-action analysis is understood to claim that the especially severe penalty for rape is more than what is deserved for the crime itself, the analysis is open to objections already made against the pragmatic analysis. Affirmative-action analysis becomes a prescription for injustice.

Affirmative-action analysis also faces other problems. The analysis supposes rape laws that are more or less sex-biased. Reforms since 1970 seem to have destroyed rape law as a means of providing *special* protection for women. Reform has made rape laws (more or less) sex-neutral. The analysis also seems to ignore the possibility that the penalty for rape might be *too* high. Some feminists have, after all, alleged exactly that. They worry that they are getting *less* protection than they would be getting if the penalties were lower. The affirmative-action analysis might well succeed in justifying some differential in punishment because of the sex of the victim without being able to justify the present huge difference. Other examples of specially severe penalty tend to confirm the hypothesis that the present huge differential (between rape and battery) cannot be justified. In Illinois, for example, the fact that the victim is a police officer turns ordinary battery into aggravated battery; the fact that a victim is under 13 years of age turns ordinary kidnapping into aggravated kidnapping; and so on. Our rape laws do not seem to have the pattern we would expect from examining analogous special protection. I conclude, therefore, that the affirmative-action analysis can no more justify the current statutory scheme than can any of the previous analyses.

RAPE AS BATTERY

I shall now sketch an argument showing a) that battery provides a statutory scheme that covers everything a rape law should cover, b) that treating rape as battery would dispose of the oddities present in most rape laws (and do it in a way that makes sense), and c) that the penalties the battery statutes now impose fit the crime of rape.

Battery in the Statutory Scheme

It is, of course, part of legal wisdom that rape is a kind of battery, though a "unique kind." What I want to show now is that the law should not treat it as in any way unique. To show that, I must, I think, begin with the obvious.

Battery is an unlawful touching. Touching another person is always unlawful without the person's consent, unless the touching is necessary to some lawful act (for example, an arrest), or the touching is an inevitable part of social life (for example, the touching necessary to get to one's seat in a crowded theater). Though it is often said that a touching is unlawful if it harms, insults, or provokes, the basis of grievance in battery seems to be the *insult* inherent in a touching that is neither necessary nor consented to. Harm and provocation seem to serve as an index of the severity of grievance rather than as alternative bases of grievance. A battery is aggravated if the batterer intentionally or knowingly causes great bodily harm, permanent disability, or permanent disfigurement; if he uses a deadly weapon; or if the battery is otherwise especially harmful, risky, or outrageous. Aggravated battery includes mayhem.

Battery is closely connected with assault. An assault is simply an offer or threat to commit battery, an inchoate battery. An assault is aggravated if the assaulter uses a deadly weapon or otherwise begins what, if completed, would be an aggravated battery. What Illinois calls "deviate sexual *assault*" might better be called "deviate sexual *battery*" since the crime cannot be committed without an unlawful touching. Assault, like any other inchoate crime, is absorbed into the completed crime if there is one. Every battery includes an assault (and so, the Model Penal Code, police departments, and many writers use "assault" to include batteries).

Sexual contact is not inherently harmful, insulting, or provoking. Indeed, ordinarily it is something of which we are quite fond. The crucial difference between ordinary sexual intercourse and simple rape is that ordinary sexual intercourse is more or less (freely) consented to while rape is not.[27] The difference between ordinary "deviate" sexual conduct and "deviate sexual assault" is the same. The contact involved is "assault" (that is, battery) only if it is *not* (freely) consented to. The line between consent and no consent is, of course, fuzzy,[28] but it is nonetheless the right line between battery and no battery. To ignore the need for consent is to treat a person as less than a person or at least as less than a full adult person. To substitute harm for absence of consent as the basis of wrong would be to turn battery (and rape) statutes into awesomely paternalistic regulations. We might find ourselves with "statutory battery" (and "statutory rape") laws for relations among competent adults as well as for relations between adults and children.

This analysis may seem to overlook three important differences between ordinary battery and "sexual battery" (that is, rape *or* deviate sexual assault). First, ordinary battery concerns contact ordinarily harmful in itself, for example, punches, kicks, or stabs, while sexual battery does not. Second (it might be said), ordinary battery does not involve violation of privacy of the sort sexual battery does. And third, ordinary battery is not an act of sexual gratification while sexual battery is. Let us take a moment to consider these three suggested differences before turning to the oddities the proposed analysis disposes of.

The first difference is, I think, plainly illusory. Friends slap one another on the back, grab one another by the shoulder, hug, and even kiss. None of these acts is harmful in itself. Though we are almost as fond of touching as of sexual intercourse, the first three usually lack sexual significance. They are pleasant intimacies that go along with being friends, the intimacies to which we tacitly consent when we become friends. Yet any of these acts can be battery if done to a stranger who has not consented to them or even if done to a friend once he has warned us off. Sexual battery is not unique among batteries in requiring acts that are not in themselves harmful. (And if it were unique in that way, that very uniqueness would provide an argument for sexual battery being *less* serious than ordinary battery, since sexual battery alone would then not necessarily add injury to insult.)

The second suggested difference between ordinary battery and sexual battery is just as illusory as the first. The suggested difference is that ordinary battery concerns areas of the body that are not particularly private (for example, the face, chest, or hands) while sexual battery does concern private areas (for example, the genitals, anus, or mouth). The suggestion must be rejected. An example will make clear why. Suppose a surgeon castrates a patient because she wants to prevent him from having children. Suppose she does this while performing an operation for hernia to which the man consented. Suppose, too, that she only uses a local anesthetic, gruffly tells the patient about the castration as soon as he has been strapped to the operating table, proceeds without concealing any part of the operation, jokes coarsely with the nurses about what she is doing, but otherwise operates properly. The surgeon would clearly be guilty of ordinary (but aggravated) battery, not "deviate sexual assault." While she would be guilty of unlawfully touching her patient's genitals (indeed, guilty of mutilating them), her act would lack the "sexual gratification" required for "deviate sexual assault." However insulting, humiliating, embarrassing, or psychologically damaging that invasion of the patient's private parts may be, the surgery remains (both by law in Illinois and to common sense generally) ordinary battery, not sexual battery. The difference between ordinary battery and sexual battery is not, then, the privacy of the parts touched or the special insult, humiliation, or the like associated with the unlawful touching of just those parts.

The third suggested difference between ordinary and sexual battery is that ordinary battery is not an "act of sexual gratification" while sexual battery is. Though this difference is not quite illusory, the suggestion must still be rejected for three reasons.

First, there certainly are acts of sexual gratification that are *not* (in Illinois or elsewhere) rape or deviate sexual assault, for example, forcing the male sex organ into the victim's armpit, navel, or ear.

Second, sexual battery does not necessarily require sexual gratification (or arousal). Some states now define rape to include forcible penetration of the vagina or rectum using a finger, dildo, bottle, or other nonsexual object. For example, for almost two decades Maryland has defined rape to include "penetration, however slight, by any object into the genital or anal opening . . . for abuse."[29] And many feminists (whether rightly or wrongly) have long downplayed the specifically sexual gratification achieved by the rapist even in rape strictly so called.

Third, some men (perhaps many) seem to get some sort of sexual gratification from beating, torturing, or mutilating their victims without touching the victim's sexual organs (or anus) or their own. Perhaps few batteries are not without their sexual overtones. Not much in life is without such overtones. Once we begin to emphasize the psychological state of the attacker rather than what he does, we may altogether lose the distinction between sexual and ordinary battery. But we began to lose the distinction much earlier. Once the traditional connection between rape, chastity, reproduction, and blood lines was broken by the introduction of deviate sexual assault into rape law, the distinction between rape and other batteries became, if not quite illusory, still hopelessly vague and impossible to defend.

Oddities Disposed Of

It is easy to see how treating rape (and deviate sexual assault) as ordinary battery would dispose of oddities such as those I pointed out earlier. There can be no rape or deviate sexual assault without sexual touching, and any sexual touching without consent (or its equivalent) would, of course, be battery. A husband, then, is guilty of battery if he forces his wife to have sexual intercourse with him or to engage in any deviate sexual contact unless he can argue that by marriage (or some other agreement) she consented to have the sexual contact in question whenever *he* wanted (or unless he can invoke some other implausible doctrine). The law of battery naturally protects even where the law of rape does not.

Similarly, a woman who uses a deadly weapon to try to get a man to have sexual contact with her commits aggravated assault whether what she tries to get is sexual intercourse or "deviate" sexual contact. The assault becomes aggravated battery if he yields to that threat, the consent won by unlawful threat being no consent at all. Changing the sex of either or both parties does not change the result. Nor does it matter whether the act in question is sexual intercourse or deviate sexual conduct, nor whether the victim has sexual contact because compelled "by force and against her will" or merely "by force or the threat of force."

Similarly, the age of neither the attacker nor the attacked is crucial. What is crucial is consent, and the question of "consent" brings us to the one oddity of which rape-as-battery does not easily dispose, that is, rape of an adult who is willing but not competent to consent. I take this failing to be a good thing (especially since in Illinois most sexual contact with such a person is not rape or deviate sexual assault). Suppose, for example, that a janitor in a mental hospital has sexual intercourse with a female patient there. Suppose too that she is quite willing but so mentally deranged that her consent is not "effective" (and even a janitor should be able to recognize her infirmity). Under Illinois law, the janitor would be guilty of rape. He could not, however, be guilty of battery. His sexual contact with her would not have been insulting. If there is any basis for grievance here, it is because of possible harm to her (and to society) if she became pregnant or contracted venereal disease. Such harm is certainly the concern of the law, but the paternalism inherent in such concern is foreign to both battery and rape. The distinction between "forcible rape" and "statutory rape" is more than a quibble. If sexual contact with a deranged patient should be prohibited even if the patient is willing (and I certainly agree that it should be at least to those with any responsibility for those patients), it should be prohibited for the same reason that we prohibit adults from taking (what Illinois once called) "indecent liberties" with a child. The basis of grievance here is not insult but the exploitation of those unable to look after themselves. A deranged woman is more like a child than she is like an unconscious but otherwise normal adult. She will not soon awake to take offense. She is like a child whether the act in question is sexual intercourse, deviate sexual conduct, or betting on the horses. The law of rape would make more sense if it were not bent to prevent exploitation as well as rape.[30]

Adequacy of Penalties

Having fit rape and deviate sexual assault into the category of battery, we must consider whether the penalties for battery are adequate for rape and deviate sexual assault. Our consideration will rest on several assumptions that I should note but cannot fully defend here. First, I assume that the penalties for simple and aggravated battery are more or less adequate for their present purpose, the punishment of ordinary battery. I may, I think, safely assume this without argument because no one is currently arguing otherwise (but I shall say something in defense of this assumption later). Second, I assume that, if we are not sure which of two evils we would rather suffer, the two evils may be treated as approximately equal; that if we *are* sure which of the two we would rather suffer, we should treat the one we would rather suffer as the less serious of the two; that the more serious the evil a statute forbids, the more serious (all else equal) the crime of violating the statute; and that severity of penalty should vary with the seriousness of crime. These assumptions combine the principle of just desert with the forced-choice analysis of seriousness.

Having assumed all that, I can quickly show that rape and deviate sexual assault are no more serious than other kinds of battery (and so show also that current penalties for sexual battery are out of proportion to the crime). For simplicity, I shall concern myself hereafter only with rape, the argument for deviate sexual assault being virtually the same. Consider the following three cases of forced choice. You (or someone for whom you care) must:

1. either (a) be compelled by brute force to have sexual intercourse (but be otherwise unharmed) or (b) be badly beaten (but without great bodily harm, permanent disability, or permanent disfigurement);
2. either (a) be compelled by threats *and* display of a scout knife to have sexual intercourse or (b) be compelled by threats and display of a scout knife to allow someone to crush your right leg by driving a car over it; and
3. either (a) be compelled by brute force to have sexual intercourse or (b) be compelled by threats and display of a scout knife to allow someone to crush your right leg by driving a car over it.

Many people would, I think, prefer to suffer 1a (simple rape) rather than 1b (simple battery with one aggravating factor), though perhaps as many would not. Many more would prefer 2a (aggravated rape) over 2b (aggravated battery).[31] Certainly almost everyone would prefer 3a (simple rape with one aggravating factor) over 3b (aggravated battery). From this it seems to follow that ordinary battery and sexual battery range over the same degrees of seriousness. Simple rape does not differ much in fearfulness from simple battery and is certainly less fearful than some aggravated battery. Aggravated rape does not seem to differ much in fearfulness from other aggravated batteries. Certainly, aggravated rape is not clearly worse than aggravated battery.[32]

Now it may seem that this way of arguing overlooks the important problem of discouraging rape when there has already been battery. We do not (it might be objected) want the mugger out for kicks to be able to say, "Well, since I've beaten her, it will cost me nothing more if I rape her too." Yet unless rape is a crime distinct from battery or one punished more severely, our mugger may sometimes correctly say that to himself and act accordingly.

This objection does point to a problem worth noting. But it is a problem for gradation of punishment generally, and that very generality makes it almost pointless here. There is a limit to how much we can punish. There is a limit to the gradation of crime we can write into law. Sooner or later, we must let the criminal get something free. The only question is when his "freebies" begin. If, for example, we treat crushing someone's leg as the most aggravated battery, the attacker can go on to cut off the victim's hands, tongue, and nose without further punishment. If we fear this eventuality enough to treat it rather than leg crushing as the most aggravated battery, we still leave the attacker free to blind his victim in addition, burn initials into the victim's cheeks, or otherwise mutilate his victim without fear of further punishment. While there are many things we do not want our mugger to do without fear of further punishment, we have no choice but to let him get away with some of them.

The penalties for battery do, however, allow us to take into account rape as an aggravating factor if we believe rape to be that important. For example, in Illinois, aggravated battery is a class-3 felony. The judge may choose a sentence of between two and five years imprisonment for anyone convicted of the crime. If we think rape (or deviate sexual assault) to be inevitably a very serious aggravating circumstance, we can save the maximum penalty in aggravated battery for those batteries that include (beside other aggravating circumstances) rape. But I suspect few of us would want to do that. We fear so many other aggravating circumstances at least as much as we fear rape. We would not want to give free rides for some of those so that we could discourage rape in particular. Rape just is not as bad as some other aggravating circumstances, for example, mutilation or torture.

The Temptation to Object

This conclusion may tempt some people to suggest that the penalties for both simple and aggravated battery are too low. Yes (some might say), a man raping a woman is not much different from a big man repeatedly kicking a small man in the genitals. But that too is very serious. Such brutality should not be punished as a mere class-A misdemeanor any more than simple rape should. Aggravated rape is (they might continue) much like crushing someone's leg by driving over it. What that shows is not that aggravated rape should be punished as a class-3 felony, but that aggravated battery should be punished as a class-X felony just as we now punish rape. We do not take crippling someone seriously enough.

Such reasoning is, I admit, tempting. The temptation is neither easy to explain nor easy to resist. Nevertheless, it can, I think, be explained and, being explained, resisted. What, then, is the explanation?

The temptation is partly a matter of nomenclature. The word "rape" makes us think of the worst rape, not the typical. The word's history may explain why. Etymologically, "rape" has more to do with violence than with sex. "Rapacious," "rapid," "rapine," and "ravenous" (as well as "rapt," "rapture," and "ravish") all have the same root as "rape." The root idea is "carrying off by force."[33] The ancient crime of "rape of the forest" consisted of "trespass committed in the forest by *violence*."[34] Saxon law did not distinguish between rape and abduction.[35] In contrast, when we think of "battery," we tend to think of simple battery. To batter is to strike repeatedly (and not necessarily with a bat). Even the adjective "aggravated" does not much change the image of battery. Illinois's statutes lost some piquancy with the substitution of "aggravated battery" for the old "mayhem." We must be careful not to let what we think of, influence what we think. Pictures are not reasons.

But pictures cannot be more than a part of the explanation for what tempts us to suppose the penalties for battery too low as soon as we include rape among batteries. The ballooning of penalty that accompanied the conversion of the old crime-against-nature statute into the modern deviate sexual assault proves that. "Crime against nature" is, if anything, more dramatic than "deviate sexual assault." The images it calls up, while not particularly sexual, are more likely to outrage than "deviate sexual assault" is. Not only the word "rape" but the *idea* of rape has a potent effect on our thinking. The idea of rape is capable of getting us to see other crimes quite differently if we associate them with rape (in the strict sense), whatever we call them. Feminists are certainly right when they claim that the "mythology of rape" leads us to do and say things about rape that we cannot rationally defend.

The power of that mythology may be gauged by the high level of agreement between some feminists and their opponents when they talk about rape. For both, rape is more than battery, more even than aggravated battery, because battery is merely an attack on someone in particular, while rape is a crime against women in general, a "sex crime" because it is a crime against the female sex, against womanhood. Women (they also seem to agree) are especially susceptible to psychic injury from forced sexual contact. A woman's rape is worse than a man's rape because women take their sexuality more seriously than men do, because women are more sexually sensitive, because in effect they *are* "the weaker sex." These feminists and their opponents agree on all this, although no evidence supports it. While the South continues to have the harshest penalties for rape, it is mostly Northern women who today provide the only intellectually respectable defense of that attitude toward rape, providing it while, perhaps, opposing the penalties that attitude implies and without quite seeing the irony of it all. Feminists cannot, I think, destroy the mythology of rape while continuing to maintain that rape is a special crime.

But even the mythology of rape does not wholly explain our temptation to think that batterer and rapist alike would get off too cheaply if convicted only of a class-A misdemeanor or a class-3 felony. We also must recognize a pervasive tendency to misread statutory penalties. Until recently, statutory penalties were something of a joke in most states. A statutory minimum term of imprisonment did not mean someone convicted of the crime would serve even that minimum term in prison. The judge had discretion to substitute probation for imprisonment. The parole board could release a convict on parole almost as soon as he arrived in his cell. Knowing that was what a statutory penalty of imprisonment often meant, we routinely discounted for judicial and administrative discretion. The results have not been happy. Statutory penalties in the United States are the most severe among industrialized countries. While the average time served in the United States is more or less the same as that in other industrialized countries, we have both the greatest percentage of criminals serving very little time and the greatest serving a very long time. In the United States, statutory penalties are not empty threats even though they are not systematically carried out. Only a few oppressive regimes have a higher rate of incarceration.[36]

Recently, our practice has begun to change. "Just deserts" has in part meant determinate sentencing, less discretion for both judge and parole board. Statutory penalties are ceasing to be a joke. We must try to remember that as we ponder the adequacy of the statutory penalties for simple and aggravated battery. We must try to take the statutory penalties literally, even if they are still applied with much discretion. The penalty for a class-A misdemeanor is imprisonment for a determinate term of less than a year; for a class-3 felony, 2-5 years imprisonment. Even six months imprisonment is a stiff sentence. Conditions in most prisons are cramped. There is no privacy, little quiet, and not much to do. The food is bad; the company, rough. A prisoner cannot go where he wants, see whom he wants, or live as he would like. There is a fair chance that other prisoners will beat or rape him at least once during his confinement. Few victims of rape would be willing to trade places with a rapist imprisoned for even six months. That is worth remembering.

It is also worth remembering what would happen if we did change the penalty for battery as we are tempted to do. If, for example, we were to change aggravated battery from a class-3 to a class-2 felony, we would also have to make many other changes. Aggravated battery is now a class-3 felony like involuntary manslaughter. A person commits involuntary manslaughter if "he unintentionally kills an individual without lawful justification . . . [by reckless acts] which are likely to cause death or great bodily harm."[37] Perhaps involuntary manslaughter is not as serious as aggravated battery. It is hard to compare the reckless taking of a life with the intentional doing of great bodily harm. But some people are troubled by treating even involuntary manslaughter as less serious than aggravated battery.

We can avoid this consequence by promoting involuntary manslaughter to class-2, although that, too, has its costs. *Voluntary* manslaughter already is in class-2. Voluntary manslaughter differs from murder only insofar as the killer acts under a sudden and intense passion resulting from serious provocation.[38] The person who commits voluntary manslaughter intends to kill and has no lawful justification. Most people therefore suppose involuntary manslaughter should not be put in the same class as voluntary.

We can avoid putting the two manslaughters in the same class by promoting voluntary manslaughter to class-1. But that, too, has consequences. Class-1 includes *attempted* murder. Just as it seemed odd to put both manslaughters in one class, it seems odd to put voluntary manslaughter in the same class as attempted murder. We can avoid that consequence by promoting attempted murder to class-X felony and creating a new class for successful murder. But then we will have to go back and consider the effect of all this on kidnapping, armed robbery, arson, and the like. When we are done, all we are likely to have done is a) increased somewhat the penalties for most crimes and b) moved aggravated battery upward in relative standing among crimes by no more than half a step or so. Much of the temptation to get tough with this or that crime disappears once we see what getting tough does to the statutory scheme.

SOME PRACTICAL ADVANTAGES
OF RAPE-AS-BATTERY

Under the common law, rape was a crime of *forced sexual intercourse*. The crime was unlawful carnal knowledge of a woman by a man (not her husband) forcibly and against her will (that is, without her consent and against her utmost resistance). If the victim consented to sexual intercourse, even though reluctantly and after some use of force, the crime could not be rape. The victim's reputation for chastity was relevant to the question of consent; the rapist's was not. While the slightest penetration constituted carnal knowledge, emission without penetration did not. The victim's testimony was not enough to establish penetration or any other element of the crime. Circumstantial evidence or testimony of other witnesses was necessary. Rape thus differed from other sex crimes by focusing on consent rather than sex; and from other crimes of force, by focusing on forced penetration rather than on force used in the situation as a whole.[39]

Reforms through 1995, whether adopted or only proposed, leave the focus of rape law more or less unchanged. We may distinguish at least seven sorts of reform (in addition to attempts to lower penalties). There is, first, making rape law sex-neutral, either by making the statutes themselves sex-neutral or by adding parallel statutes for males. Second, penetration of the female's organ by the male's is no longer necessary for rape. In some states, for example, one can now commit rape by forcing a bottle into female or male anus, provided the act is for sexual arousal or abuse. Third, there has been a change of nomenclature. Increasingly, "rape" does not appear in the statutes at all. Instead, we find "sexual battery," "sexual assault," "forcible sexual intercourse," or the like. "Rape" is becoming a term of the past even if rape is not becoming a crime of the past. Related to this is a fourth reform. Rape (whatever the nomenclature) is being divided. There may be special statutes for "date rape," rape by spouse, aggravated rape, "gang rape," and so on. In part this reform is a response to what seems the popular view that rape (so-called) can only occur between strangers; in part, it is a response to differences in the actual gravity of the offense. Fifth, there have been attempts to distinguish consent from mere submission. The required resistance has been much lessened. Many jurisdictions require no more resistance than is reasonable under the circumstances. Under some circumstances, perhaps even mere words would be force enough to make further resistance unreasonable (and so unnecessary). Related to this reform is a change in the laws of evidence. Evidence of "unchasteness" is often inadmissible or admissible only where it has some special bearing on consent. Last, the laws of evidence and procedure have been changed so as to shield the victim from publicity, rough-handling in court, and invasion of privacy unwarranted by the particular facts of the case.[40]

These reforms, though substantial, leave rape a crime of *forced penetration*. The penetration is no longer necessarily of anyone's sex organ, by anyone's sex organ, or for anyone's sexual gratification. In some states, rape is in effect no longer a sex crime at all. The reforms together make rape much more like battery. But they do not make rape an ordinary battery. Rape cannot be that while the forcibleness of the penetration itself remains the crucial element of the crime. Requiring forced penetration leaves the focus of rape law where it has always been: on what goes on just before penetration. The victim still needs a lawyer's counsel during the rape. A word or gesture just before or during penetration can make irrelevant all the horrors of an evening. The victim could destroy a good case by saying, "Come on, let's get it over with" or even just, "Okay." The rapist can still argue (as he always has) that this victim really did consent. Because intent to force penetration (or at least knowing that one is forcing penetration) is necessary for the crime, the rapist can also argue that the victim at least seemed to him to have consented by such words (or that he reasonably supposed her to have consented) and that he would not have had sexual intercourse with her if she had not.

The rapist may be telling the truth when he says that he thought the victim consented. But even if he is lying, the burden of proving intent (or its equivalent) falls upon the prosecution. The rapist, not the prosecution, gets the benefit of any reasonable doubt. Given the severity of the penalty for rape, judge or jury may find many doubts reasonable that they would not find reasonable were the possible penalty much less severe. All this is as it should be. There can be no rape if there is consent to penetration, and perhaps none even if the rapist only thought (or reasonably thought) there was consent. There can be no rape because rape law, however reformed, must focus on the forcibleness of the penetration itself. If there is consent to the penetration, there can be no rape. When a necessary element of the crime is missing, events leading up to the consent become irrelevant for proof of the crime.

To focus on consent to penetration seems to throw the crime (whatever we call it) out of focus. When did the crime begin? It began (we want to say) when the rapist made his first threat, when he first grabbed his victim's arm, or when he first did some other unlawful act with the intention of forcing penetration. The actual penetration makes worse what was already bad enough, but it is not the essential fact. Even if his victim really did consent to the penetration itself, whatever the reason, the crime (we want to say) is not much changed. Consent to penetration simply makes what he did a little less wrong. The basis of grievance is not the penetration itself but his getting to penetrate by this or that unlawful act. If the rapist is to have a full defense by appeal to consent under this analysis, he must somehow show that his victim ratified all unlawful acts from the first through penetration. But as long as we distinguish rape from ordinary battery, we cannot analyze rape in this way. Penetration, not the surrounding battery, remains the focus of proof.

The unavoidable disadvantage of rape law, however reformed,

is that it makes forced penetration the crucial element. Threats, beatings, use of a deadly weapon, and the like are necessarily reduced to evidence or to aggravating circumstances. They become relevant, if they become relevant at all, only to prove the forcibleness of penetration or once the forcibleness is proved. Rape-as-battery, in contrast, makes the beating, threat, weapon, or the like relevant from the beginning. If, for example, the rapist choked his victim, even a little, there is battery. The question becomes how bad was it. Consent to subsequent penetration is, at most, relevant to whether the penetration itself was an aggravating circumstance. The fact that the choking was intended to force sexual intercourse would be a distinct aggravating circumstance, as would anything else the rapist did to force consent. Rape-as-battery thus changes the focus of proof so that much more evidence becomes relevant to proving the basic crime. Proving the basic crime becomes much easier.

That shift of focus may also make proof of the basic crime easier for another reason. Feminists are probably right that judges and jurors have peculiar views about women and rapists. Indeed, feminists are probably right that our thinking about sex in general is often quite peculiar. There do not, however, seem to be similar peculiarities in our thinking about being threatened, beaten, or choked. Rape-as-battery shifts the focus of proof away from the "sexual" moment to the first use of threat or force. Rape-as-battery tends to downplay the sex just as rape-as-forced-penetration tends to play it up. Our views about consent to battery are likely to be far more reliable than our views about consent to sexual intercourse. Everyone is supposed to like sex (except when some special circumstance destroys its attraction). No one is supposed to like being threatened, beaten, choked, or the like (unless he is a masochist). We can easily imagine ourselves deliberately precipitating a sexual encounter while protesting otherwise. It is far harder to imagine ourselves deliberately precipitating a frightening threat, beating, or choking. Rape-as-battery thus tends to focus on those elements of the crime for which a defense of consent seems least plausible.

The shift of focus has its costs. To substitute battery (and assault) statutes for rape statutes is to give up the possibility of punishing most rapists as severely as we now can. The rapist who merely threatens his victim with bodily harm if she does not do as he says may be able to get off with only a month of imprisonment for the class-C misdemeanor of assault if he makes good a defense of consent to the penetration itself. The one month would be the maximum, given because he apparently intended to force penetration. If the rapist cannot make good the defense of consent, he would receive a somewhat heavier sentence, perhaps three or four months, for a battery in which there were no aggravating circumstances beyond the sexual form of the unlawful touching. If the rapist actually grabbed his victim roughly, struck her, choked her, or otherwise showed significant brutality, he could receive a sentence up to the maximum one-year imprisonment. If the rape was exceedingly brutal, did great bodily harm, caused permanent disfigurement, or the like, it would be possible to prosecute the rape as a class-3 felony. The sentence could reach the range of 2-5 years imprisonment. Only if the rapist displayed a handgun or similar deadly weapon would it be possible (in Illinois) to prosecute the rape as a class-X felony. Only then could the sentence reach the range of 6-30 years. Rape-as-battery is not a recipe for incapacitation or exemplary punishment. The typical rapist probably would not receive a sentence of more than six-months imprisonment.

But rape-as-battery *may* be a recipe for relatively certain punishment of rapists. That is worth keeping in mind. The reforms of the last decade have not made rape prosecution much more likely to succeed. In 1977 (the last year the FBI published such figures), forty-five percent of all prosecutions of adults charged with rape ended with acquittal or dismissal.[41] No one has suggested that that statistic reflects any tendency of prosecutors to prosecute persons probably innocent or to adopt standards for charging less rigorous than for crimes generally. The statistic reflects an opposite reality. Judges and juries (but especially juries) are slow to convict persons accused of major felonies except where the evidence is unanswerable and the crime egregious. Punishing rape less severely might make punishment more certain.

But (it may seem) substituting rape-as-battery for rape-as-class-X-felony-of-forced-penetration is hardly the way to make punishment more certain. Rape-as-battery is already on the books (as ordinary battery or assault). What I have actually argued for is repealing the rape statutes. Such repeal may seem unnecessary. It would be enough to have prosecutors charge rapists with battery as well as with rape. What would be gained by denying prosecutors the tool of rape-as-class-X-felony? Surely (it may seem), such a tool gives prosecutors considerable power in plea bargaining that they would not otherwise have.

Prosecutors often do charge rapists with ordinary battery as well as with rape. To what effect? Every tool has its costs. What are the costs of rape-as-class-X-felony-of-forced-penetration? One cost is in appearances. So long as rape is treated as a very serious crime, any rapist eventually convicted of "mere" battery (or assault) instead of rape will believe himself to have gotten away with rape (more or less). He can look with relief upon even a year's imprisonment. The public impression is likely to be similar. A year for battery is almost invisible beside a "not guilty" for rape. The public will understandably suppose the rapist to have gotten away with rape.[42] If, however, no class-X conviction were possible for simple rape, the rapist would have no grounds for relief. The public impression would have to be that he was tried for what he did, convicted, and punished. Justice was done. The rapist did not get away with anything.

The costs of rape-as-class-X-felony-of-forced-penetration are, however, not all in appearances. Though a prosecutor may always charge a rapist with battery or assault as well as with rape, such multiple charging may not be as effective as simply charging battery alone. The charge of battery has a tendency to get lost. In 1977, only thirteen percent of adults prosecuted for rape were convicted of some lesser offense (even though forty-five percent won outright acquittal or dismissal, and only forty-two percent were convicted on the original charge).[43] We may, I think, safely assume that in general the "lesser offense" was battery of some sort.

Why should the charge of battery so often get lost? I can only guess. The complexities of rape prosecution may cause long delays. Such delays would make the evidence of battery go stale along with the evidence of rape. A good case of battery might be ruined in order to prosecute a good case of rape eventually lost. Prosecution for rape may also so distort the focus of trial that battery will not seem proved either. Evidentiary rules for rape, unless fully reformed, permit impugning the victim's testimony in ways otherwise impermissible. Perhaps, too, seeking

conviction for a crime with a very severe penalty makes convicting the accused of battery seem trivial, anticlimactic, hardly
worth bothering about. The lesser charge may be thrown out almost absent-mindedly once the judge or jury decides the greater
charge is not proved.

Whatever the explanation, there seems to be some truth to
the claim that our rape laws are part of a "protection racket."
That prosecutor's "tool" seems to protect rapists from conviction of battery if they are simultaneously prosecuted for rape. Is
it not at least plausible that if conviction for rape-as-class-X-
felony-of-forced-penetration were not possible, prosecutors would
have little trouble getting quick conviction for the battery?

CONCLUSION: STATUTORY PENALTY
AS DESCRIPTION OF CRIME

Two more arguments for rape-as-battery require mention.
Both arguments assume that statutory penalties do more than
set punishment. Both assume that statutory penalties teach something (that is, carry information). Rape-as-battery, I would argue, teaches what we want to teach; rape-as-class-X-felony
does not.

To classify a certain crime as deserving a severe penalty is, it
seems to me, to say in effect that the crime is heinous. If the
crime does not *look* all that bad, judges and juries are likely to
begin quietly redefining the crime so that it fits the classifica-
tion. They will read aggravating circumstances into the statutory
description. The typical rape does not look all that bad to most
people. That may be one reason that juries have trouble convicting rapists when the penalty is severe. How can *this* act be *that*
crime? There is an analogous problem with the typical rapist.
He is usually quite ordinary, not at all what you would expect a
class-X-felon-sex-fiend to be. How can *he* deserve that penalty?
By making rape a major felony, we help to define rape in a way
that makes it likely that only the cruelest rapes will be punished
at all and then only if committed by social outcasts.

We may also be helping to keep rape a crime that women
especially fear in prospect and some men especially relish committing. Women have, in fact, more reason to fear the prospect

of battery than rape. Aggravated battery of women is three times more common than rape; simple battery, eight times more common.[44] But the message that the rape statutes send is that rape should be feared far more than battery. People who batter you are only misdemeanants or minor felons, but rapists are just about the worst felons there are (except for murderers). Rape statutes themselves help to maintain an unrealistic picture of rape and rapists. They contribute to the very mythology of rape that feminists believe oppresses women. Would women be any more afraid to go out at night than men are if women thought of rape the way men think of battery? After all, men are assaulted twice as often as women (and suffer injury twice as often, too).[45]

That unrealistic picture may also have something to do with why some men rape. There will doubtless be some rapes as long as there are people who want to humiliate others. The forced intimacy of rape is just too obvious a means of humiliation to go unused. But is it not at least possible that some men rape because the law itself helps to maintain the myth that rape is somehow special, more like murder or some other great crime than like dishonorable bullying? To be a rapist, our laws now say, is to be very bad. Might there not be fewer rapes if the law made it clear that rape is just another battery, not a sex crime or a great crime, just another way to make a helpless victim suffer?

Lest all this sound like heresy to some feminists, let me conclude with a quotation from Susan Brownmiller's famous book: "Since man first equated rape with ruination of his wholly owned property," she wrote,

> . . . he reflected his own concern most thunderously in the punishments that this law could impose . . . A modern perception of sexual assault that views the crime strictly as an injury to the victim's bodily integrity, and not as an injury to the purity or chastity of man's estate, must normalize the penalties for such an offense and bring them in line more realistically with the penalties for aggravated assault, the crime to which a sexual assault is more closely related.[46]

All I have argued here is that such a "modern perception" makes special laws for rape unwise as well as unnecessary once the penalties for rape are "[brought] in line."

NOTES

Work on this chapter was funded in part by an Organized Research Grant from Illinois State University for June 1982. An early version of this chapter was presented at the Annual Meeting of the Academy of Criminal Justice Sciences, Louisville, Kentucky, 24 March 1982. I should like to thank Michael Gorr, Mortimer Kadish, Sue LaSeure, Pat Murphy, Clark Zumbach, and Debra Zumbach, among others, for helpful comments on one or another draft.

1. *Annotated California Codes* (St. Paul, Minn.: West Publishing Co., 1983)—hereafter referred to as *Cal. Penal Code*—secs. 264 (Rape) and 451 (Arson). The penalty for arson that causes great bodily harm is five, seven, or nine years; for arson of an inhabited structure (even if no injuries in fact ensue), two, five, or seven years. The penalty for simple rape thus falls between these two forms of aggravated arson. By contrast, the penalty for assault with caustic chemicals is two, three, or four years (*Cal. Penal Code* sec. 244); for mayhem, two, four, or six years (sec. 213); and for spouse abuse, two, three, or four years (sec. 273.5).

2. See, for example, Kathleen Quenneville, "Will Rape Ever Be a Crime of the Past?: A Feminist View of Societal Factors and Rape Law Reform," *Golden Gate University Law Review* 9 (1978–79): 581–607, especially 590.

3. Federal Bureau of Investigation, U.S. Department of Justice, *Crime in the United States* (Washington, DC: U.S. Government Printing Office, 1980)—hereafter *FBI Uniform Crime Reports*—6, 14, 20, percent 23. The ratio is about 8 assaults or 48 burglaries to every one rape. Because rape is so often described as the most underreported crime, I should, I think, point out that this ratio does not compare apples and oranges. Aggravated assaults and burglaries both seem to go unreported about as often as rape does. The figures are 49% unreported for rape as against 46% for aggravated assaults and 52% for burglary. U.S. National Criminal Justice Information and Statistics Service, *Sourcebook of Criminal Justice Statistics* (Washington, DC: U.S. Government Printing Office, 1980), 228.

4. Barbara Babcock, et al., *Sex Discrimination and the Law* (Boston: Little Brown, 1975), 863 n. 57.

5. *Coker v. Georgia*, 433 U.S. 584, 97 S.Ct. 2861, 2869 & 2876 (1977).

6. Babcock, n. 56.

7. *Illinois Criminal Law and Procedure* (St. Paul, Minn.: West Publishing Company, 1983)—hereafter referred to as *Ill. Rev. Stat.*—Chap. 38, sec. 11–1, 11–2, and 11–3.

8. *Ill. Rev. Stat.*, secs. 11–4 and 11–5. These two crimes are descendants of the old "statutory rape." They differ only in that a person charged with the class–1 felony may defend himself (or herself) by showing either that he reasonably believed the child to be 16 years or older or that the child had previously been married, while a person charged with the misdemeanor cannot defend in that way. A curious distinction, is it not? What is the difference between a willing (or unwilling) child and a willing (or unwilling) but deranged adult? Why have two statutes concerning virtually the same crime? Why are the penalties so different?

9. *Ill. Rev. Stat.*, secs. 5–8–1, 9–1 (Murder), 10–2 (Aggravated Kidnapping), 18–2 (Armed Robbery), 20–1.1 (Aggravated Arson), 9–2 (Voluntary Manslaughter), 9–3 (Involuntary Manslaughter).

10. *Ill. Rev. Stat.*, secs. 10–1 (Kidnapping), 12–4 (Aggravated Battery), 12–2 (Aggravated Assault), 12–4.1 (Heinous Battery), and 33A–3 (Armed Violence).

11. *Ill. Rev. Stat.*, secs. 11–16 (Pandering), 11–7 (Adultery), and 11–8 (Fornication).

12. Rape and deviate sexual assault are now lumped together as "criminal sexual assault"; a distinction has been drawn between "[ordinary] criminal sexual assault" (a class–1 felony on the first offense, a class–X felony thereafter) and "aggravated criminal sexual assault" (a class–X felony); and some of the oddities listed here have disappeared.

13. Manachem Amir, *Patterns of Forcible Rape* (Chicago: University of Chicago Press, 1971); Sedelle Katz and Mary Ann Mazur, *Understanding the Rape Victim* (New York: John Wiley & Sons, 1979); A. Nicholas Groth, *Men Who Rape* (New York: Plenum Press, 1979). Much of this (and other) research is conveniently and critically summarized in Mary Beard Deming and Ali Eppy, "The Sociology of Rape," *Sociology and Social Research* 65 (July 1981): 357–80. My debt to them is obvious.

14. For example, Welsh S. White, "Disproportionality and the Death Penalty: Death as a Punishment for Rape," *University of Pittsburgh Law Review* 38 (Winter 1976): 145–83; Vivian Berger, "Man's Trial, Woman's Tribulation: Rape Cases in the Courtroom," *Columbia Law Review* 77 (January 1977): 1–101; Note, "*Coker v. Georgia*: Disproportionate Punishment and the Death Penalty," *Columbia Law Review* 78 (December 1978): 1714–30; Quenneville; and Note, "Rape Laws, Equal Protection, and Privacy Rights," *Tulane Law Review* 54 (February 1980): 456–79.

15. Pamela Foa, "What's Wrong with Rape?" in *Feminism and Philosophy*, ed. Mary Vettering–Braggin et al. (Totowa, NJ: Littlefield, Adams & Co., 1977), 347–59.

16. Susan Rae Peterson, "Coercion and Rape: The State as a Male Protection Racket," in *Feminism and Philosophy*, 362.

17. Peterson, 368–70.

18. Carolyn Shafer and Marilyn Frye, "Rape and Respect," in *Feminism and Philosophy*, 333–46.

19. This "most" is, of course, a finding of my informal survey that I invite others to replicate. The questions must, however, be carefully put. Because of the special power of the word "rape" to call up a picture of a badly beaten, bleeding, and hysterical victim, one must describe in detail what is meant by "simple rape." Indeed, it is best to avoid the word altogether. The sociological data summarized above may be helpful here.

20. Raymond Belliotti, "A Philosophical Analysis of Sexual Ethics," *Journal of Social Philosophy* 10 (January 1979): 8–11.

21. I should like to thank Michael Gorr, Clark Zumbach, and others who noticed that I overlooked this analysis in an earlier version of this chapter. Prospect analysis probably represents one common-sense notion of seriousness of crime. See, for example, Thorsten Sellin and Marvin Wolfgang, *The Measurement of Delinquency* (New York: John Wiley & Sons, 1964), especially 289 and 381, which develop a scale of seriousness based on responses to a questionnaire. "Forcible rape" came in second to murder, well ahead of armed robbery and "aggravated assault" (that is, aggravated battery). The questionnaire asked respondents to decide how serious each of a long list of crimes was. The crimes were described in reasonable detail, not just named, but the only interpretation given the respondent for the term "seriousness" was that "seriousness" was not necessarily what the law or courts might say it was. While the results of this ingenious study (and its successors as well) are interesting because they demonstrate a surprising consensus on how to rank crimes by "seriousness" (whatever that term means), they are not necessarily interesting as a measure of which crimes are most feared as such and so not necessarily relevant to that sense of "seriousness" required for deciding what a crime *deserves*. The importance of this point should not be underestimated. How far the Sellin-Wolfgang methodology may take us from justice can be gauged by considering a more recent study by Peter Rossi et al., "The Seriousness of Crimes: Normative Structure and Individual Differences," *American Sociological Review* 39 (April 1974): 224–27. According to this study, most people thought that "forcible rape after breaking into a home" was about as serious as the "planned killing of an acquaintance" and considerably worse than "forcible rape of a stranger in a park" or "assassination of a public official." "Forcible rape of a former spouse" fell far down on the list, between "neglecting to care

for own children" and "manufacturing and selling autos known to be dangerously defective" (237). A similar survey in which the questions were put in terms of the forced-choice analysis below would, I think, yield different results.

22. As in note 19 above, I here urge care in putting the question.

23. I owe this analysis to Pat Murphy, who pointed it out to me in private conversation (without, however, endorsing it herself).

24. I argue for the unlikelihood of ever having such a calculus in *To Make the Punishment Fit the Crime*, chapter 4, 73–77.

25. No doubt one of the reasons that it is hard to convict a man of rape when the victim lacks a "reputation for chastity" is that he seems far less an ogre than the man who would rape a woman of the "old school." Reforms ruling out inquiry into reputation for chastity may suppress the question without getting it out of the courtroom altogether. That is as it should be. The question, while not relevant to determination of guilt, is relevant to the question of whether in this case the jury (or judge) should nullify the statute because even its minimum penalty is out of proportion to the crime in question.

26. I owe this analysis to Mortimer Kadish.

27. When I first wrote this, it seemed too obvious for argument. Since then Catherine MacKinnon (quoting this sentence in a footnote) has suggested that "the wrong of rape has proved so difficult to define because the unquestionable starting point has been that rape is defined as distinct from intercourse, while for women it is difficult to distinguish the two under conditions of male dominance." *Toward a Feminist Theory of the State* (Harvard University Press: Cambridge, Massachusetts, 1989), 174. While I find much to disagree with in MacKinnon's radical critique of heterosexual intercourse (in this and virtually all other actual societies), I think she is right in supposing that my analysis of rape must be wrong on this level—or not at all. We disagree only insofar as I think what is problematic is the concept of rape *rather than*, as she does, the concept of heterosexual intercourse. Most writing on rape proceeds, in contrast, as if neither rape nor heterosexual intercourse were a problematic concept.

28. See, for example, Susan Griffin, "Rape: The All-American Crime," in *Philosophy and Feminism*, 318–319; Quenneville, 586–597; E. M. Curley, "Excusing Rape," *Philosophy & Public Affairs* 5 (Summer 1976): 325–60; and Leigh Bienen, "Mistakes," *Philosophy & Public Affairs* 7 (Spring 1978): 224–45.

29. Note, "Legislation: Rape and Other Sexual Offense Law Reform in Maryland 1976–1977," *Baltimore Law Review* 7 (Fall 1977): 151–70, especially 160–61.

30. Compare Note, "Unlawful Sexual Intercourse: Old Notions and

a Suggested Reform," *Pacific Law Review* 12 (January 1980): 217–33; and Note, "Criminal Law—Equal Protection—Gender-Based Statutory Rape Provision Held Invalid," *Washington University Law Quarterly* 59 (Spring 1981): 310–17.

31. For an example of how not to respond to this argument, see Lynne Henderson, "Rape and Responsibility," *Law and Philosophy* 11 (February–May 1992): 127–178, especially 174–175: "In developing his argument against serious penalties for rape, Davis ignores the terror of rape victims when he poses the question: Which would you choose, being compelled by brute force to have sexual intercourse or being badly beaten without permanent harm?" I do not *ignore* the terror, the pain, the embarrassment, or anything else; I simply leave it to my informant to evaluate them. Henderson, in contrast, allows her ideology to determine how women (and men) should weight all that. My claim "strikes her as false" just because she has not put it to the test.

32. Note that the argument here is independent of the probability of the event (whether perceived probability or objective) because the fear-based analysis used here is forced-choice rather than prospect.

33. Eric Partridge, *Origins* (New York: The Macmillan Company, 1959), 550.

34. Henry Campbell Black, *Black's Law Dictionary*, revised 4th ed. (St. Paul, Minn.: West Publishing Co., 1968), 1427.

35. Frederick Pollock and Frederic Maitland, *History of English Law*, 2nd ed. rev. (London: Cambridge University Press, 1968), 490.

36. *Fair and Certain Punishment: Report of the Twentieth Century Fund Task Force on Criminal Sentencing* (New York: McGraw-Hill, 1976), 6–7 (without citation of source); and Irvin Waller and Janet Chan, "Prison Use: A Canadian and International Comparison, *Criminal Law Quarterly* 17 (1974): 47–71.

37. *Ill. Rev. Stat.* chap. 38, sec. 9-3.

38. *Ill. Rev. Stat.* chap. 38, sec. 9-2.

39. See, for example, *American Jurisprudence*, 2nd ed. (Rochester, New York: Lawyers' Cooperative Publishing Co., 1972), secs. 1–26 under "Rape"; or Babcock, 820–63.

40. See generally references in note 15; Note, "Rape Reform Legislation: Is It the Solution?" *Cleveland State Law Review* 24 (Summer 1975): 463–503; and Note, "Rape in Illinois: A Denial of Equal Protection," *John Marshall Journal of Practice and Procedure* 8 (Spring 1975): 457–96.

41. *FBI Uniform Crime Reports* (1977), 216. Because so much has been made of this disturbing fact about rape prosecution, I should point out that much the same seems to be true of some other major crimes.

The corresponding figure for robbery is 46 percent of charges against adult defendants ending with acquittal or dismissal; for aggravated assault (including aggravated battery), 43 percent; and for arson, 42 percent. Only the figures for murder and the lesser crimes are less disturbing: for murder (including non-negligent manslaughter), 29 percent; for burglary, 23 percent; for larceny-theft, 21 percent; for motor-vehicle theft, 33 percent; for vandalism, 32 percent; for weapons possession, 27 percent; and so on. Apparently, rape is not the only crime with penalties so severe that conviction has become difficult. (These figures have, I understand, been much criticized. They nevertheless remain, as far as I can tell, the only ones we have on conviction rates generally. If rape is a special case, the evidence for its being so has yet to be provided. Feminist literature discussing conviction rate often cites this table (or its predecessors) without mentioning the comparable figures for robbery, aggravated assault, and so on. See, for example, Berger, 5 (and note 26).

42. The same argument can be made about the death penalty. In states where the death penalty is on the books but seldom imposed, or imposed but seldom carried out, the public may think of any penalty less than death as getting away with murder. Better for both deterrence and moral education not to have a death penalty than to have it but hardly ever use it. Of course, this argument assumes that people pay attention to what courts do. For some empirical evidence that they do *not*, see Nigel Walker, *Why Punish?* (Oxford: Oxford University Press, 1991), 27–28.

43. *FBI Uniform Crime Reports* (1977), 216.

44. *Sourcebook*, 234. "Underreporting" will not explain away these figures. See Note 4 above for comparison of reporting rates.

45. *Sourcebook*, 234.

46. Susan Brownmiller, *Against Our Will* (New York: Simon and Schuster, 1975), 379.

Eleven

Punishing the Bad Samaritan

"Bad samaritan" is now shorthand for any stranger who fails to offer help to someone in immediate danger of death or serious bodily harm when he (the bad samaritan) knows (or should know) that he can help without substantial cost or danger to himself and without breach of any substantial duty to another. Among the best-known bad samaritans are thirty-eight residents of Kew Gardens, a quiet, middle-class neighborhood of Queens, New York. While a neighbor, Kitty Genovese, was stabbed to death on the street one March night in 1964, they looked out their windows, hearing her cry for help for more than half an hour. Able to help simply by lifting the phone, dialing the police, and telling what they knew, they did nothing.[1]

Most discussions of the bad samaritan concern one of three questions: a) whether he violates a moral duty or right or is instead guilty of some lesser moral failing; b) whether he should be civilly liable for the harm that occurs because of his failure to render aid; and c) whether bad samaritanism should be punishable as a crime.[2] While discussion continues, the predominant view seems to be that, whether or not we have a moral right to the bad samaritan's help in a life-threatening emergency, our common interest in avoiding harm suffices to justify a statute making bad samaritanism a crime. The liberty such a statute takes is small, since we seldom have an opportunity to help in an emergency; the security the statute gives may compensate for that loss, since unwanted death is a great evil. "Bad-samaritan laws" are a form of social insurance, as justifiable as a tax for fire or police protection.[3]

This chapter will assume that bad-samaritan laws are morally permissible (whatever the reason). Its question is what the penalty for violating a bad samaritan law should be. Since this seems to be the first sustained effort to answer that question, I should briefly explain what makes the question worth answering.

WHAT MAKES THE QUESTION WORTH ANSWERING

Russia adopted the first bad samaritan statute in 1845. Over the next century or so, more than twenty European states followed, including Spain, Italy, Germany, the Netherlands, and all of Scandinavia except Sweden.[4] But until 1967, no common-law jurisdiction did anything similar. In that year, Vermont became the first to adopt such a statute. A quarter century later, Vermont remains the only common-law jurisdiction with a bad-samaritan statute, though at least four other American states have recently made criminal failure to report certain crimes (and Minnesota has made the bad samaritan civilly liable for any harm her inaction causes).[5]

Most bad-samaritan statutes set the maximum penalty for violation relatively low. Vermont has one of the lowest penalties. Violation of its bad-samaritan statute is only a misdemeanor punishable by a fine not to exceed $100. Most other jurisdictions set the maximum at a year of imprisonment (usually with the alternative of fine, public censure, or other lesser penalty). France's statute is exceptional, setting the maximum penalty at five years imprisonment. This exception is, however, more apparent than real. The French statute also serves to punish homicide by omission (for example, where a jailer allows a prisoner in his care to starve to death), a crime for which the higher penalty seems appropriate.[6]

This narrow range of penalties suggests that common sense (or, more exactly, the consensus of legal institutions) considers bad samaritanism to be a relatively minor crime, no worse than, say, petty theft or simple battery. If, then, any theory of punishment were to recommend a much higher penalty (or none at all), its defenders would have only two unattractive options. They could try to show that common sense was wrong, presumably (to avoid begging the question) on grounds independent of their theory. Or, instead, they could admit that their theory departed from common sense in one respect.

While such an admission is not the same as giving up the theory, it is nonetheless an admission of weakness. If, in addition, other theories do not depart from common sense in that respect, the theory is, in that respect, at a competitive disadvantage. The piling up of such disadvantages would eventually bury the theory.

This chapter is part of a larger undertaking consisting in the piling up of such disadvantages as a way of winning support for the theory of criminal desert that I favor.[7] Bad-samaritan laws interest me primarily because different theories of punishment seem to give radically different recommendations concerning the maximum penalty for violation. I shall now illustrate how different the recommendations can be using three theories I intend to ignore hereafter: incapacitation, deterrence, and (traditional) *lex talionis*.

Incapacitation theory understands punishment as primarily concerned with preventing crime by disabling criminals (for example, by holding them in prison until they are no longer likely to commit crimes). For incapacitationists, the point of preventing crime is to make society safer, more prosperous, or otherwise better off (in a consequentialist way). Since the bad samaritan's crime consists in a failure to act (a nondoing when there is a legal duty to act), putting a bad samaritan in prison or otherwise disabling him would seem to be a uniquely inappropriate strategy. While prison (or some other disablement) might reduce his opportunities to be a bad samaritan (that is, to violate his legal duty), it would do so only by default (that is, only by also denying him the opportunity to help). Since bad samaritans are otherwise no more likely to commit crimes than the average citizen, society will be no safer with bad samaritans in prison than out. The bad samaritan can "do nothing" anywhere. Bad-samaritan statutes thus bring out the inherent incompleteness of incapacitation as a theory of how much to punish. Incapacitation can justify no punishment for bad samaritanism (or other omissions).[8]

Like incapacitation theory, deterrence theory seeks to prevent crime. But deterrence theory recommends setting penalties not to incapacitate but to make the crime less attractive than following the law. Deterrence theory would, then, recommend punishing the bad samaritan only as much as necessary to deter failure to render aid in appropriate circumstances. Since, by definition, the bad samaritan can act without much cost, the penalty for inaction need not be high. For example, even in the Genovese case, the statutory penalty need not have been much more than the cost in time of a phone call (perhaps adjusted downward to allow for the probable prompting of conscience or upward for any perceived improbability of enforcement). Deterrence theory thus seems to yield a maximum penalty in the same moderate range as common sense does (though we cannot be sure without empirical evidence that we are unlikely to get).[9]

Lex talionis, in contrast, would seem to require the severest penalty that the legal system allows. The general principle of *lex talionis* (as traditionally understood) is *equivalence* between harm done and punishment imposed. The punishment is not for an act as such, for what was intended or risked, but for what was done ("an eye for an eye," as the Bible says). So, for example, to kill someone, even "by accident," would justify the same penalty—"blood money" or death—as would killing deliberately. Traditional *lex talionis* is not so much a theory as a slogan. No theorist defends it without amending it to reduce the importance that moral luck would otherwise play in punishment.

What punishment would *lex talionis* impose on bad samaritans? The harm done Kitty Genovese included fear, pain, physical injury, and (eventually) death. Genovese suffered violent death in part because thirty-eight bad samaritans did nothing to help her. They had it in their power to help and instead (consciously) chose to do something else. The choice of each was a cause (a necessary condition) of her violent death.[10] True, her attacker was the primary agent of harm, but his responsibility does not reduce theirs. Responsibility for harm can be divided among many participants without reducing anyone's responsibility. So it seems that *lex talionis* would require us to punish each bad samaritan who let Genovese die much as we would punish her murderer. Death, or at least decades of imprisonment, is as close as we can come to making them suffer the death that she suffered because of what they did.

But, it might be objected, *lex talionis* would not require so harsh a punishment. We were able to draw the conclusion we did only because we treated a failure to act ("omission") as if it were a positive act ("commission"). The objection is correct in pointing out that we have been arguing as if omissions (conscious nondoings) differed in no morally important way from commissions (conscious doings). The objection is, however, wrong in assuming that making the distinction will save *lex talionis* from a result contrary to common sense or, at least, that it will save it from that result without committing it to other results equally contrary to common sense.

If punishment must be for commissions, not omissions, then the bad samaritan cannot be punished at all—and the bad samaritan is not the only one. The parent who deliberately lets her infant starve to death when there is plenty of food in the house also cannot be punished. She too kills by a nondoing. Since that result seems contrary enough to common sense to require us to allow punishment for omissions, we are left with the question what that punishment might be—if the result is to be different from the one we already derived from *lex talionis*. We must, it seems, punish an omission by another omission (or its equivalent). What omission would be equivalent to what Kitty Genovese suffered? Being-left-alone does not seem right. But being-left-alone-where-you-stand-a-good-chance-of-being-killed does (for example, by being made to spend a night in a lion's den). Would not that penalty be roughly equivalent to a sentence of death or several decades in prison?

Seldom will one find a statutory crime where these old workhorses of theory pull in such different directions. I am, however, not interested in these three but in three others.[11] Each is retributive; that is, each is a theory setting statutory penalties according to some notion of criminal desert. One, the fairness theory, is my own. The other two are, first, a modern version of *lex talionis*, one combining considerations of harm with other factors and, second, "character theory" (as I shall call it), which measures criminal desert by a nonlegal feature of the *criminal* (rather than of the crime). I shall show that the fairness theory does a better job of setting the statutory maximum penalty for bad samaritanism than do the other two. Though I shall not discuss other criminal omissions, what I do say should apply to them as well. For my purposes, bad samaritanism is just a special case of criminal omissions.

A MODERN VERSION OF *LEX TALIONIS*

Hyman Gross has argued that criminal desert is a function of
four features of the criminal conduct: harm, dangerousness, control, and right.[12] His approach resembles (traditional) *lex talionis*
in making harm central to determining deserved punishment; it
differs from *lex talionis* only in not allowing harm to be decisive. Gross's approach resembles that of a number of other contemporary theorists, including Andrew von Hirsch and Robert
Nozick.[13] Gross differs from these primarily in the care with
which he explores the role of factors other than harm. That care
is the reason I give his exposition pride of place in this section.
I shall first explain his approach and then apply it to setting the
maximum penalty for bad samaritanism.

For Gross, "harm" refers to any state of affairs that the law
seeks to prevent. Several crimes may share the same harm. For
example, the harm in murder, voluntary manslaughter, involuntary manslaughter, and even attempted murder is the same, violent death. For some crimes, such as murder, the state of affairs
that the law seeks to prevent is an element of the offense itself.
For others, such as attempted murder, it is not. For Gross, this
distinction is *not* important. The "harmfulness" of an act is determined in prospect, by what it risks, not in retrospect, by what
it does. All else equal, the more harmful the conduct is, the more
severe the punishment should be. So, for example, murder, whether successful or merely attempted, should have a higher penalty
than theft, whether successful or merely attempted.[14]

Closely related to harm is "dangerousness." Conduct is dangerous insofar as it makes occurrence of a certain harm more or
less probable. Like harmfulness, dangerousness is independent of
actual outcome.[15] For example, whatever happens, pulling the
trigger of a gun believed to be loaded is (all else equal) more
dangerous than pulling the trigger of one believed to be unloaded. That is so because (as a matter of fact) guns believed to be
loaded go off more often than guns believed to be unloaded. The
more dangerous an act, the more punishment it deserves (all else
equal).

For Gross, "control" is an ability to direct the course of events.
Control is relevant to criminal desert because we "want to attribute to those we accuse only the harms and dangers they have

brought about or allowed within those parts of the world that are (or should be) under their control."[16] Punishment should be for what we do (or risk), not merely for what happens. The distinction between act and omission is irrelevant; the crucial distinction is between what the criminal could control and what he could not control.[17] Could he, under the circumstances, have avoided what happened?

"Control" is Gross's version of *mens rea*, "mental state," or "responsibility" (and so includes "self-control"). Control is a matter of degree. For example, we have more control of what we do recklessly than of what we do negligently. Since recklessness is conscious negligence, the reckless are aware of their negligence (aware, that is, that they are not acting with due care). That awareness puts them in position to avoid the consequences of negligence in ways they could not, or could not as easily, were they unaware of it. They are in a better position than the negligent to direct the course of events. In much the same way, we have more control of what we do purposely than of what we do recklessly. To avoid doing an illegal harm on purpose, one need only give up that illegal purpose; but, to avoid doing an illegal harm recklessly, one may have to give up one or more lawful purposes (as well as an unlawful means). Giving up such purposes demands (all else equal) more control (at least more self-control). The more control a criminal has over the course of events constituting his crime, the more punishment he deserves for the crime (all else equal).

The last feature of conduct Gross considers relevant to criminal desert is "right." Right differs from these other features. Right is not an element of criminal conduct as such (as harm, danger, and control are), but a basis for justifying what would otherwise be criminal conduct (or at least for reducing the conduct's culpability). So, for example, even if I intentionally shoot someone, killing him, I am not guilty of murder if the killing was (justified) self-defense; that is, if I had a right to shoot him under the circumstances in order to save myself from death or serious bodily harm.[18]

Applying this analysis to bad-samaritan statutes, we get a result not much different from that (traditional) *lex talionis* gave. The bad samaritan has, by definition, considerable control. He must be able to help without substantial cost or danger to himself and without breaching any substantial duty to another; and he must know that (or at least be in a position where he should have known it). He does not, however, have the control of someone trying to bring about the harm in question. The bad samaritan is reckless, not intentionally harmful.

The harm that bad-samaritan statutes seek to prevent is among the greatest, that is, death or serious bodily harm. And the bad samaritan's conduct can be quite dangerous. For example, in the Genovese case, the inaction of the thirty-eight residents of Kew Gardens eventually made Genovese's violent death virtually certain. The thirty-eight were—except for the murderer—all that stood between Genovese and death. In this respect at least, the Genovese case is not unusual. Bad samaritan laws usually require that help be given only in situations involving immediate danger.

So, on Gross's analysis, disobeying a bad-samaritan law must be very serious. But how serious? The answer is: as serious as reckless homicide. The bad samaritan can be and generally is reckless; knowing what she should do, she does something else. She risks the same harm (violent death) as anyone else who commits homicide. The bad samaritan is also as dangerous as many who commit homicide, for example, the jailer who lets a prisoner starve to death before his eyes. Indeed, given Gross's dismissal of the distinction between act and omission, there can be, on his analysis, no interesting difference between that jailer and the residents of Kew Gardens who let Genovese die. So, according to Gross, it seems, the maximum penalty for bad samaritanism should be as severe as for other forms of reckless homicide. How severe is that? In Illinois, reckless homicide is a class-3 felony, punishable by up to five years imprisonment.[19] Five years imprisonment is five times the maximum penalty for simple battery or petty theft, well beyond the range common sense sets for bad samaritanism.

How might Gross respond to this apparent inconsistency between his analysis and common sense? He might just accept the inconsistency—but at the cost of weakening his theory's appeal. He would, in effect, have to admit one departure from common sense, the renunciation of the distinction between act and omission, had committed him to another. His theory would be on its way to fantasy.

Gross might, then, prefer to argue that we have misapplied his analysis. There is (he might say) an important difference between even the bad samaritans who let Genovese die and the jailer who lets a prisoner die. The same statute that punishes bad samaritans imposes the duty to help. The bad samaritan's duty to help is not an independent legal duty (whether or not it is an independent moral duty). In contrast, the duty of the jailer arises from his special position of responsibility, his office under another statute, not from the homicide statute that punishes him. The harm that the law seeks to prevent in a case like the jailer's is different from that it seeks to prevent in the case of a bad samaritan.

Let us agree that the two harms are different. Mere difference does not make one crime more serious than another. For Gross, one class of crime is more serious than another (danger, control, and right being held constant) only if the harm one statute seeks to prevent is greater than the harm the other statute seeks to prevent. So for us, the question must be whether someone like the jailer does (or risks) greater harm than someone like a resident of Kew Gardens in the Genovese case (not whether the harm one does is different from the harm the other does). Does the jailer do *greater* harm? The answer seems to be that he does only if death-resulting-from-breach-of-some-independent-legal-duty is a greater harm than death-resulting-from-breach-of-a-duty-the-statute-in-question-imposes. But how could we show the first harm to be greater than the second?

I know of only one way: ask which harm we would prefer to avoid—prefer for ourselves, if we can suffer the harms ourselves, and otherwise, prefer for someone or something we care about. Harm A is worse than harm B if, and only if, we prefer B to A (all else equal) when forced to choose between them. Since I can see no reason (all else equal) to prefer suffering death-resulting-from-breach-of-some-independent-legal-duty over suffering death-resulting-from-breach-of-a-duty-the-statute-in-question-imposes or, indeed, suffering death of the second sort rather than death of the first sort, I must conclude that they are equally bad. So, Gross cannot defend his analysis by claiming that the harm the jailer does is worse than what the bad samaritan does because the harm the jailer does is a breach of an independent legal duty, while what the bad samaritan does is not.

Can Gross defend his analysis by claiming instead that the jailer's omission is worse than that of the residents of Kew Gardens because the jailer is the last human capable of intervening while Genovese's *murderer* has that status in her case, not the residents of Kew Gardens? I think not. Bad-samaritan statutes do not generally distinguish between "natural emergencies" (such as a child drowning in a shallow pond after accidentally falling in) and "criminal emergencies" (such as Genovese's). That is not surprising. The harm in question is much the same: a painful and unnecessary death. Reckless homicide (as such) cannot be more harmful than bad samaritanism just because some element of the causal chain is human rather than natural (or, indeed, natural rather than human).

I am, of course, not denying that the jailer is morally worse than the bad samaritan. He may be. Nor am I denying that he deserves more punishment than the bad samaritan. I believe he does. Rather, I am simply arguing that considerations of control, dangerousness, harm, and right do not distinguish the jailer from the bad samaritan. Like traditional *lex talionis*, Gross's modern version seems to leave out an important consideration. What? It is time to look at the fairness theory.

FAIRNESS

"The fairness theory" (as I understand it) is not a theory of the purpose, justification, or function of the criminal law in general or of punishment in particular. It is not even a theory of how much criminals should be punished, all things considered—that is, taking into account mercy, public expense, or the like. Rather, it is a theory of criminal desert, of how much one can legally punish a criminal before exceeding what he deserves for his crime (that is, for his doing what the law forbids).

The theory is often criticized for giving a misleading picture of crime or the grounds of punishment (of confusing the criminal law with the rules of a gentleman's club). The theory does not deserve that criticism. As a theory of criminal desert, it leaves to theories of legislation the explanation of why the law should forbid certain acts and not others and to general theories of punishment the explanation of why the law should assign penalties to doing what the law forbids. The fairness theory purports only to explain a certain aspect of criminal justice: the limits on legal punishment imposed by considerations of criminal desert. The fairness theory is only a theory of side-constraints.

The fairness theory can best be understood as deriving from a presupposition of retributivism. Because retributive theories are, as such, theories of *just* punishment (rather than, as utilitarian theories are, of efficient punishment), they presuppose something approximating a just legal system. Indeed, the idea of "just punishment," or even "deserved punishment," is of little use outside such a system. (Consider, for example, what punishment, if any, would be just, or deserved, if an Auschwitz inmate were to violate a camp rule by stealing food from a storehouse or by killing a guard while trying to escape.)

The fairness theory of criminal desert depends on three characteristics of a just legal system:

(a)   that providing for punishment if someone disobeys a law is justified, in part at least, because (in a relatively just legal system) so providing helps to assure that the laws will be obeyed—and so that justice will be maintained;

(b)   that punishing someone for a particular act of disobedience (in such a legal system) is justified only if the punishment is no more than what the act deserves (and so, no more than what justice allows); and

(c)   that giving the criminal what he deserves for his crime (in such a legal system) tends to maintain a just balance between the benefits of obedience to law and the burdens of such obedience (by, for example, helping to maintain the system or by undoing unfair advantage).

With these three characteristics in mind, we can easily see why the fairness theory of criminal desert sets a maximum penalty for bad samaritanism much lower than does Gross's theory.[20]

The criminal law protects a society from what its legislators fear would happen if no laws forbid certain acts. For our purposes, it does not matter whether the object of legislative fear is (or should be) harm to individuals only, harm to society, the moral disolution of society, or some combination of these or other

concerns. The object of legislative fear is relevant only to setting the boundaries of the criminal law (for example, to the decision to adopt a bad-samaritan statute). What *does* matter now
is that, in a relatively just legal system, the criminal law protects each person subject to it from some of what she fears others would do (or not do) otherwise. The criminal law can do
that for each person only insofar as everyone else does what the
law requires.

How does the criminal law get people to do what they otherwise would not do? While each person may want to require this
or that act because she fears that she (or someone or something
she cares about) will suffer if others do not do it, she cannot
generally obey the law for that reason. (Most of the people the
law protects are people about whom she does not care.) Insofar
as people are of good character, they may obey the law simply
because doing otherwise is unthinkable. Insofar as they are morally self-conscious agents, they may obey because doing otherwise (in a relatively just legal system) would be morally wrong.
Only insofar as people are potential criminals will they obey, if
they do, because they fear detection and punishment. Punishment
(of others) is one means, but only one means, of assuring each
person that she may reasonably do as the law says.

Whatever the reasons people have for doing as the law says,
this much seems plain. Generally, if the criminal law requires
an act (for example, helping in an emergency), some people would
find the act unattractive enough to omit—were it not for the law
requiring it. Legislators may sometimes be moved by analogy,
false fears, or inertia to require what no one would omit. But
we may safely ignore that possibility; it will rarely be realized
and, when it is, will never lead to punishment (except through
error or conspiracy).

We may then assume that any act the criminal law requires
(for example, helping in an emergency) is one some of the law's
subjects would otherwise omit. To assume that is, however, not
to assume that the act is unattractive to everyone or equally unattractive to those who would omit it but for the law. No two
subjects of the law need be legally moved to do exactly the same
acts, moved by the same reasons, or moved to the same degree,
nor need they benefit from the obedience of others in the same

way or to the same degree. What matters is the *overall* balance of protection and restraint. The criminal law is a single system benefiting each by guiding the rest. So long as each subject gains more from the criminal law's protection than she loses by its restraint, the criminal law may be a good bargain for her.[21] So long as the criminal law is a good bargain for everyone, it is justified.

Disobeying the criminal law while others obey is (generally) advantageous to the person disobeying (provided, of course, the disobedience does not bother conscience too much, lead to punishment, or otherwise turn out badly). (In other words, people generally have interests that conflict with interests of others that the law protects.) The advantage of disobeying the law would, however, *not* necessarily be the same were there no law. Indeed, the advantage must exist, at least in part, because the criminal law is a system of cooperation. Criminal advantage is parasitic on that cooperation. By his crime, the criminal takes some fruits of cooperation to which he is not entitled, while depending on others not to do something similar. The bad samaritan who, for example, watches a murder rather than calling the police, can do that because few people break into apartments, guns blazing, to wreck, rob, and kill. The very security that the law provides makes it possible to be a bad samaritan—rather than another hunted animal who could come to Genovese's aid only at great personal risk.

Obeying the law while others do not is, in contrast, disadvantageous (all else equal). One must bear a burden that one would not otherwise bear while others, those not doing what they are supposed to do, bear no such burden. So, for example, in Vermont, someone who rescues a latter-day Kitty Genovese must disrupt his plans. However small that burden, it is still larger than the burden of someone who does what he wants instead of doing as Vermont's bad-samaritan law requires.

The advantage so taken will (generally) be *unfair* advantage (provided the law is part of a relatively just legal system). That will be true even if the law does not enforce a preexisting moral duty. Consider an analogy. Suppose that I deliberately make an illegal move during a chess game—say, castle out of check. That move is morally wrong (all else equal). Yet it is not morally

wrong because a moral rule says, "Don't castle out of check" or
even, "Obey the rules of chess." No moral duties attach directly
to moving pieces on a board or to chess as such. The relevant
moral rule is, "Obey the rules of any morally permissible cooperative practice in which you participate." Castling out of check
is (ordinarily) morally wrong because chess is (ordinarily) a
morally permissible cooperative practice, and castling out of
check is a violation of its rules.[22] In the same way, a crime is
the taking of *unfair* advantage (within a relatively just legal system) because the crime violates a rule of a morally permissible
cooperative practice, the legal system itself. If we understand
"cheating" to be disobeying the rules of a morally permissible
cooperative practice, the advantage that one gets by disobeying
the criminal law as such is the advantage that one gets by a certain sort of cheating, whatever the cheating itself ultimately ac-
complishes.

This "cheater's advantage" may be thought of as corresponding to a "license" the obedient do not "take." The problem of
determining the relative seriousness of a particular crime may
then be thought of as a problem of determining the relative value of the corresponding "license," that is, its value relative to
other licenses. The more valuable the license, the more serious
the crime. While any fair, orderly, and efficient procedure for
setting prices should serve to set an appropriate value on such
(imagined) licenses, I have found a certain permanent auction,
something like a bond market (or stock exchange), to serve best
when I am trying to gauge the relative value of the unfair advantage of a particular (class of) crime.

Imagine a society much like ours, except that anyone subject
to the criminal law may bid on "licenses" to disobey. Each license allows for one violation of a particular statute (or in complex statutes, for the violation of a particular section or rule).
Each license may be used only once (after the criminal has been
captured, tried, and convicted of the crime in question), but may
be resold in the market any number of times until the final pur-
chaser decides to use it (just as a bearer bond can be resold until
cashed in).

The number of these licenses must be limited, if they are not
all to sell for a penny. Let us imagine the number to be limited
much as the number of licenses to hunt duck or deer is limit-

ed—that is, by considering both how much income the society can raise by offering a certain number of licenses and how much "hunting" can be done without leaving less to "hunt" in years to come. The society would, of course, try to maximize income over the long run. We must, then, imagine either that no "poaching" is possible or, more realistically, that "poachers" would be subject to a special (humane) penalty, one severe enough to make "poaching" of any sort rare (say, mandatory death or permanent exile to outer space). To be sure that this "metapenalty" does not bias market price, we must suppose it to be the same no matter what is "poached."

This metapenalty introduces some injustice into the legal system that we are imagining (or at least a disproportion between the harm some poaching does and the penalty it receives). But given the availability of licenses through a fair procedure, the metapenalty cannot produce enough injustice to undermine our assumption that the society in question is relatively just. The criminal always has the option of avoiding the crime or buying a license rather than risking the metapenalty, and in a relatively just society, should generally have the means to pay for the license.

The analogy between price and punishment may seem wild. It is not. To be worth its cost, the criminal law must maintain a certain level of "social well-being" ("order," "security," or the like). This level of well-being, which corresponds to the animal population of concern to game wardens, can only be maintained if society pays for it, whether by public expenditures for schools, poor relief, police, and the like, or by individual expenditures for burglar alarms, bars on windows, private security guards, and the like. The trade-off between the cost of crime control in our society and the benefits corresponds to the trade-off in our imagined society between the income from selling licenses and the costs of the licensed crimes. The calculations of the society we are imaging are not so different from those that the society we live in actually makes (or, at least, should make).

Because a specific license pardons only a specific violation of a specific criminal statute, "cashing in" a license leaves all other legal and moral relationships as they were. So, for example, even if a thief "pays her debt to society" with a "theft license," she is still liable to civil suit for return of the property she stole or for damages for any harm she caused. She also remains open to moral criticism. Though pardoned as a criminal, she remains a thief.

Because the license only pardons a specific violation of a criminal statute, and because our imagined market is a fair procedure, market prices should be a good *index* of the value of unfair advantage taken simply by violating the criminal law in question (though not of the actual value of the crime to the criminal, whether in prospect or in retrospect). To say that the market price is a good index of the value of the unfair advantage taken is, however, not to say that the price has any significance apart from the market. Like the price of any commodity anywhere, the price of a license in our market has significance only relative to other prices within the same price system. Our imagined market will yield only a fair *ranking* of crimes, not anything we could reasonably treat as the appropriate table of "prices" in our society. We need a separate argument to set penalties in our society.

We may, then, translate the problem of determining how much punishment bad samaritans deserve into three simpler problems: (1) distinguishing the special unfair advantage one takes by disobeying a bad-samaritan statute; (2) using the market we have imagined to determine the relative value of that advantage (the price that the appropriate license would fetch); and (3) using that relative value to place bad samaritanism within the penalty scale of our own society.

The special advantage that one gains simply by disobeying a bad-samaritan statute is the advantage of being able to do anything other than help out in a serious emergency, even though helping would be relatively easy, safe, and morally unproblematic. How much would such an advantage be worth? The market price of a bad-samaritan license will depend in part on what other licenses are selling for, how likely one is to need a license, how many other bidders there are, how much they are willing to bid, and so on. Such considerations can be quite important in determining the price of some licenses. But so long as we make no unreasonable assumptions, they are not crucial for bad-samaritan licenses.

What is crucial is the "cost" of complying with the statute. Buying a license can be rational only if, in prospect, the cost of owning a license is less than the cost of not owning it. Since market price tends to approximate that sort of rationality, bad-samaritan statutes should sell for less than the (prospective) cost of obeying the statute. But obeying a bad-samaritan statute is *always* relatively cheap. Unlike most criminal statutes, bad-samaritan statutes are designed to make obeying cheap. The statute demands nothing unless the risk, cost, and moral burden of obeying are all "insubstantial." The price of a license to disobey must, then, be "insubstantial," too.

To see how this argument translates into a relatively low penalty for bad samaritanism, we need only compare the (worst) bad samaritan with our jailer. The jailer's recklessness is a conscious failure of reasonable care. The duty of reasonable care is much more burdensome than the bad samaritan's duty to aid in an emergency. The duty of reasonable care may require our jailer to take substantial risks, bear substantial costs, or breach a substantial duty in order to provide food for a starving prisoner. So, someone seeking a license to commit reckless homicide should be willing to pay substantially more than someone seeking a license to commit bad samaritanism. The actual market price of the licenses should reflect this difference. Reckless-homicide licenses should cost much more than bad-samaritan licenses.

Our imagined market has, it seems, reminded us of a consideration not on Gross's list: the cost of compliance. Though perhaps overemphasized in deterrence theory, this consideration is absent from all forms of *lex talionis*. Its absence is, I think, not an oversight. For *lex talionis*, the cost of compliance can only be an excuse; as an excuse, it must work in a way opposite to the way it works when setting the crime's maximum penalty. The *higher* the cost of compliance, the stronger the excuse. Why can the cost of compliance only be an excuse in *lex talionis*, with the strength of the excuse declining as the cost of compliance does?

Historically, the appeal of *lex talionis*, however amended, has been its ability to mirror morality in an important respect. We blame people more for harmful acts than for harmless ones, more for relatively dangerous acts than for acts less so, more for harms over which people have considerable control than for those over which they have less, and more for acts that people have no right to do than for acts they have a right to do. If punishment is simply moral blaming carried on by other means, moral blaming should give the measure of legal punishment. Since we also generally blame people more for omitting what they could easily do than for omitting what they could do only at substantial cost or risk, or by ignoring a substantial duty, morality tells us to blame the bad samaritan more than the jailer. Bad-samaritan statutes thus provide a relatively clear case where standards of moral blaming are not mirrored in criminal punishment.

Though this is not the place for a detailed explanation of why standards of moral blaming might differ from those of criminal punishment, the outline of such an explanation is plain enough. Law and morality are quite different undertakings. Legal systems are much more formal than morality and much more expensive to operate. Their penalties can be much more severe, their procedures much less sensitive to individual differences. Laws can be passed by a majority of one in a legislature of a hundred; morality requires much more agreement to impose its standards. Indeed, law and morality differ so much that the interesting question is why anyone would suppose that even a relatively just legal system would mirror morality in any but the most general way.

Because amending *lex talionis* to fit the criminal law's treatment of compliance costs would sacrifice *lex talionis'* connection with morality and, with that, its intuitive appeal, *lex talionis* cannot simply be amended to take compliance cost into account as the fairness theory does. Insofar as *lex talionis* is true to morality, it must contain features foreign to the criminal law.

What then, according to the fairness theory, is the appropriate penalty for bad samaritanism in "this society" (whether Vermont, Denmark, Ethiopia, or some other actual legal entity)? Our imagined market has shown that whatever the maximum penalty for reckless homicide is, the maximum penalty for bad samaritanism should be much lower. How much lower? That will depend on three other features of the legal system.

One feature is how much the bad-samaritan statute in fact demands. Different legal systems may interpret even identical statutes differently; "risk," "cost," or "duty" (or their equivalents) may demand less in one jurisdiction than in another. The less demanding the statute as interpreted, the less unfair advantage one would take by violating the statute and the lower the maximum deserved penalty would be.

A second feature relevant to how much below the maximum

penalty for reckless homicide the maximum penalty for bad samaritanism should be is the number of steps on the penalty scale.
If, for example, the penalty scale only had three steps, and reckless homicide were on the middle step, bad samaritanism would
have to be on the bottom step. If, instead, the penalty scale had
eight steps, and reckless homicide were on the fourth (with murder on the first, attempted murder on the second, and voluntary
manslaughter on the third), then bad samaritanism could be placed
on the eighth, seventh, or even sixth step. Where bad samaritanism should in fact be depends on how similar bad samaritanism
is to crimes already on those steps.

So, a third feature relevant to how much below the maximum penalty for reckless homicide the maximum penalty for
bad samaritanism should be is the penalty for similar crimes.
The lower the maximum for similar crimes, the lower the penalty for bad samaritanism should be. If crimes at the low end
of the scale bear little resemblance to bad samaritanism, arguments from similarity (and dissimilarity) may be indecisive.
Desert will then leave the legislator free to choose any one of
those low steps. This, I think, is consistent with (and may well
explain much of) the actual diversity among maximum penalties
for bad samaritanism.

CHARACTER

I now want to consider briefly a third approach to setting penalties, one that virtue theorists may find tempting: "character theory." I want to consider it because character theory might be
confused with some forms of *lex talionis*. To avoid seeming to
leave myself open to certain objections that rely on character
theory, I must address that theory directly.

What distinguishes "character theory" from theories we have
discussed so far is a focus on the criminal rather than the crime.
In this respect, character theory resembles traditional (utilitarian) "reform theory" and (nonutilitarian) "education theory." It
differs from these in being a theory of desert rather than of cure
or moral improvement. Bad character deserves punishment, when
it does, not because the punishment may cure or otherwise im-
prove the criminal, but—according to character theory—because

the world is a morally better place when bad character suffers.[23] While the criminal law can, by definition, only punish those legally guilty of crime, deserved punishment has little to do with the crime. The measure of deserved punishment is morally blameworthy character, not morally blameworthy conduct.

"Character" in such a theory refers to relatively fixed dispositions of a person, that is, to virtues and vices. Even a relatively good person can, by mischance or misunderstanding, be led to do something morally wrong. Such a wrong does not, according to character theory, deserve punishment. Indeed, character theory has built into it a distinctive theory of excuse. For character theory, excuses distinguish those features of a crime that arise from the criminal's bad character from those that are mere accidents (or derive from essentially good dispositions). Crime that derives from accidents (or the criminal's good character) should *not* be punished. Bad character as such, even if due to disease or misfortune, should be. Bad character is precisely what deserves punishment.

What can such a theory tell us about how much to punish the bad samaritan? The answer seems to depend on how bad a character the bad samaritan is. The philosophical literature makes the bad samaritan sound pretty bad, much worse than a petty thief or someone likely to commit simple battery. Jeffrie Murphy's judgment on the bad samaritan—"moral slime"—is well known. Paul Hughes recently concurred in a calmer tone: "[the bad samaritan is, by definition,] a person lacking in the degree of compassion, sympathy, kindness, or fellow-feeling that we take to be among the standard equipment of minimally decent human beings."[24] If we take such judgments seriously, the worst (standard) bad samaritan would seem to be morally no better, and perhaps worse, than the worst (standard) reckless homicide.[25] One can, it seems, commit reckless homicide and still be a minimally decent human being (whether or not one can be a bad samaritan and be minimally decent). Consider, for example, a driver whose speeding causes a fatal accident or the hunter who shoots another hunter, taking him for a deer. Any assessment of their relative depravity must take into account both that the law demands much more of the potential reckless homicide than of the potential bad samaritan (reasonable care all the time rather than a little help in an emergency) and that (all else equal) judgments of character become less harsh the harder it is to do the right thing.

Like the appeal of *lex talionis*, the appeal of character theory is its connection with moral blaming. The only difference in appeal is that character theory assumes that criminal punishment is analogous to blaming *persons* while *lex talionis* makes the same assumption concerning *acts*. So like *lex talionis*, character theory must have trouble accommodating the way we punish bad samaritanism.

Or rather, it must *if* it ever develops a full-fledged theory of criminal desert. It may not—even if it does develop a full-fledged theory of what justifies punishment as an institution. Character theory seems ill-suited to setting statutory penalties. Indeed, like reform theory, it seems positively adverse. The purpose of statutory penalties (for retributivists) is to help the legislature limit what judges can do when sentencing. But legislators see only the crime, while the judge sees the criminal, and for character theory, it is the criminal who deserves punishment, not the crime. The setting of statutory penalties thus seems extrinsic to, if not inconsistent with, character theory.

CONCLUSION

My conclusion is that the fairness theory of criminal desert does a better job of setting the statutory maximum for bad samaritanism than does either retributive alternative. "Do a better job" here means doing better at (a) giving a definite answer, (b) giving an answer consistent with common sense (the uncontroversial practice of legal institutions), and (c) giving an answer that brings out significant factors we might otherwise overlook. *Lex talionis*, however modernized, seems destined to fail to do a better job in the second or third way. Character theory seems destined to fail in the first way, too.

NOTES

1. Or more accurately, did nothing to help. It is surprising how much else the thirty-eight did. Martin Gansberg, "37 [sic] Who Saw Murder Didn't Call the Police: Apathy at Stabbing of Queens Woman Shocks Inspector," *New York Times*, Friday, 27 March 1964, 1, 38.

2. For discussion of the moral right to aid or the moral duty to rescue, see Peter Singer, "Famine, Affluence, and Morality," *Philosophy and Public Affairs* 7 (Spring 1972): 229–243; Alan Gewirth, *Reason and Morality* (Chicago: University of Chicago Press, 1978), 217–230; Patricia Smith, "The Duty to Rescue and the Slippery Slope Problem," *Social Theory and Practice* 16 (Spring 1990): 19–41; John M. Whelan, "Charity and the Duty to Rescue," *Social Theory and Practice* 17 (Fall 1991): 441–456; and David Copp, "Responsibility for Collective Inaction," *Journal of Social Philosophy* 22 (Fall 1991): 71–80. For discussion of civil liability for bad samaritanism, see Frank E. Denton, "The Case Against a Duty to Rescue," *Canadian Journal of Law and Jurisprudence* 4 (January 1991): 101–132. For discussions focused on the criminal law, see Eric Mack, "Bad Samaritanism and the Causation of Harm," *Philosophy and Public Affairs* 9 (Spring 1980): 230–259; Joel Feinberg, *Harm to Others* (New York: Oxford University Press, 1986), 126–186; David Conter, "Feinberg on Rescue, Victims, and Rights," *Canadian Journal of Law and Jurisprudence* 4 (January 1991): 133–144; and Alison McIntyre, "Guilty Bystanders? On the Legitimacy of Duty to Rescue Statutes," *Philosophy and Public Affairs* 23 (Spring 1994): 157–191.

3. Note that the question of legal punishment for bad samaritanism is distinct from the question of the moral wrongness of bad samaritanism, law or no law. So, for example, just because much of the moral criticism of bad samaritanism turns on denial of the distinction between acts and omissions, it does not follow that a bad-samaritan statute must be justified in that way. The law seems properly to require many positive acts that morality does not, for example, payment of sales tax or service on a jury. It is important in what follows not unthinkingly to turn questions of what the law should be into questions of what morality is.

4. F. J. M. Feldbrugge, "Good and Bad Samaritans: A comparative Survey of Criminal Law Provisions Concerning Failure to Rescue," *The American Journal of Comparative Law* 14 (1966): 630–657, especially 635–657 (Appendix); and Gilbert Geis, "Sanctioning the Operation of Portugal's New 'Bad Samaritan' Statute," *International Journal of Victimology* 1 (1991): 297–313.

5. Susan J. Hoffman, "Statutes Establish a Duty to Report Crimes or Render Assistance to Strangers: Making Apathy Criminal," *Kentucky Law Journal* 72 (1983–84): 827–865, at 839 and 858. New York did, however, have a statute requiring citizens to notify authorities of a death. Gansberg, 38.

6. Poland and Bulgaria, with three-year maximums, also have statutes that combine failure to rescue and homicide by omission. Feldbrugge, 646–648.

7. See chapters 8 and 10; *To Make the Punishment Fit the Crime* (Boulder, CO: Westview Press, 1992), especially chapters 3–9; and "Postscript: In Fairness of Condemnation," *Israel Law Review* 25 (1991 Summer/Autumn): 581–594.

8. "Rewiring" a bad samaritan, or otherwise improving him, is, of course, reform (or rehabilitation) rather than incapacitation. My point here concerns incapacitation as a theory distinct from reform. If the distinction between disabling and reforming cannot be made, then incapacitation collapses into reform, and my comments here become uninteresting. That, however, is incapacitation's problem, not mine.

9. Of course, it is open to a critic of deterrence to argue that, on the contrary, the perceived probability of enforcement is (relative to other crimes) so low that the penalty necessary to compensate would have to be very high, perhaps death, to have any significant deterrent effect. Such critics remind us of how much deterrence theory depends on empirical information we lack, a point I have made elsewhere at some length. See, especially, *To Make the Punishment Fit the Crime*, 75–77 and 86–90. Such criticism of deterrence, though deserved, has been made often enough elsewhere to need no rehearsal here. I mention deterrence only to illustrate how different its response to bad samaritanism would seem to be.

10. Note that I am not claiming any of the thirty-eight was *the* cause (or even that anyone's *conduct* was). We seem to reserve the term "the cause" for a sufficient condition (when we do not simply mean the appropriate object of blame, the causal factor most easily controlled, or the causal factor whose part may shed the most light). I am using "cause" in the way the law generally does, that is, as a but-for circumstance. There is no doubt that, but for the failure of each and everyone of the thirty-eight to act, Kitty Genovese would not have been murdered.

11. For those who think that I have been too quick to dismiss these old workhorses, see my review of Nigel Walker's *Why Punish?* in *Law and Philosophy* 12 (November 1993): 51–63; as well as *To Make the Punishment Fit the Crime*, 3–17.

12. The theory is stated more or less in full in Hyman Gross, *A Theory of Criminal Justice* (New York: Oxford University Press, 1979). In what follows, I generally cite the later (and more readily accessible) summary of the theory in: Hyman Gross, "Culpability and Desert," *Archiv Fur Rechts Unter Sozialphilosophie* 19 (1984): 59–69, reprinted in *Philosophy of Law*, 4th ed., ed. by Joel Feinberg and Hyman Gross (Belmont, CA: Wadsworth Publishing Company, 1991), 669–676.

13. Andrew von Hirsch and Nils Jareborg, "Gauging Criminal Harm: A Living-Standard Analysis," *Oxford Journal of Legal Studies* 11 (Spring 1991): 1–38 (as well as von Hirsch's older work); Robert

Nozick, *Philosophical Explanations* (Cambridge, MA: Harvard University Press, 1981), especially 363–365.

14. Though I think Gross's equation of attempts and corresponding complete crimes wrong, it still represents the majority view among writers on criminal justice. I shall ignore it hereafter because it does not directly concern us (except insofar as it would require us to punish bad samaritans whose inaction in fact did not cause harm as severely as those whose inaction did). For an extended criticism of Gross's view, see *To Make the Punishment Fit the Crime*, 101–120.

15. Gross, "Culpability and Desert," 671.

16. Gross, "Culpability and Desert," 672.

17. Gross specifically dismisses the distinction between act and omission in *Theory of Criminal Justice*, 61–65. For a more recent defense of the centrality of control (rather than of "guilty mind"), see Douglas N. Husak, *Philosophy of Criminal Law* (Totowa, NJ: Rowman & Littlefield, 1987), especially 97–111. I have no quarrel with substituting "control" for "mens rea" in the "elements of the crime."

18. Gross, "Culpability and Desert," 672.

19. *Illinois Criminal Law and Procedure* (St. Paul, Minn.: West Publishing Company, 1991), chap. 38, sec. 9-3 (Reckless Homicide), sec. 16-1 (Petty Theft), sec. 12-3 (Simple Battery), sec. 1005-8-1 (Penalties for Felonies), sec. 1005-8-2 (Penalties for Misdemeanors).

20. What follows is, of course, more a proof sketch than a complete proof. Though space forbids me to do more here, those who want more should see my *To Make the Punishment Fit the Crime* for a general exposition of the fairness theory (though without application to bad samaritanism), and chapter 12 below for defense of the theory against recent objections.

21. The system of criminal law in question *is* a good bargain if, in addition to being better than no criminal law, it is better than any alternative actually available (taking into account the cost of conversion as well as the cost of operation). Generally, the costs of conversion are so high—or hard to determine—that even a pretty poor system is a good bargain.

22. We are, of course, assuming that the "principle of fairness" ("Don't cheat") is a moral rule. For those who have doubts about its moral status, see my "Nozick's Argument *for* the Legitimacy of the Welfare State," *Ethics* 97 (April 1987): 576-594; and Richard Arneson, "The Principle of Fairness and Free-Rider Problems," *Ethics* 92 (July 1982): 616–633. We are also assuming normal conditions, for example, that we have not changed the rules by agreement, that we are trying to play chess. Under normal conditions, chess is a cooperative game because people play in order to exercise their skill at chess,

to beat their opponents at chess, or the like. Under normal conditions, a cheating opponent ruins the game even if he cheats so badly that he loses. He may, however, compensate for ruining the chess game by allowing one to play the "game" of poetic justice.

23. Compare G.E. Moore, *Principia Ethica* (London: Cambridge University Press, 1966), 213–214.

24. Paul M. Hughes, "Bad Samaritans, Morality, and the Law," *International Journal of Applied Philosophy* 7 (Winter 1992): 9–13, at 11.

25. Because philosophers have been so hard on bad samaritans, it is worth thinking more carefully about how bad samaritans come to be bad samaritans. See, for example, Stanley Milgram and Paul Hollander, "The Murder They Heard," *Nation* 198 (15 June 1964): 602–604.

Twelve

Criminal Desert and Unfair Advantage

By "the fairness theory," I mean that theory of criminal desert proportioning the (maximum) legal punishment for a crime to the unfair advantage the criminal takes by the crime. This chapter is a response to one criticism of that theory. Though the criticism has a history almost two decades long, I shall be concerned only with the form it has taken in the last few years. The criticism might be cast as a syllogism:

1. A satisfactory theory of criminal desert would proportion the criminal's (maximum) legal punishment only to the crime's seriousness (and the criminal's culpability).
2. Considerations independent of a crime's seriousness (and the criminal's culpability) determine the unfair advantage the criminal takes.

So: any theory of criminal desert that proportions (maximum) legal punishment even in part to the unfair advantage the criminal takes cannot be satisfactory.

I shall argue that premise 2 is false. There is an attractive analysis of unfair advantage to which seriousness is conceptually related in the appropriate way.

RECENT WORK

David Dolinko's recent assault on retributivism will serve both to illustrate the importance of my thesis and to introduce certain

257

needed distinctions.[1] Dolinko distinguishes between those "bold" retributive theories that make giving the criminal what he deserves "the whole point of the institution of punishment" and those "more modest theories" that make desert necessary for a morally permissible institution of punishment (while remaining silent concerning the institution's justifying aim). A bold theory purports to show punishment to be *"rationally* justified" (that is, something reason requires): modest theories, only that punishment is *"morally* justified" (that is, something both reason and morality allow).[2] Dolinko devotes most of his article to modest retributivism.

Of the three "modest" theories that Dolinko identifies, the fairness theory is, he says, "probably the most influential." Herbert Morris's seminal article, "Persons and Punishment," is Dolinko's first target.[3] For Morris, punishing a person is morally justified if the punishment restores the equilibrium of benefits and burdens (in a relatively just legal system) by taking from the criminal what she owes—the unfair advantage she gained simply by breaking the law. The criminal deserves punishment if she has taken unfair advantage. The punishment is justified if it takes back or cancels that advantage. Having thus sketched the fairness theory, Dolinko objects:

> This account bridges the gap between "X deserves punishment" and "Punishing X is morally justified" only to the extent that we understand what "unfair advantage" criminals derive from their crimes. So what, precisely, is that advantage?[4]

Since (according to Dolinko) Morris does not answer that question, Dolinko turns to three retributivists who do: John Finnis, Jeffrie Murphy, and George Sher. Dolinko begins with Finnis (exiling Murphy to a footnote as one who "endorsed a similar view"). Finnis describes the unfair advantage that the criminal takes as, for example, "'indulging a (wrongful) self-preference' instead of exercising self-restraint."[5] For Finnis, Dolinko concludes, "the advantage the criminal obtains from his crime ought to be proportional to the burden of self-restraint that others carry but that he has thrown off."[6] The unfair advantage a particular criminal takes will depend, then, on how tempting people generally find the crime in question. If people were tempted more by a lesser crime like tax evasion than by the more serious crime of murder, tax evasion would have to be punished more severely than murder. That conclusion is, Dolinko thinks, enough at odds with common sense to write *finis* to this version of the fairness theory.[7]

Dolinko then turns to Sher. Sher understands the unfair advantage the criminal takes as "freedom from the demands of the moral prohibitions he violates," with the magnitude of the benefit being determined by the strength of the moral prohibition violated.[8] Dolinko rejects this analysis for two reasons. First, many crimes, including tax evasion, do not seem to violate any moral prohibition. They are mere *mala prohibita*. So, unless "moral prohibition" includes a prohibition of breaking the law, Sher's analysis would leave much criminal desert unexplained. If, however, the only moral prohibition in question (for *mala prohibita* at least) is "Don't break the law," the strength of the prohibition would fail to distinguish between crimes in the way we commonly do. The analysis could not explain why some *mala prohibita* should be punished more severely than others.

That is Dolinko's first reason for rejecting Sher's analysis. His second is that Sher cannot provide a convincing analysis of the "freedom" the criminal actually gains. "Though the criminal has in fact done what is prohibited," Dolinko notes, "this in no way dissolves or abrogates the obligation he, like everyone else, is under not to do the act."[9] Insofar as freedom is reduced by obligation, the criminal is no freer than the law-abiding. Both have the same obligation to obey the law. But insofar as freedom is (in part) the power to act against obligation, the criminal is still no freer than the law-abiding. The criminal has simply used the power, while the law-abiding have not. Either way, the criminal does not gain freedom by his crime.

Dolinko concludes his discussion of the fairness theory with this observation:

> [There] does seem to be truth in the underlying notion that the wrong-doer enjoys "an unfair advantage" as compared to his law-abiding fellow citizens. Unlike them, the criminal enjoys the benefit conferred by the self-restraint of other people (freedom from aggression and interference) without having paid the price everyone else pays for the benefit (restraining his own aggressive impulses). But if the

wrongdoer's "unfair advantage" is his enjoying a benefit he has not paid for, the "advantage" can be removed just as readily by taking away the benefit as by exacting the unpaid "price."[10]

I find this concluding observation perverse. Dolinko clearly feels the attraction of the fairness theory. He nonetheless rejects it for a reason suggesting that he does not understand his own feelings. Literally removing the benefit the criminal took by committing the crime would require undoing the past—or something equivalent. Taking back the money the tax evader took neither undoes the past nor does the equivalent. The tax evader has broken the law, lied on his tax forms, and reaped the unlawful use of the money from the time he should have paid the tax till the time the government seized his assets. He had a good chance of getting away with the crime. Merely giving back the money would not even constitute full compensation were the government to sue as a private person in a civil action. The tax evader would owe lost interest, court costs, and the like. Why then should merely giving back the money leave the tax evader no unpaid "price" to be repaid by punishment?

To this question, Dolinko might respond: "Unfair! I've just shown there is no way to cash out that price. You have an appealing metaphor, not a workable theory."[11] If that is Dolinko's response, it is Dolinko who is unfair. He has failed to consider one more version of the fairness theory, one that explicitly claims to answer the objection he raises, one that I find more attractive than those he has considered, my own. His failure to consider it at this crucial point in the argument is no mere oversight. Ten pages earlier, Dolinko notes its existence but dismisses it because "he argues [that his version] could be accepted even by someone who justifies the institution of criminal punishment on purely utilitarian grounds."[12]

Dolinko apparently forgot his own distinction between bold and modest retributivism. A "bold retributivist" who thought that even a utilitarian could accept his theory would indeed be irrelevant to Dolinko's project. Such a "retributivist" would hardly be a retributivist at all. But a modest retributivist could well leave open the question of whether the aim of punishment is utilitarian, claiming only that considerations of desert constitute side-constraints (constraints that even a utilitarian should accept for utilitarian reasons). Such a modest retributivist would need to answer precisely the question Dolinko claims Finnis and Sher could not answer. Dolinko's own way of posing the question thus forbids him to dismiss my answer simply because utilitarians (as well as retributivists) might accept it.[13]

Dolinko has left his flank badly exposed, but three retributivists—R. A. Duff, Don Scheid, and Andrew von Hirsch—have (unwittingly) come to his aid.[14] Writing at about the same time as Dolinko, each argued that my version of the fairness theory fails for the same reasons that, according to Dolinko, the versions of Finnis and Sher do. Von Hirsch put the objection this way: "[the] ratings Davis's model would assign to crimes . . . are problematic . . . and the model [itself] . . . emphasizes quite alien features of criminal conduct."[15]

We may distinguish two objections: first, that the actual rankings my version of the fairness theory produces are subject to counterexamples (such as Dolinko's involving murder and tax evasion); and second, that my version cannot be right because unfair advantage (as I interpret it) is "alien" to criminal desert. Let us consider the second objection first.

A PROBLEM FOR MY ANALYSIS

Starting with my 1983 paper, "How to Make the Punishment Fit the Crime," I have been working with two conceptions of seriousness. One is a descendant of Mabbott's method for setting penalties. I summarized it in seven steps:

1. Prepare a list of penalties consisting of those evils (a) that no rational person would risk except for some substantial benefit and (b) that may be inflicted through the procedures of the criminal law.
2. Strike from the list all inhumane penalties.
3. Type the remaining penalties, rank them within each type, and then combine rankings into a scale.
4. List all crimes.
5. Type the crimes, rank them within each type, and then combine rankings into a scale.

6. Connect the greatest penalty with the greatest crime, the
   least penalty with the least crime, and the rest accordingly.

7. Thereafter, type and grade new [humane] penalties as in
   step [3] and new crimes as in step 5, and then proceed
   as above.[16]

This summary does not mention "unfair advantage." Though
a detailed explanation follows each step, those explanations also
fail to mention "unfair advantage." For example, part of step 5,
crucial here, is explained in this way (though in more detail):
Crimes are typed by the minimum object they would normally
have in view. They differ only in means. Crimes of the same
type are ranked by placing lowest in the list of crimes of that
type the crime that most people would prefer to have happen to
themselves (or someone or something they care about) if forced
to choose between that one and any other of that type. The next-
lowest crime (of that type) would be the one most people prefer
to suffer if forced to choose between it and any other of that
type still unranked, and so on.[17]

Given no mention of "unfair advantage" in this procedure, we
naturally ask: What does this procedure have to do with the fairness theory? To answer that question, I imagined—as in chapter
11—an auction of pardon-like "licenses" to commit crimes.[18] The
auction was intended not as a real possibility but as a model
allowing us to use what we know about markets to gauge unfair
advantage. A fair-market price should be an index of the value
of the unfair advantage that a criminal takes simply by committing a particular crime. I then argued that the market would produce the same results as my seven-step method. Apparently, the
argument proved too sketchy for Duff, Scheid, and von Hirsch.

While I have varied the details of the market over the years,
I have always had the same purpose: to offer a model that makes
the price of licenses an index to their objective (or social) value. The concept of objective value should not be controversial.
We all recognize the difference between what we should pay for
something in a store, its objective value as commodity, and what
we might be willing to pay for it—its subjective value, its value
to us. A price can be too high even if we are willing to pay it,

or too low even if we are unwilling to pay it. The fair price of something is not its value to us (or even the cost of making or replacing it), but what a willing (and rational) buyer would pay a willing (and rational) seller in a relatively fair, efficient, and orderly market. That is all I mean by "objective value."

Eventually, I concluded that the best model for understanding the objective value of the unfair advantage that the criminal takes by a crime would be a certain continuing auction, a stock market for criminal licenses. Each license would specify a single crime (the license following the language of the statute). Each license could be used ("cashed in") only once but, like a bearer bond, could be bought and sold until "cashed in." Even non-criminals might rationally "invest" in such a license if its present price seemed too low given long-term trends in supply and demand. Price would track "market fundamentals."[19]

As noted in chapter 11, the prices generated in this way do not translate directly into punishments. They merely generate a ranking (an ordinal scale) within a type. This ranking must be combined with other rankings generated in the same way for other types. The resulting complex must then be set beside a scale of penalties (itself an ordinal ranking). We are free to draw lines between crimes and penalties so long as lines do not cross, not too many lines meet any one crime or penalty, and the crime ranked lowest receives a penalty lower than most other crimes receive. The market corresponds to step 5 of the seven-step method. Why should the market give the same results as step 5?

To answer that question, we must consider the social background presupposed when we talk of *criminal* desert rather than of simple moral desert. The "criminal" in "criminal desert" presupposes criminal laws; "desert," the relative justice of the legal system to which those laws belong. Talk of "criminal desert" outside a legal system is both rare and metaphorical. And even such talk within seems out of place if the system is not at least relatively just. What, for example, could an inmate of a concentration camp deserve in criminal punishment for picking a guard's pocket or striking a work leader?

The criminal law generally creates a framework of cooperation. Whatever benefit the criminal law offers an individual—Dolinko's "freedom from aggression and interference"—depends in large part on what others do. The burdens of the system do not. Each subject of the law owes obedience whether others obey or not. She contributes to legal order, if she does, whether others do or not. In any relatively just legal system, each subject has reason to want every other to obey, reason enough to make it worthwhile for each to obey as well if that were necessary to get others to do the same. Except under extraordinary circumstances, no rational person could prefer "the state of nature" to a relatively just legal system. She could not even choose her own official exemption from the law's demands if the price of that exemption were the loss of legal protection.

In this respect, the criminal law of any relatively just legal system resembles a voluntary cooperative practice. While doing as the law says may not always be rational, it is rational both to demand that others (generally) obey and to claim the law's protection for oneself. A rational person would endorse, accept, and generally support the criminal law (of a relatively just legal system) whether or not he himself intended to obey strictly (or at all).

Of course, subjection to the criminal law of even a relatively just legal system is not voluntary. Individuals cannot throw off the obligation to obey even by renouncing the law's protection. They can only flee its jurisdiction. Even so, the criminal law (of any relatively just legal system) has a voluntary aspect. The law can achieve its benefits only if those who *can* get away with crime generally do not try, even though they would try if they believed so many others were already committing crimes that the law was no longer able to guarantee the benefits that come from general obedience. Without cooperation, the system would either dissolve into disorder or maintain order only by demanding an enormous share of society's resources for police, hidden cameras, prisons, and the like. In any ordinary legal system, the law's subjects exercise significant self-restraint in the belief that others are doing the same. They cooperate voluntarily.

To cheat is to violate the rules of a voluntary cooperative practice. Insofar as the criminal law is a voluntary cooperative practice, crime is cheating (whatever else it might be). Cheating takes unfair advantage and, in a relatively just practice, is morally wrong for that reason (all else equal). So in a relatively just legal system (all else equal), the criminal takes unfair advantage by his crime (whatever else he may gain by it). To Dolinko's question, "So what, precisely, is that advantage?" we can answer, "Cheater's advantage."[20]

Cheater's advantage is, as such, always a violation of the same moral rule. Cheating is cheating. But the *value* of the advantage can vary from crime to crime. For example, the market price for a license to engage in illegal possession of a narcotic might be higher (or lower) than the market price for a license to engage in illegal possession of a firearm—even though both crimes are *mala prohibita*. My analysis is, then, not prey to Dolinko's objection to Sher's analysis. We need not fall back on a blanket obligation to obey the law; what we do fall back on, the value of cheater's advantage, is not necessarily the same for all *mala prohibita* (even though there is at least one moral rule that all violate).

Is this analysis also secure against Dolinko's objection to Finnis? In one way, it plainly is. We can easily explain why cheater's advantage is not necessarily proportional to the self-restraint that the law-abiding are exercising or the criminal would have exercised but for the crime in question. While the difficulty of self-restraint will certainly be one factor contributing to the value of the unfair advantage a certain crime will take, so may other factors such as the supply of licenses.

Of course, this answers Dolinko only if step 5 and the market in fact do scale crimes in the same way. We have not yet shown that and, on first impression, there seems no reason to think they do. Why should a method involving the sale of pardons-in-advance to would-be criminals (our market) produce the same results as a method emphasizing what people fear happening (step 5)? We must now face Duff, Scheid, and von Hirsch.[21]

THE PROBLEM SOLVED

We must begin with step 5. Duff, Scheid, and von Hirsch all seem to have misunderstood it. Step 5 does not require ranking all crimes along a single dimension, only ranking them within each type and connecting types to create something resembling the map of a complex subway system (crimes corresponding to stops and types corresponding to lines). This "map" takes on the appearance of a unidimensional scale only after it is connected with a unidimensional scale of penalties (for example, years in prison). Only in connection with such a scale does it make sense, for example, to describe armed robbery as twice as bad as grand theft. And even then, the description is misleading—much as would be describing as "twice the car" a car that sells for twice the price of another.[22]

If two crimes are of the same type, they are both acts that a potential criminal with a certain motive could choose (under normal circumstances). So, for example, battery and theft are not of the same type. A potential batterer will not normally consider theft as another means of harming his victim. A would-be thief is equally unlikely to consider battery as another means of getting property. Tax evasion, on the other hand, is of the same type as theft. Like theft, its purpose is to get property.

Ranking within a type has its counterparts in the market. Each type of crime will correspond to a group of potential bidders. These bidders will share a single motive—for example, getting the property of others for themselves. Though each may have a different crime in mind, each can choose from the same set (theft, tax evasion, and so on). Bidders may, however, differ in the amount they are willing to spend for the license they want (even if we assume equal wealth). Those more skilled at tax evasion than burglary should, for example, be willing to spend more for a license to evade taxes than for a license to burgle.

Bids will nonetheless follow a pattern. They will tend to be lower where the risks involved in committing the crime are greater, where the absolute return on any particular offense is likely to be small, where the chance of having to use the license the first time one commits the crime are high, and so on. A license to beat someone with a lead pipe (aggravated battery) will, for example, tend to go for more than a license to beat someone with only one's bare hands (simple battery); a license to commit grand theft, for more than a license to commit petty theft; and so on.

Since they can work against each other, these tendencies must be resolved. The market's way of resolving them corresponds to step 5's connecting of type to type (the "transfer stops" on a subway line). The market brings different types of crime into relation by forcing otherwise distinct groups of bidders to compete. For example, thieves (or more exactly, "property takers") might bid against thugs for a license to rob (use force or the threat of force to deprive others of property). For thieves, such a license would be for a special property crime, one using force. The license would be attractive insofar as using force would make it possible to take property otherwise beyond a thief's grasp. For thugs, the same license would be for a special violent crime, one using force to take property. Instead of earning money by hiring themselves out to scare, wound, or kill people, thugs could now use force to take property. They would not have to wait till someone hired them. They could go into business for themselves.

We can now see how, contrary to first impression, step 5 builds in the (rational) criminal's perspective in a way corresponding to the market. One way I defended the seven-step method, the way I hoped would appeal even to utilitarians, was by pointing out that, since the criminal law presupposes the criminal's rationality, society would (in effect) discourage crime generally by providing for punishment of crime and discourage most those crimes that society wants least by punishing those crimes most severely. The seven-step method could hardly do that without taking into account how (rational) criminals choose crimes.

When I say that the seven-step method takes the criminal's perspective into account, of course I do not mean that anyone using the method must consciously take into account what criminals think. I mean just the opposite. Because the seven-step method has a certain structure, a structure that implicitly fits the criminal's perspective, anyone using the method need only consciously take account of what the method says to take account of—which crimes rational people fear most, which penalties rational people fear most, and so on. Doing that is, in effect, taking the criminal's perspective into account.

Indeed, the seven-step method takes the criminal's perspective into account in two ways. One is step 5's ranking (both within each type and between types). The ranking captures the structure of "demand." The other way the seven-step method takes the criminal's perspective into account is by arranging penalties so that the more severe penalties go to the more serious crimes (that is, the crimes that rational people fear more); the less severe, to the less serious. The seven-step method is, in effect, a procedure for guiding "consumption of crime" into those channels society is most willing to tolerate. In this respect too, it resembles the market. Markets guide consumption (whatever their participants intend).

I have now shown that the seven-step method is much more like the market than critics have supposed. The central features of the method—ranking within type, connecting of types, and connecting with penalties—correspond to central features of the market. This structural isomorphism means that the criminal's perspective will have a place in the seven-step method equivalent to its place in the market. I shall now show that, though the market may seem to take account only of the criminal's perspective, it in fact takes as much account of society's perspective as the seven-step method does. The two procedures are in fact equivalent.

As I imagine the market, society only offers a certain number of licenses for each crime. The number is determined by the amount of that crime the society is willing to tolerate. For example, the society might offer only 1,000 robbery licenses each week but 10,000 burglary licenses. A society's willingness to tolerate crime will depend on at least two factors. One is the amount of income produced by licenses for that crime. The other is how much people fear the crime. The more people fear a crime, the higher society's probable "return" on a license will have to be for it to offer the license for sale. The society will seek to maximize net return (subject perhaps to certain distributive constraints).

Talk of such calculations may strike many otherwise sympathetic readers as sufficiently odd to discredit the whole analysis. I urge them to reconsider. Any society will make similar calculations. For example, if "too many" burglaries occur in a given neighborhood, the police may increase patrols, go door-to-door advising residents how to discourage burglars, and perhaps set up a fencing operation nearby to ensnare some of the burglars. The criminal law's resources are always limited (and usually fully employed). Distributing those resources so as to discourage burglary in this neighborhood rather than robbery in another may force the burglary rate in the one neighborhood back "into line" while allowing the robbery rate in the other to remain where it is or even continue to rise. The calculation upon which such decisions depend, whether implicit or explicit, is the practical counterpart of the market calculation determining whether to offer 100 more licenses to burgle or 10 more licenses to rob.

That is one kind of calculation any society makes. Another determines the share of total resources to devote to controlling crime. We could have less crime than we now have if we were willing to do more. We have the amount of crime we do because we are unwilling to allow more intrusive police surveillance, to use money now devoted to farm subsidies to increase welfare payments, to legalize recreational use of cocaine, heroin, and marijuana, and so on. The income from sale of licenses corresponds to the resources made available in our society by not doing more to control crime.

That, I hope, is enough to dispel the impression that our imagined market is too contrived to help us understand the criminal law (either as it is or as it should be).

AN OBJECTION FROM
CRIMINAL DESERT

We have now shown that our imagined market and the seven-step method each reproduce the structure underlying the other. Contrary to what critics claimed, we have no reason to expect the two procedures to produce inconsistent results. The two are alternate ways of doing the same thing. The advantage of the market over the seven-step method is that it spotlights the criminal's calculations. The advantage of the seven-step method over the market is that it spotlights society's efforts to guide the consumption of crime.

We have shown the seven-step method and the market to be more or less equivalent, but have we done that in a way that makes the market useless for gauging criminal desert? Scheid thinks so:

> To the extent that prices go up or down with supply, they do not accurately reflect unfair advantages [the basis of criminal desert]. Rather, the prices reflect the irrelevant factor of different supplies of licenses for different crimes which differences are, in turn, reflections of a pre-auction notion of seriousness of the

different crimes. Thus, the prices will be biased indicators of
the amount of punishment that should be attached.[23]

Why does Scheid think the effect that supply has on price
biases measurement of criminal desert (the value of the unfair
advantage the criminal takes by a crime)? "[Price should]," Scheid claims, "reflect which crimes the bidders regarded as more
valuable, without also reflecting variations in supplies of different crime licenses."[24] Scheid's objection thus presupposes that
the value of the unfair advantage a criminal takes is to be
measured solely by how much the bidders value what they bid
on, ignoring supply. The value of unfair advantage is, according
to Scheid, subjective (in this sense).[25] That, I think, is a mistake. Objective rather than subjective value is the proper measure of the unfair advantage a criminal takes simply by
committing a particular crime. The market we have imagined
measures what it should.

There are two ways to show this. One is to point out that (as
we have just seen) the seven-step method should give the same
results as the market does. Since neither Scheid nor any other
critic has yet objected to the seven-step method, none should
object to the market, either. Unfortunately, this *ad hominem* argument is unlikely to be decisive. Though no critic has yet objected to the seven-step method, many, including Scheid, might
object once convinced that it mirrors the market.[26]

The other way to show that the market measures what it should
is to show that objective rather than subjective value is crucial
to a (rational) criminal's choice of crime. Subjective value, having only a subsidiary role in the choice of crime, cannot determine what the criminal deserves for that choice. Objective value,
being crucial to that choice, can. I shall now show that.

I begin with the obvious. A rational criminal deciding which
crime to commit will take into account how society routinely
deploys all its resources (not just statutory penalties). All else
equal, he will prefer "easy pickings." If he nonetheless commits a riskier crime, he will do it because the advantage of
getting away with it is (in prospect) greater than the advantage of getting away with any less risky alternative. Consider
this example:

All else equal, robbery may or may not be more attractive
than theft to a particular criminal. But if getting away with rob-

bery is harder than getting away with theft, a potential criminal can rationally choose robbery over theft only if the probable return at least makes up for the greater risk. For the probable return to make up for the greater risk, getting away with robbery must be more advantageous than getting away with theft. The value of the unfair advantage the robbery takes must be greater than the value of the unfair advantage the theft takes.

That is not because robbery is necessarily riskier than theft. It is not. Robbery is riskier than theft only if a social decision makes it so. In this society, robbery is riskier than theft because, for example, we devote proportionally more resources to hunting down robbers than to hunting down thieves. In this society, then, a criminal cannot rationally commit robbery unless getting away with it is worth more than getting away with theft. The crime he can rationally commit is (in part) a function of what the society fears, not simply of what he happens to value.

The crime he can rationally commit is also a function of other objective factors. A would-be criminal must decide how much effort (and other resources) to put into a crime. While he cannot rationally invest more than the advantage he expects from it (after discounting for risk), he might well invest considerably less. Insofar as he is rational, he will invest no more than necessary. So, how much he actually invests in committing a crime would indicate the minimum value of the unfair advantage he expected (discounted for risk), not the actual value to him.

How much that is will, in turn, depend on more than what he happens to regard as valuable. He should take into account both legal and illegal alternatives to the crime in question, "the opportunity costs" of the crime. Among the factors determining opportunity costs are what other criminals are doing. For example, the more bank robberies there are, the more resources a would-be robber will have to invest in a bank robbery to get the same return. (A bank robbed too often becomes a fortress or disappears.) If too many others have already chosen to rob banks, the advantages of bank robbery will not be enough to pay for the effort necessary to succeed. Our would-be robber will have been "outbid." He will have to choose another crime or go straight. Subjective evaluation plays only a small part in the (rational) criminal's choice of crime. In this respect, our society does not differ from the one in which we imagined the auction.

Yet one question remains. A license bought at our auction guarantees only that if the holder commits the appropriate crime and is then captured, tried, convicted, and sentenced, she can hand in the license and be excused from punishment. The license pardons. It does not guarantee success (for example, that a thief will get to keep what she has stolen for more than an instant). The value of the license must, then, depend on the possibilities that the crime in prospect opens up. These are possibilities closed off while the would-be criminal obeys the law. Cheater's advantage necessarily consists of only these possibilities—not of freedom, the profits of a particular crime, or the subjective pleasure of doing as one wishes. Cheater's advantage is what the criminal gets simply by breaking the law in question. Can the market measure the value of this advantage?

It can, but only if we exclude all irrelevant factors. So, for example, we must imagine that the society hosting the market punishes all *un*licensed crime the same—as "poaching" (or instead, that poaching is impossible in that society). That assumption filters out the bias that differential punishment for poaching would otherwise introduce.[27] Once all irrelevant factors are excluded, the maximum a potential criminal could rationally bid for a certain license should correspond to the value of the unfair advantage she takes simply by committing the crime. The more valuable the unfair advantage, the more she could rationally bid.

What can a bidder rationally bid? That depends in part on what others bid. The bidder should offer no more than necessary to get the license she needs. In other words, she should offer no more than necessary to outbid for the last license. So, insofar as bidders are rational, the market price of a certain license will tend to approximate what is necessary to win the bidding on the last license of that kind. Since the winning bidder might well have been willing to pay much more than necessary, what the criminal paid for a license indicates only the *minimum* she thinks it worth, not its full value to her. The price she pays will in a large part be an indication of what she supposes it rational for others to bid for the last license of that kind.

We have now shown that what bidders can rationally bid for a license is objective in a way that how much they (rationally or irrationally) value it is not. What we have shown will, I think, be true in any market that is at least as acceptable a model of the criminal law as the one we have imagined. Earlier we showed that allowing society to control the supply of licenses in our imagined market makes the market more like the criminal law of any society much like ours than disallowing it would. Rational criminals do in fact take "supply" into account in determining which crimes to commit. So, since the (rational) criminal's choice determines criminal desert (at least for retributivists), our market, not Scheid's subjective alternative, should gauge criminal desert better.

Scheid is mistaken about the market as we imagined it. It does not merely reflect society's "pre-auction notion of seriousness." Society cannot control prices simply by controlling supply. Another factor, the criminal's rational expectation of advantage, also figures in. In this world, that expectation includes how much crime society is willing to tolerate. But, as in the market, it includes more—the alternatives to the crime in question (including other crimes) and the conduct of other criminals. Society's fear of crime, while relevant enough to criminal desert not to be inherently "biasing" when allowed to constrain supply, is not so relevant to market price that the market becomes a mere reflection of that fear. So, as we have imagined the market, price is an unbiased indicator of criminal desert.

A "COUNTEREXAMPLE" COUNTERED

I have, I believe, now refuted the general criticism that Duff, Scheid, and von Hirsch made of the market as a measure of criminal desert. I shall conclude by disposing of one putative counterexample. The ease with which I do that should add authority to the argument already given and provide a pattern for disposing of similar objections.[28]

One way von Hirsch tries to show how "alien" the market is to criminal desert is by asking us to compare two crimes, "aggravated assault" (threatening or actually attempting aggravated battery) and "[grand] theft" (theft of a "fairly substantial sum," say, $300). As von Hirsch correctly observes, "Most people would rate the former the more serious conduct because the interest it intrudes upon—the victim's physical safety—is deemed more important than the monetary interests that theft threatens."[29] But measured by benefit to the criminal (as the market does in part), not assault but theft would seem the more serious crime. Since "people do not generally judge the gravity of crimes by talking about how much they would pay to be permitted to engage in conduct," von Hirsch concludes that aggravated assault, not grand theft, deserves the more severe punishment.[30] The market cannot be a good guide to criminal desert.

This argument includes no reference to a criminal code, a curious omission in a writer who, like von Hirsch, has actually had a hand in writing the sentencing provisions of more than one. What would we find if we actually consulted such a code? In Illinois, aggravated assault is a class-A *misdemeanor*, punishable by less than a year in jail, while theft of more than $300 is a class-3 *felony*, punishable by two to five years in prison.[31] Even aggravated battery is ranked no higher than theft of more than $300.[32] In Illinois, at least, practice is against von Hirsch.

What has gone wrong? The market helps to explain. Von Hirsch has assumed that how people rate their interests in property and physical safety is the *sole* factor determining criminal desert (culpability aside). He has overlooked the connection between such interests and how the criminal chooses a crime. One advantage of the market is that it reminds us to consider the criminal's perspective, "demand," as well as society's perspective, "supply." Because the market takes demand into account as well as supply, it explains actual statutory schemes better than von Hirsch's alternative.

This is not to say that the market requires that grand theft be punished more severely than aggravated assault. What the market requires depends a good deal on the statutory scheme (on the number of stops on each line as well as where the lines intersect). For example, let us suppose a statutory scheme with seven classes of penalty (for example, A, B, and C misdemeanors and 1–4 felonies). If theft were divided into five classes (theft under $100, theft of $100-$300, theft above $300 but less than $1000, and so on), theft of $300 would rank lower relative to aggravated assault than if theft were divided into only two classes (say, petty theft, under $300, and grand theft, $300 or more). Theft and assault come into relation through connections at the upper end of the penalty scale, beginning, say, with robbery. If each class of theft is assigned a different penalty (the point of having such classes), the effect of having five classes of theft instead of two is to reduce the maximum penalty permissible for a theft of $300. Given enough classes of theft, von Hirsch's intuition might be realized—but not for the reason that he gives.[33]

Though the market will in fact give this result, the seven-step method gives the same result more quickly. Our intuitions about ranking within type of crime and about connecting types are generally much clearer than our intuitions about the market. The market is an alternative to intuitions, a model forcing us to make our reasoning explicit. That, I think, is why (as von Hirsch says) in practice people generally decide how much to punish crime without talking about how much they would pay to engage in this or that crime. The market becomes useful only when our intuitions are not clear, or we wonder whether our intuitions are reliable. The market is a tool of theory.[34]

I began with a general criticism of the fairness theory. I refuted certain recent versions of that criticism, beginning with Dolinko's. I hope that one effect of these refutations is to raise doubts about the criticism itself. Crime, or at least the criminal law, presupposes a social background. Why should that social background not guarantee a connection between unfair advantage and seriousness in something like the way I have suggested? Critics of the fairness theory of criminal desert have yet to address the question with any care.[35]

NOTES

I should like to thank Don Scheid, R. A. Duff, and participants in the Philosophy Colloquium, Illinois Institute of Technology, 16 October 1991, for helpful comments on early drafts of this chapter.

1. David Dolinko, "Some Thoughts about Retributivism," *Ethics* 101 (April 1991): 537–59. For Dolinko's response to the argument made here, see his "Mismeasuring 'Unfair Advantage': A Response to Michael Davis," *Law and Philosophy* 13 (November 1994): 493–524; for my reply, see "Method in Punishment Theory," *Law and Philosophy*, forthcoming.

2. Dolinko, 539.

3. Dolinko, 545.

4. Dolinko, 545.

5. Dolinko, 545.

6. Dolinko, 545.

7. Dolinko, 545–46.

8. Dolinko, 546.

9. Dolinko, 547–48. Dolinko seems unaware of Richard Burgh's well-known paper, "Do the Guilty Deserve Punishment?" *Journal of Philosophy* 790 (April 1982): 193–210. He might have benefited from reading it. Burgh distinguishes four possible interpretations of unfair advantage, while Dolinko only manages two (both versions of Burgh's second).

10. Dolinko, 548.

11. Dolinko responded to this interpretation, "Mismeasuring," 497: "Davis has misunderstood me; I nowhere asserted that confiscating the proceeds of a crime would count as 'removing the benefit the criminal took.' That 'benefit,' on the view whose appeal I admitted, is supposed to lie in the criminal's enjoying freedom from aggression and interference by others. Removing the benefit would therefore mean permitting others to interfere at will with the criminal's interest, not merely compelling the restitution of ill-gotten gains." In other words, what Dolinko found attractive was the idea of outlawing the criminal (whatever her crime). That unproportionate response strikes me as considerably less attractive than the interpretation I suggest here. I have therefore left it just in case anyone else finds it attractive.

12. Dolinko, 539n.

13. Dolinko now agrees: "The Davis version of the fairness theory, I now concede, *should* be examined by those of us who take a dim view of retributivism." "Mismeasuring," 494.

14. R. A. Duff, "Auctions, Lotteries, and the Punishment of Attempts," *Law and Philosophy* 9 (February 1990): 1–37; Don E. Scheid, "Davis and the Unfair-Advantage Theory of Punishment: A Critique," *Philosophical Topics* 18 (Spring 1990): 143–70; and Andrew von Hirsch, "Proportionality in the Philosophy of Punishment: From 'Why Punish?' to 'How Much?'" *Criminal Law Forum* 1 (Winter 1990): 259–90.

15. Von Hirsch, 266–67. Compare Duff, 15–16 ("we can have no confidence that the auction will generate a ranking of crimes . . . which matches at all closely what we would regard as a plausible ranking according to their seriousness"); and Scheid, 158 ("it does not rectify what standard principles of corrective justice require"). See also Hyman Gross, "Fringe Liability, Unfair Advantage, and the Price of Crime," *Wayne Law Review* (Summer 1987): 1395–411, especially 1401.

16. Michael Davis, "How to Make the Punishment Fit the Crime," *Ethics* 93 (July 1983): 736–37 (brackets indicate changes made to clar-

ify). Scheid, 169 (note 51), remarks the resemblance between this procedure and that found in John Kleinig, *Punishment and Desert* (The Hague: Martinus Nijhoff, 1973), chapter 7. John Braithwaite and Philip Pettit, *Not Just Deserts* (Oxford: Clarendon Press, 1990), 150, do the same. The two procedures should not be confused. Like Mabbott's, the parent of both, mine is designed for justified criminal punishment (and close relatives), not (as Kleinig's is) for *any* morally justified punishment. Some details, especially ranking by type, are new (and as I will soon show, important). Compare J. D. Mabbott, "Punishment," *Mind* 48 (April 1939): 152–67, especially 162. (I am embarrassed to say that I did not come across Kleinig's book until 1988.)

17. Note that my analysis of seriousness of crime (what rational people fear) differs from the common retributivist analysis in terms of "harm." For the importance of this difference, see *To Make the Punishment Fit the Crime*, chapter 3. For an (unintended) illustration of the disadvantages of harm, see Andrew von Hirsch and Nils Jareborg, "Gauging Criminal Harm: A Living-Standard Analysis," *Oxford Journal of Legal Studies* 11 (Spring 1991): 1–38. Von Hirsch here limits himself to crimes with identifiable victims (a small part of the criminal law) and to sentencing within a statutory scheme rather than to setting statutory penalties. This, of course, is by far the easiest part of the problem of determining just deserts. Even so, he promises much while delivering little.

18. "How to Make the Punishment Fit the Crime," 742–46.

19. *To Make the Punishment Fit the Crime*, chapter 10.

20. I owe this convenient term to Scheid, 157. Note his observations that "[Davis has provided] a fifth possible meaning . . . to be added to Burgh's list [of four]."

21. While not the only objection these three writers make in the papers cited, it is the only one I shall be concerned with here—both because space does not allow me to do much more and because I believe that I have dealt adequately with the remaining important ones elsewhere. See "Postscript: In Fairness to Condemnation," *Israeli Law Review* 25 (Summer-Autumn 1991): 581–94; and *To Make the Punishment Fit the Crime*, chapters 9 and 10.

22. Compare Scheid, 163: "[The fairness] theory requires more than simple ordinal matching and more than proportional matching." It requires matchings that exactly annul, that is, absolute matching. Scheid is mistaken only in thinking absolute matching a problem for the fairness theory. Scheid thinks it a problem because he assumes matching must be a *natural* fact (analogous to the energy necessary to change ice to water). In fact, "absolute matching" is, like "full payment," not a natural fact but a social relation presupposing conventions for set-

ting "prices" and making "payment." Criminal desert presupposes a complex social relation, the criminal law of a relatively just society (including both a list of crimes and a list of penalties). The fairness theory provides a means for *constructing* a system of exact matching *within the bounds of justice*, not for discovering it in nature. Those who look for just punishment in nature will find nothing but scattered boulders waiting the hand of architect and mason. Those who look for it within the complex social relations of the criminal law will find a structure enough like the market's to make the market a useful model for determining what justice allows (or, in some cases, requires).

23. Scheid, 148–149.

24. Scheid, 149.

25. Compare Scheid, 147–148: "Strictly speaking, the amount of money would-be criminals pay for crime licenses under the model will reflect their (aggregate) *perception* of the (unfair) advantage they expect to gain by committing the crime, rather than the unfair advantages that actually accrue. Nevertheless, while crime-license prices will reflect subjective perceptions, the relative ranking of actually-accruing advantage might well come out the same, especially under an on-going market arrangement."

26. Dolinko has now objected in "Mismeasuring 'Unfair Advantage': A Response to Michael Davis," *Law and Philosophy* 13 (November 1994): 493–524. Scheid has demurred in "Davis, Unfair Advantage Theory, and Criminal Desert," *Law and Philosophy* 14 (November 1995): 375–409.

27. Compare Duff, 12–13, with *To Make the Punishment Fit the Crime*, chapter 10, especially, 244–247. One of the reviewers at *Law and Philosophy* raised a related objection: "The 'supply' of crimes is determined by looking at the resources we currently devote to preventing various crimes and thus to the level of each type we are willing to tolerate. But among other things that determine supply is the severity of punishment we mete out for each crime. We can reduce crime either by devoting more resources to the police, etc., *or* by increasing the severity of punishment. Therefore the supply of crime is a function of the severity of punishment we choose. But the 'price' of crime—and therefore the unfair advantage it represents—is a function of its supply (as well as of demand). And the 'price' is a measure of criminal desert. Thus, it seems to follow that criminal desert is a function of the severity of the punishment we choose! But this can't be correct . . ." It isn't. The point of the assumptions defining the market is to filter out irrelevant factors. If an argument (such as this one) reveals an irrelevant factor, then I will try to filter it out. But there is no need to do that this time. The critic has simply con-

fused the model with what it models. He is right that, *in the model*, supply is determined by a social decision, one presumably made by looking at the resources the society wants to devote to prevention. But he is wrong that severity of punishment is a factor in determining supply in a way threatening the model. I originally avoided that threat by recognizing "poaching" as a possible metacrime to be punished in the *same* way *whatever* the corresponding license would be. For those who find "poaching" troublesome, I offered instead the less plausible (but still workable) assumption that no crime will be committed without a license (so long as licenses are not too few). Either way, the differentials in demand for crime will not be a function of differentials in severity of punishment for those crimes. Only in this world (rather than in the model) does "price" (severity of punishment) affect "demand" (incidence of crime). How much effect is, of course, a vexed question. But whatever it is, in this world, desert should be figured ignoring that effect (as it is in the seven-step method).

28. For example, Duff, 9–10; and Scheid, 160–161.

29. Von Hirsch, 267.

30. Von Hirsch, 267.

31. *Illinois Criminal Law and Procedure* (St. Paul, Minn.: West Publishing Company, 1991), ch. 38 sec. 12–2 and sec. 1005-8-3; ch. 38 sec. 12–3 and sec. 1005-8-1.

32. *Illinois Criminal Law*, ch. 38 sec. 16-1.

33. We can quickly respond to Dolinko's counterexample to Sher in the same way. Murder, a violent crime, will have to be ranked against other violent crimes like battery, aggravated battery, armed robbery, and so on. Given a choice between being robbed at gunpoint and being murdered (with or without robbery), most of us would choose being robbed. So, murder must be ranked higher than armed robbery. Given a choice between suffering armed robbery (in ourselves or through those we care about), most of us would choose to suffer tax evasion. So, tax evasion must be ranked lower than armed robbery. And so, contrary to what Dolinko supposed, the fairness theory would rank tax evasion below murder, not above it (even though they never come into direct comparison).

34. I make this point explicitly in *To Make the Punishment Fit the Crime*, 66. For an example of how the seven-step method might be used to settle a controversy, see chapter 11. For examples of the use of the market on more complex issues, see *To Make the Punishment Fit the Crime*, chapters 5 (attempts), 6 (habitual offender statutes), and 7 (strict liability).

35. Perhaps this is the place to deal summarily with a related criticism that von Hirsch, 269, citing Duff, makes. There is, he thinks,

something artificial about explaining the sentence of a convicted murderer or robber only by the unfair advantage he took. We should also refer to the harm he did, to the rights he violated, or to other morally interesting features. I agree. So? As I understand the sentencing process, any reference to relative unfair advantage is appropriate only to explain why the maximum legal punishment for that crime is deserved. The judge is free to refer to the harm the criminal did, to the rights he violated, and so on, to explain the crime's relative rank, since such matters are relevant to "supply" decisions (as I have been at pains to argue) and so to unfair advantage. The judge is also free to refer to such things for other purposes, for example, to explain why she did not show mercy, to remind the criminal of the nonlegal reasons for not committing the crime, or simply to express her outrage at the crime. The fairness theory does not forbid carrying out such other purposes during sentencing (though it does limit how such purposes can be carried out). Much the same would be true of legislative discussions.

Bibliography

American Law Institute, *American Jurisprudence*, 2nd ed. Rochester, New York: Lawyers' Cooperative Publishing Co., 1972.

American Medical Association. *Code of Medical Ethics: Current Opinions of the Council on Ethical and Judicial Affairs of the American Medical Association.* Chicago: American Medical Association, 1992.

American Medical Association. "Physician Participation in Capital Punishment (Resolution 5, I-91)," Report A of Council on Ethical and Judicial Affairs, Chicago: American Medical Association, December 1992.

Amir, Manachem. *Patterns of Forcible Rape.* Chicago: University of Chicago Press, 1971.

Annotated California Codes. St. Paul, Minn.: West Publishing Co., 1983.

Arneson, Richard J. "The Principle of Fairness and Free-Rider Problems." *Ethics* 92 (July 1982): 616–633.

Babcock, Barbara et al., *Sex Discrimination and the Law.* Boston: Little, Brown, 1975.

Baird, Robert M. and Stuart E. Rosenbaum, editors. *Philosophy of Punishment.* Buffalo, NY: Prometheus Books, 1988.

Bedau, Hugo Adam. *The Courts, the Constitution, and Capital Punishment.* Lexington, Mass.: D.C. Heath, 1977.

———. *Death is Different: Studies in the Morality, Law, and Politics of Capital Punishment.* Boston: Northeastern University Press, 1987.

———. "How to Argue about the Death Penalty." *Israel Law Review* 25 (Summer-Autumn 1991): 466–480.

———. "Thinking About the Death Penalty as a Cruel and Unusual Punishment." *U.C. Davis Law Review* 18 (Summer 1985): 873–925.

————. "The Death Penalty as Deterrent—Argument and Evidence." *Ethics* 81 (April 1972): 205–217.

————, ed. *The Death Penalty in America: An Anthology*, 3rd. ed. New York: Oxford University Press, 1982.

Bedau, Hugo Adam and Chester M. Pierce, eds. *Capital Punishment in the United States*. New York: AMS Press, 1976.

Belliotti, Raymond. "A Philosophical Analysis of Sexual Ethics." *Journal of Social Philosophy* 10 (January 1979): 8–11.

Berns, Walter. *For Capital Punishment: Crime and the Morality of the Death Penalty*. New York: Basic Books, 1979.

Berger, Vivian. "Man's Trial, Woman's Tribulation: Rape Cases in the Courtroom." *Columbia Law Review* 77 (January 1977): 1–101.

Bienen, Leigh. "Mistakes." *Philosophy & Public Affairs* 7 (Spring 1978): 224–245.

Bonnie, Richard J. "The death penalty: When doctors must say no." *British Medical Journal* 305 (15 August 1992): 381–382.

————. "Medical Ethics and the Death Penalty." *Hastings Center Report* (May/June 1990): 12–18.

Braithwaite, John and Philip Pettit. *Not Just Deserts*. Oxford: Clarendon Press, 1990.

Brandt, Richard B. "The Morality and Rationality of Suicide." In *A Handbook for the Study of Suicide*, ed. Seymour Perlin. New York: Oxford University Press, 1975.

British Medical Association. *Medicine Betrayed: The Participation of Doctors in Human Rights Abuses*. London: Zed Books, 1992.

Brownmiller, Susan. *Against Our Will*. New York: Simon and Schuster, 1975.

Burgh, Richard. "Do the Guilty Deserve Punishment?" *Journal of Philosophy* 790 (April 1982): 193–210.

Coker v. Georgia, 433 U.S. 584, 97 S.Ct. 2861 (1977).

Conter, David. "Feinberg on Rescue, Victims, and Rights," *Canadian Journal of Law and Jurisprudence* 4 (January 1991): 133–144.

Conway, David A. "Capital Punishment and Deterrence," *Philosophy and Public Affairs* 3 (Summer 1974): 431–443.

Cooper, David D. *The Lesson of the Gallows*. Athens, Ohio: Ohio University Press, 1974.

Copp, David. "Responsibility for Collective Inaction." *Journal of Social Philosophy* 22 (Fall 1991): 71–80.

Federal Bureau of Investigation, *Crime in the United States.* Washington, D.C.: U.S. Government Printing Office, 1980.

Curley, E. M. "Excusing Rape." *Philosophy & Public Affairs* 5 (Summer 1976): 325–360.

Curran, William and Ward Casscells. "The Ethics of Medical Participation in Capital Punishment by Intravenous Drug Injection." *New England Journal of Medicine* 302 (24 January 1980): 226–230.

Davis, Michael. "Brandt on Autonomy." In *Rationality and Rule-Utilitarianism*, ed. Brad Hooker. Boulder, CO: Westview Press, 1993, 51–65.

———. "Death, Deterrence, and the Method of Common Sense." *Social Theory and Practice* 7 (Summer 1981): 145–177.

———. "Do Cops Need a Code of Ethics?" *Criminal Justice Ethics* 10 (Summer/Fall 1991): 14–28.

———. "How to Make the Punishment Fit the Crime." *Ethics* 93 (July 1983): 736–737.

———. "The Moral Authority of a Professional Code." *NOMOS* 29 (1987): 302–337.

———. "The Moral Status of Dogs, Forests, and Other Persons." *Social Theory and Practice* 12 (Spring 1986): 27-59.

———. "Method in Punishment Theory." *Law and Philosophy*, forthcoming.

———. "Professionalism Means Putting Your Profession First." *Georgetown Journal of Legal Ethics* 2 (Summer 1988): 352–366.

———. "Postscript: In Fairness to Condemnation." *Israel Law Review* 25 (Summer-Autumn 1991): 581–594.

———. "Review of *Why Punish?*" *Law and Philosophy* 12 (November 1993): 51–63.

———. "Thinking Like an Engineer: The Place of a Code of Ethics in the Practice of a Profession." *Philosophy & Public Affairs* 20 (Spring 1991): 150–167.

———. "Nozick's Argument *for* the Legitimacy of the Welfare State." *Ethics* 97 (April 1987): 576–94.

———. *To Make the Punishment Fit the Crime.* Boulder, CO: Westview Press, 1992.

————. "Treating Patients with Infectious Diseases: An Essay in the Ethics of Dentistry." *Professional Ethics* 2 (Spring/Summer 1993): 51–65.

————. "The Use of Professions." *Business Economics* 22 (October 1987): 5–10.

————. "Vocational Teachers, Confidentiality, and Professional Ethics." *International Journal of Applied Philosophy* 4 (Spring 1988): 11–20.

Deming, Mary Beard and Eppy, Ali. "The Sociology of Rape," *Sociology and Social Research* 65 (July 1981): 357–380.

Denton, Frank E. "The Case Against a Duty to Rescue." *Canadian Journal of Law and Jurisprudence* 4 (January 1991): 101–132.

Dolinko, David. "Mismeasuring 'Unfair Advantage': A Response to Michael Davis." *Law and Philosophy* 13 (November 1994): 493–524.

————. "Some Thoughts about Retributivism." *Ethics* 101 (April 1991): 537–559.

Duff, R. A. "Auctions, Lotteries, and the Punishment of Attempts." *Law and Philosophy* 9 (February 1990): 1–37.

————. *Trials and Punishments*. Cambridge: Cambridge University Press, 1985.

Durkheim, Emile. "Two Laws of Penal Evolution," *Economy and Society* 2 (1973): 285–308. This is a translation by T. Anthony Jones and Andrew Scull of an essay originally published in *Année Sociologique* 4 (1899–1900).

Ehrlich, Isaac. "The Deterrent Effect of Capital Punishment: A Question of Life and Death," *American Economic Review* 65 (June 1975): 397–417.

Ellis, Ralph D. and Carol S. Ellis. *Theories of Criminal Justice*. Wolfeboro, New Hampshire: Longwood Academic, 1989.

Entman, Howard. "First Do No Harm." *Journal of the American Medical Association* 261 (6 January 1989): 134.

Fair and Certain Punishment: Report of the Twentieth Century Fund Task Force on Criminal Sentencing. New York: McGraw–Hill, 1976.

Feinberg, Joel. *Harm to Others*. New York: Oxford University Press, 1986.

Feldbrugge, F. J. M. "Good and Bad Samaritans: A Comparative Survey of Criminal Law Provisions Concerning Failure to

Rescue." *The American Journal of Comparative Law* 14 (1966): 630–657.

Furman v. Georgia, 408 U.S. 238, 92 S. Ct. 2726 (1972).

Gansberg, Martin. "37 Who Saw Murder Didn't Call the Police: Apathy at Stabbing of Queens Woman Shocks Inspector." *New York Times*, Friday, 27 March 1964, 1, 38.

Geis, Gilbert. "Sanctioning the Operation of Portugal's New 'Bad Samaritan' Statute." *International Journal of Victimology* 1 (1991): 297–313.

Gert, Bernard. *The Moral Rules*. New York: Harper Torchbooks, 1973.

Gewirth, Alan. *Reason and Morality*. Chicago: University of Chicago Press, 1978.

Gross, Hyman. "Culpability and Desert." *Archiv Für Rechts Unter Sozialphilosophie* 19 (1984): 59–69.

———. "Fringe Liability, Unfair Advantage, and the Price of Crime." *Wayne Law Review* (Summer 1987): 1395–1411.

———. *A Theory of Criminal Justice*. New York: Oxford University Press, 1979.

Groth, A. Nicholas. *Men Who Rape*. New York: Plenum Press, 1979.

Hallie, Phillip P. *Cruelty*. Middletown, CT: Wesleyan University Press, 1982.

Hampton, Jean. "The Moral Education Theory of Punishment." *Philosophy & Public Affairs* 13 (Summer 1984): 208–238.

Hart, H. L. A. "Murder and the Principles of Punishment: England and the United States." *Northwestern Law Review* 52 (September 1957): 433–461.

Henderson, Lynne. "Rape and Responsibility." *Law and Philosophy* 11 (February–May 1992): 127–178.

Hillman, Harold. "An unnatural way to die." *New Scientist* (27 October 1983): 276–278.

Hoffman, Susan J. "Statutes Establish a Duty to Report Crimes or Render Assistance to Strangers: Making Apathy Criminal." *Kentucky Law Journal* 72 (1983–84): 827–865.

Hornum, Finn. "Two Debates: France, 1791; England, 1956." In *Capital Punishment*, ed. Thorsten Sellin. New York: Harper & Row, 1967.

Hsieh, Dennis S. "Physicians Should Give Injections." *Journal of the American Medical Association* 261 (6 January 1989): 132.

Hughes, Paul M. "Bad Samaritans, Morality, and the Law." *International Journal of Applied Philosophy* 7 (Winter 1992): 9–13.

Husak, Douglas N. *Drugs and Rights.* New York: Cambridge University Press, 1992.

———. "Is Drunk Driving A Serious Offense?" *Philosophy & Public Affairs* 23 (Winter 1994): 52–73.

———. *Philosophy of Criminal Law.* Totowa, New Jersey: Rowman & Littlefield, 1987.

Illinois Criminal Law and Procedures. St. Paul, Minn.: West Publishing Company, 1983.

Illinois Criminal Law and Procedures. St. Paul, Minn.: West Publishing Company, 1991.

Jacobs, Susan L. "Legal Advocacy in a Time of Plague." *Journal of Law, Medicine, and Ethics* 21 (Fall–Winter 1993): 383–389.

Kadish, Sanford. "Complicity, Cause, and Blame: A Study in the Interpretation of Doctrine." *California Law Review* 73 (March 1985): 323–410

Karwath, Rob. "Death's arrival one of precision." *Chicago Tribune*, 11 September 1990, 6.

Karwath, Bob and William Grady. "Walker becomes 1st execution in 28 years." *Chicago Tribune*, Wednesday, 12 September 1990, 1.

Katz, Sedelle and Mary Ann Mazur. *Understanding the Rape Victim.* New York: Wiley, 1979.

Kennedy, Daniel B. "A Public Guardian Represents a Fetus: Court refuses request for a C-section and boy is born apparently healthy." *American Bar Association Journal* (March 1994): 27.

Kevorkian, Jack. "Medicine, ethics, and execution by lethal injection." *Medicine and Law* 4 (July 1985): 307–313.

Kipnis, Kenneth. "Heath Care Ethics: Establishing Standards of Professional Conduct." *Corrections Today* 54 (October 1992): 92–95.

Kleinig, John. *Punishment and Desert.* The Hague: Martinus Nijhoff, 1973.

LaFave, Wayne R. and Austin W. Scott, Jr. *Criminal Law.* St. Paul, Minn.: West Publishing Co., 1972.

Leiser, Burton M. *Liberty, Justice, and Morals*, 2nd ed. New York: Macmillan, 1979.

Levine, Robert J. *Ethics and Regulation of Clinical Research*, 2nd. ed. New Haven: Yale University Press, 1988.

Mabbott, J. D. "Punishment." *Mind* 48 (April 1939): 152–167.

Mack, Eric. "Bad Samaritanism and the Causation of Harm." *Philosophy & Public Affairs* 9 (Spring 1980): 230–259.

MacKinnon, Catherine. *Toward a Feminist Theory of the State.* Harvard University Press: Cambridge, Massachusetts, 1989.

McIntyre, Alison. "Guilty Bystanders? On the Legitimacy of Duty to Rescue Statutes." *Philosophy & Public Affairs* 23 (Spring 1994): 157–191.

Milgram, Stanley and Paul Hollander. "The Murder They Heard." *Nation* 198 (15 June 1964): 602–604.

Mill, John Stuart. "Speech in Favor of Capital Punishment." In *Philosophy of Law*, ed. Joel Feinberg and Hyman Gross. Encino, CA: Dickenson Publishing Company, 1975.

Moore, G. E. *Principia Ethica.* London: Cambridge University Press, 1966.

Moore, Kathleen. *Pardons.* New York: Oxford University Press, 1989.

Morris, Herbert. "A Paternalistic Theory of Punishment." *American Philosophical Review* 18 (October 1981): 263–271.

———. "Persons and Punishment." *Monist* 52 (October 1968): 475–501.

Morris, Norval. *Madness and the Criminal Law.* Chicago: University of Chicago Press, 1982.

Morse, Stephen J. "Excusing the Crazy: The Insanity Defense Reconsidered." *Southern California Law Review* 58 (March 1985): 777–836.

Nathanson, Stephen. *An Eye for an Eye? The Immorality of Punishing by Death.* Lanham, MD.: Rowman & Littlefield, 1987.

Note. "*Coker v. Georgia*: Disproportionate Punishment and the Death Penalty." *Columbia Law Review* 78 (December 1978): 1714–30.

Note. "Rape Laws, Equal Protection, and Privacy Rights." *Tulane Law Review* 54 (February 1980): 456–479.

Note. "Rape Reform Legislation: Is It the Solution?" *Cleveland State Law Review* 24 (Summer 1975): 463–503.

Note. "Rape in Illinois: A Denial of Equal Protection." *John Marshall Journal of Practice and Procedure* 8 (Spring 1975): 457–496.

Note. "Legislation: Rape and Other Sexual Offense Law Reform in Maryland 1976–1977." *Baltimore Law Review* 7 (Fall 1977): 151–70.

Note. "Unlawful Sexual Intercourse: Old Notions and a Suggested Reform." *Pacific Law Review* 12 (January 1980): 217–33.

Note. "Criminal Law—Equal Protection—Gender–Based Statutory Rape Provision Held Invalid." *Washington University Law Quarterly* 59 (Spring 1981): 310–17.

Nozick, Robert. *Philosophical Explanations*. Cambridge: Harvard University Press, 1981.

Parker-Gwilliam, Dai. "M.D. fights 'execution's assistant' role." *Loyola Magazine* (Spring 1993): 82.

Partridge, Eric. *Origins: A Short Etymological Dictionary of Modern English*. New York: Macmillan, 1958.

Peck, Jon K. "The Deterrent Effect of Capital Punishment: Ehrlich and his Critics." *Yale Law Journal* 85 (January, 1976): 359–367.

Perutz, M. F. "The White Plague." *New York Review of Books* 41 (26 May 1994): 35–39.

Pollack, Barry. "Deserts and Death: Limits on Maximum Punishment." *Rutgers Law Review* 44 (1992): 985–1019.

Pollock, Frederick and Frederic Maitland. *History of English Law*. 2nd ed. revised. London: Cambridge University Press, 1968.

Primoratz, Igor. *Justifying Legal Punishment*. Atlantic Highlands, NJ: Humanities Press Internation, 1989.

———. "Punishment as Language." *Philosophy* 64 (April 1989): 187–205.

Quenneville, Kathleen. "Will Rape Ever Be a Crime of the Past?: A Feminist View of Societal Factors and Rape Law Reform." *Golden Gate University Law Review* 9 (1978–79): 581–607.

Reiman, Jeffrey. "The Death Penalty, Deterrence, and Horribleness: A Reply to Michael Davis." *Social Theory and Practice* 16 (Summer 1990): 261–272.

———. "Justice, Civilization, and the Death Penalty: Answering van den Haag." *Philosophy and Public Affairs* 14 (Spring 1985): 115–148.

Rossi, Peter et al. "The Seriousness of Crimes: Normative Structure and Individual Differences." *American Sociological Review* 39 (April 1974): 224–227.

Ruthven, Malise. *Torture: The Grand Conspiracy.* London: Weidenfeld and Nicolson, 1978.

Schabas, William A. *The Abolition of the Death Penalty in International Law.* Cambridge, UK: Grotius Publications Limited, 1993.

Scheid, Don E. "Davis and the Unfair-Advantage Theory of Punishment: A Critique." *Philosophical Topics* 18 (Spring 1990): 143–170.

———. "Davis, Unfair Advantage Theory, and Criminal Desert." *Law and Philosophy* 14 (November 1995): 375–409.

Schoeman, Ferdinand D. "On Incapacitating the Dangerous." *American Philosophical Quarterly* 16 (January 1979): 27–35.

Sellin, Thorsten. *The Death Penalty.* Philadelphia: American Law Institute, 1959.

Sellin, Thorsten and Marvin Wolfgang. *The Measurement of Delinquency.* New York: John Wiley & Sons, 1964.

Sidel, Victor W., Ernest Drucker, and Steven C. Martin. "The Resurgence of Tuberculosis in the United States: Societal Origins and Societal Responses." *Journal of Law, Medicine and Ethics* 21 (Fall-Winter 1993): 303–316.

Simmons, A. John et al., eds. *Punishment.* Princeton: Princeton University Press, 1995.

Singer, Peter. "Famine, Affluence, and Morality." *Philosophy & Public Affairs* 7 (Spring 1972): 229–243

Skillen, A. J. "How to Say Things with Walls." *Philosophy* 55 (October 1980): 509–523.

Skolnick, Andrew A. "Health Professionals Oppose Rules Mandating Participation in Executions." *Journal of the American Medical Association* 269 (10 February 1993): 721–723.

Smith, Patricia. "The Duty to Rescue and the Slippery Slope Problem." *Social Theory and Practice* 16 (Spring 1990): 19–41.

Summer, L. S. "A Matter of Life and Death." *Nous* 10 (May 1976): 153–163.

U.S. National Criminal Justice Information and Statistics Service, *Sourcebook of Criminal Justice Statistics.* Washington: Government Printing Office, 1980.

van den Haag, Ernest. "On Deterrence and the Death Penalty." *Ethics* 78 (July 1968); 280–289.

van den Haag, Ernst. *Punishing Criminals.* New York: Basic Books, 1975.

Vettering-Braggin, Mary et al, eds. *Feminism and Philosophy.* Totowa, NJ: Littlefield, Adams & Co., 1977.

von Hirsch, Andrew. *Past or Future Crimes.* New Brunswick, NJ: Rutgers University Press, 1985.

―――. "Proportionality in the Philosophy of Punishment: From 'Why Punish?' to 'How Much?'" *Criminal Law Forum* 1 (Winter 1990): 259–290.

―――. "Prediction of Criminal Conduct and Preventative Confinement of Convicted Persons." *Buffalo Law Review* 21 (Spring 1972): 717–758.

von Hirsch, Andrew and Nils Jareborg. "Gauging Criminal Harm: A Living-Standard Analysis." *Oxford Journal of Legal Studies* 11 (Spring 1991): 1–38.

Walker, Nigel. *Why Punish?* Oxford: Oxford University Press, 1991.

Walker, Peter N. *Punishment: An Illustrated History.* New York: Arco Publishing Company, 1973.

Waller, Irvin and Janet Chan. "Prison Use: A Canadian and International Comparison." *Criminal Law Quarterly* 17 (1974): 47–71.

Whelan, John M. "Charity and the Duty to Rescue." *Social Theory and Practice* 17 (Fall 1991): 441–456.

White, Welsh S. "Disproportionality and the Death Penalty: Death as a Punishment for Rape." *University of Pittsburgh Law Review* 38 (Winter 1976): 145–183.

Index

About the Author

Michael Davis is Senior Research Associate at the Center for the Study of Ethics in the Professions, Illinois Institute of Technology. Before coming to IIT in 1986, he taught at Case-Western Reserve, Illinois State, and the University of Illinois at Chicago. In 1985-86, he held a National Endowment for the Humanities fellowship. He has held a number of National Science Foundation grants, including one to integrate ethics into technical courses (1991-95). Davis has published more than seventy articles, including two dozen on criminal justice, authored one other book (*To Make the Punishment Fit the Crime*, Westview, 1992), and coedited two others (*Ethics and the Legal Profession*, Prometheus, 1986, and *AIDS: Crisis in Professional Ethics*, Temple, 1994). He received his Ph.D. in philosophy from the University of Michigan in 1972.